Conflict of Interests
The Politics of American Education

Conflict of Interests

The Politics of American Education

THIRD EDITION

Joel Spring

State University of New York,
College at New Paltz

Boston, Massachusetts   Burr Ridge, Illinois   Dubuque, Iowa
Madison, Wisconsin   New York, New York   San Francisco, California   St. Louis, Missouri

McGraw-Hill

*A Division of The **McGraw·Hill** Companies*

CONFLICT OF INTERESTS
The Politics of American Education

Copyright © 1998 by the McGraw-Hill Companies, Inc. All rights reserved.
Copyright © 1993, 1988 by Longman Publishing Group. All rights reserved.
Printed in the United States of America. Except as permitted under the United
States Copyright Act of 1976, no part of this publication may be reproduced or
distributed in any form or by any means, or stored in a data base or retrieval
system, without the prior written permission of the publisher.

This book is printed on acid-free paper.

2 3 4 5 6 7 8 9 0   FGR FGR   9 0 9 8

ISBN 0-07-060579-3

This book was set in Palatino by Graphic World, Inc.
The editor was Beth Kaufman;
the production supervisor was Kathryn Porzio.
The cover was designed by John Hite/Joan O'Connor.
Project supervision was done by Tage Publishing Service, Inc.
Quebecor Printing/Fairfield was printer and binder.

Library of Congress Cataloging–in–Publication Data

Spring, Joel H.
    Conflict of Interests : the politics of American education / Joel
Spring.—3rd ed.
        p.   cm.
    Includes bibliographical references and index.
    ISBN 0-07-060579-3 (alk. paper)
    1. Education and state—United States.   2. Politics and education—
United States.   I. Title.
LC89.S66   1998
379.73—dc21   97-14052

http://www.mhhe.com

About the Author

JOEL SPRING, professor of education at the State University of New York–College at New Paltz, received his Ph.D. in educational policy studies from the University of Wisconsin. His major research interests are history of education, multicultural education, Native American culture, and the politics of education.

Professor Spring is the author of many books including *The Cultural Transformation of a Native American Family and Its Tribe 1763–1995: A Basket of Apples; Images of American Life: A History of Ideological Management in Schools, Movies, Radio, and Television; American Education (now in its eighth edition); Wheels in the Head: Educational Philosophies of Authority, Freedom, and Culture from Socrates to Paul Freire; and the Intersection of Cultures: Multicultural Education in the United States; and Political Agendas for Education: From the Christian Coalition to the Green Party.*

Contents

8   Local Politics of Education   133

9   The Knowledge Industry   161

10   The Political Uses of the Courts   179

11   The Political Control of Education in a Free Society   195

Preface

This third edition includes a new first chapter, "Educational Politicians and the Doctors of Spin." The chapter examines the impact of President Bill Clinton's New Democratic politics on educational policies and the influence of the Christian Coalition on the Republican Party. In the 1996 election, there was an important realignment of educational policies between the two political parties. The Christian Coalition's control of the educational sections of the 1996 Republican National Platform curtailed Republican advocacy of Goals 2000. The Republican platform called for the end of the Department of Education and Goals 2000. Elected with a promise to fulfill their *Contract with America*, the Republican Congress led by Newt Gingrich also proclaimed its desire to reduce federal involvement in education. Forced to abandon Goals 2000, Republican campaign statements on education were limited to discussions of school choice and privatization.

Assuming leadership over federal education policies, President Clinton applied the strategies advocated by New Democrats. A key element in this strategy is winning back to the Democratic Party white middle-class voters who were alienated by the party's previous focus on helping the poor and minority groups. In making this appeal, Clinton promised to use a combination of federal grants and tax deductions to make the first two years of post-secondary education available to all high school graduates. These education proposals were part of a general New Democratic economic policy to reduce declining wages and job insecurity for the middle class.

I updated chapters to reflect the new era of education politics. In Chapter 4, I added a section, "The Revolt Against Bureaucracy," explaining the ideological origins of attacks on educational bureaucracies. Beginning with the influence of Austrian economics in the 1950s, conservatives identified the problem with public schools to be bureaucratic control. Their solution was the application of free market economics. Out of this thinking came the first proposals for school choice. New Democrats incorporated these ideas into a call for reinvention of schools. I discuss this in a new section to Chapter 6, "Reinventing the Schools."

Joel Spring

CHAPTER 1

Educational Politicians and the Doctors of Spin

"Oh, listen, honey, I know . . . I'm sorry . . . we got stuck here. But great news. Real progress with the teachers," apologized the presidential-candidate Governor Jack Stanton over the phone to his wife after being delayed by a romantic interlude with Ms. Baum, a member of the regional board of a New York City teachers' union.[1] Governor Jack Stanton, from a small state in the South, is the main character in the popular 1996 novel *Primary Colors* whose author, listed as Anonymous on the title page, was later revealed to be *Newsweek*'s columnist Joe Klein.[2]

Opening with Governor Stanton's visit to Ms. Baum's literacy program in Harlem and their brief tryst in a New York City hotel, the novel provides insight into the role of educational issues in politics, and the behind-the-scenes struggles over campaign strategy and media images. For example, discouraged after losing the Democratic primary in New Hampshire, Governor Stanton describes to his wife, Susan Stanton, a conversation with a preschool teacher during one of his table-to-table campaign visits in a New Hampshire restaurant. Governor Stanton told the teacher of the wonderful education projects started in his state—Bill Clinton was known as the education Governor in Arkansas—and his interest in Head Start. The teacher replied that she would never have guessed his interest in education issues from the New Hampshire campaign. Governor Stanton concludes from the encounter, "We gotta figure out how to communicate what we *love* about what we do."[3]

Today, communicating to voters involves manipulation of media images and giving the correct spin to events. The doctors of spin have the responsibility of interpreting events so that they sound favorable to their candidate. For instance, Governor Stanton's spin doctors interpreted his second-place showing in the New Hampshire primary as a victory rather than a defeat. It was a victory, the spin doctors claimed, because they didn't expect Governor Stanton to do well in New Hampshire and, as a result, his second-place position proved he was a strong candidate.

Mary Matalin and James Carville were campaign managers and spin doctors for President George Bush and Governor Bill Clinton, respectively, in the 1992 presidential campaign. "When you're spinning a reporter," Carville states in their coauthored book—they married after the campaign—"you're telling them how to look at a story. Or you're telling them they're covering it wrong."[4] Mary Matalin describes preparation for spinning reporters after a Bush–Clinton debate in 1992. During the debate, Bush's pollsters continually monitored a focus group for their reaction to topics discussed by Bush. Those topics receiving high and low marks along with four or five issues to emphasize with reporters were distributed in a one-page list to Bush's political spinners just before the end of the debate. The purpose of the list was to ensure that all spinners emphasized the same points. The spinners then rushed into a room—the spin session for this debate was held in a cavernous gym at Washington University—and were met by a shouting crowd of reporters from television and newspapers. The job of the spinners was to project the most positive image of their candidate to the news media. Here, Republican spinners stated that in the debate George Bush personified an experienced leader, while Clinton appeared as just another politician. In addition, the spinners emphasized Bush's position on health issues because they received a high rating by pollsters during the debate.[5]

In recent years, education has become an important issue for campaign managers and the doctors of spin. In 1988, presidential candidate George Bush rallied educational supporters of the Republican party with the announcement, "I want to be the education president, I want to lead a renaissance of quality in our schools." Three years later, his claim to be "education president" backfired when he was criticized for not getting his educational initiatives through Congress. A. Graham Down, president of the Council of Basic Education, said in 1991 regarding Bush's educational efforts, "I would give him [President Bush] a C-minus, maybe a D-plus. I mean, he hasn't really done much except talk, and talk is cheap."[6] In the 1992 and 1996 campaigns Bill Clinton adopted the image of education president.

Politicians, including presidential, congressional, gubernatorial, and state legislative candidates, find educational topics appealing because they project the image of a person who cares about human values. In addition, politicians can tie education to economic concerns and, therefore, can claim that investment in education contributes to economic growth.

Of course, as I will discuss throughout this book, education is also a contentious topic. Issues of values, multiculturalism, school organization, and financing divide members within political parties and are reflected in the ideology of the Democratic and Republican parties.

As illustrated by *Primary Colors*, educational politicians hope to appeal to various interest groups. Governor Jack Stanton wanted to capture teachers' votes which often means appealing to the two teachers' unions. President Bill Clinton, as I will describe below, also sought the support of the business sector for his educational policies. Opposing Clinton were special-interest groups representing the religious right.

CONFLICTING POLITICAL GROUPS IN EDUCATION

In this chapter, I am focusing on the major actors in the politics of education. As indicated in Table 1-1, I subdivide these categories into a range of often-conflicting groups. Under the category of government officials, I am including educational politicians, administrative politicians, boards of education, and the courts. The category of politicians includes elected officials in federal, state, and local governments. Because of the educational focus of this book, I am considering boards of education as a separate category, though most members are elected and could be considered educational politicians.

My intention is to explain the role of each group in the politics of education. You should keep in mind that conflicts of interest are not necessarily negative. Conflict is often the dynamic force that drives political systems to seek new solutions. On the other hand, conflict does result in losers and winners. It is a struggle over control of the educational system. Depending on your own political ideology, you might be pleased or distressed by the losers and winners in the U.S. educational system.

POLITICIANS

In 1996, *USA Today*/CNN/Gallup found that education was the major concern of the U.S. public. When asked to identify the issues on which they would vote for president, 67 percent responded the quality of K-12 education, while 66 percent identified crime, and 64 percent chose the economy. This poll shows the importance for politicians of projecting a positive image regarding education.[7]

I need to emphasize the issue of "a positive image" because many voters are unclear about the political debate over education. As pollster Mark Mellman states, "[Education] is sort of vague at the federal level, but it's a for-it-or-against-it kind of thing. And if you're against it, you're in trouble."[8]

As a case study of an educational politician, I am going to explore Bill Clinton's evolution from the "educational" governor of Arkansas to the Chair of the National Governors Conference to his tenure as an "educational" President. Clinton's story reflects the use of a positive educational image in building a political career.

TABLE 1-1. The Major Political Groups in Education

Major Government Actors	Special-Interest Groups
Politicians	The Big Three
Administrative politicians	Teachers' unions
School boards	Corporate sector
	Foundations
	Other interest groups

Education became a focus in Clinton's political career after having won the governorship of Arkansas in 1978. He lost it in the 1980 election. The 1982 election returned Clinton to the governor's mansion under the banner that education was the key to Arkansas's economic revival. He called for emphasizing the teaching of basic skills, expansion of educational opportunities for the poor, and emphasizing vocational and high-technology programs.

"Hillary Clinton," Meredith Oakley, the editor and political columnist of the *Arkansas-Democrat Gazette*, states, "was responsible for her husband's decision to emphasize education reform above all other matters in his second term."[9] After his second election, Bill, Hillary, and his advisors decided that during his first term he projected a confused public image by trying to do too much. It would be best, they concluded, to emphasize educational reform and create a public image of Bill Clinton as the "education governor."

In adopting this approach to public image-building, other Southern governors who would also affect educational politics and policies in the 1990s joined Clinton. During the 1980s, Tennessee's Governor Lamar Alexander and South Carolina's Richard Riley stressed educational reform as the key to the economic development of their states. In 1996, Lamar Alexander attempted to follow in Clinton's footsteps by running in the Republican presidential primary.

[margin note: Clinton's SECT of Ed]

Clinton, Alexander, and Riley were to play leading roles in the National Governors Association and the creation of Goals 2000. In 1986, Bill Clinton was elected to the vice chair of the National Governors Association. The chair of the organization was Lamar Alexander of Tennessee. In 1989, President Bush asked the National Governors Association to develop what would become the Goals 2000 agenda.[10] The request by President Bush was part of his promise to be the "education president." In 1990, Bush presented these goals to Congress in his 1990 State of the Union address. Lamar Alexander, whom President George Bush eventually appointed Secretary of Education, pushed the Goals 2000 agenda. After President Clinton's election in 1992, Clinton signed the Goals 2000: Educate America Act.

Hillary's role in building Bill Clinton's educational image is extremely important. Beginning with her involvement as a lawyer in the Children's Defense Fund in the 1970s to the publication of her book, *It Takes a Village: And Other Lessons Children Teach Us* (1996), she has been an important crusader for educational reform.[11] During Bill Clinton's second gubernatorial term, he appointed Hillary chair of the state's Education Standards Committee that Arkansas's Quality Education Act of 1983 created. Other members of the Education Standards Committee agree that the final report reflected Hillary's agenda.[12]

The idea of statewide education standards for educational reform would haunt educational politics throughout the 1990s. The assumption is that creating academic standards for student performance will force local school districts to improve instruction. Schools, it is assumed, will raise student achievement to the level of the state standards.

Creating standards to reform schools has a great deal of political appeal because it doesn't necessarily require raising taxes to increase educational spending. The underlying message of the educational standards movement is that the primary problem with education is that local school districts and teachers are not working hard enough to increase student achievement. The whip of high state achievement standards, it is assumed, will drive school districts and teachers to reform instruction.

Bill Clinton would eventually advocate the idea of standards as the key to educational reform at meetings of the National Governors Association. By the time of his presidency, Bill Clinton was advocating world and national standards as the key to the economic development of the United States.

The major result of Clinton's campaign in Arkansas for educational reform was increased ratings in the polls.[13] His doctors of spin proclaimed that educational reform had resulted in a victory for the people of Arkansas. In the public mind, he was now the "education governor." With his popularity running high, Clinton spent little time campaigning in 1984. With the subsequent passage of legislation giving Arkansas governors four-year terms, Clinton's position was secure.

The 1992 presidential election between Bush and Clinton promised to be an "education election." In 1991, the year before the election, the Bush administration created the New American Schools Development Corporation. Officials within the Bush administration admitted that plans for the establishment of the corporation were part of a larger strategy to ward off criticism during the 1992 presidential election campaign that the Bush administration lacked a coherent domestic agenda. Against this background of criticism, Bush unveiled plans to reform American education and to fulfill his 1988 pledge to be the "education president." This reform package included the creation of model schools, incentives for parental choice of schools, and, of course, Goals 2000. Highlighting the political nature of the Bush reform package was its development and supervision by the highly skilled educational politician Secretary of Education Lamar Alexander, Clinton's former Republican colleague in the National Governors Association and the former "education governor" of Tennessee.[14]

On the other side, Clinton planned to attack President Bush for not carrying through on his promise to enact the Goals 2000 agenda. In their 1992 campaign book, *Putting People First: How We Can All Change America*, Bill Clinton and Al Gore wrote, "Government fails when our schools fail. For four years we've heard a lot of talk about 'the Education President' but seen little government action to invest in the collective talents of our people."[15] Clinton and Gore promised to enact Goals 2000 within their first 100 days in the White House (in this campaign document it is called the 1989 Education Summit's "National Education Goals"), including national examinations and national standards.[16]

Of course, the importance of education as a campaign theme depended on the doctors of spin and the image makers. The problem facing President Bush in 1992 and the Republican presidential candidate in 1996, Bob Dole, is the sharp division within the Republican Party between moderates and the right wing. In Chapter 2, I will examine the divisions within the Republican and Democratic parties over education issues. What I want to stress here is the difficulty for national Republican leaders to please the different constituencies within their party.

As a moderate Republican, Bush faced the problem in 1992 of creating a national campaign theme that would unite the various elements of his party. One item not supported by right-wing Republicans were Goals 2000 because of possible increased federal intrusion in local schools. In a haphazard manner, the Bush media managers latched onto the theme of "Family" to unite the party.

Mary Matalin tells the following story of how "Family" emerged as the campaign theme. During the 1992 primary, Matalin and others were flying aboard Air Force One trying to complete a speech for Bush to deliver upon landing. A former Louisiana Representative, Henson Moore, strolled through the cabin suggesting a nice sound bite "Jobs, Family, Peace." They put it in the speech but not as part of a central strategy. It was just to be a good sound bite.[17]

As media managers know, television news programs look for short statements in speeches that can be easily featured. Television news programs are limited in time they can focus on any one topic. Therefore, the perfect sound bite is one that allows for quick and easy use by the media. The media jumped on the sound bite and emphasized "Family." Matalin claimed that the campaign would have preferred an emphasis on "Jobs" and "Peace." There was no intention in the campaign to stress "Family."[18]

Bush's running mate and representative of the more conservative faction of the Republican Party, Dan Quayle, added to focus on the family by singling out the television program *Murphy Brown* as representing how television, movies, and liberals were undermining traditional family values. Quayle's criticism of *Murphy Brown* caught Republican strategists by surprise. In fact, Matalin reported that at a White House senior staff meeting she was the only one who actually knew the program. To support Quayle, the White House staff members decided to spin the line that Quayle's statement was related to a general breakdown of the family caused by government programs and television.[19]

The episode with Quayle and Bush's sound bite left the impression that family values were the central message of the Republican campaign. In Matalin's words, "No one believes this, but *there never was a strategy to place family values at the center of our message.*[20] Consequently, the whole third night of the 1996 Republican convention was devoted to the "Family." The emphasis on the family and family values appealed to right-wing Republicans and conveyed to the public that the right-wing, as opposed to the moderate-wing, was in control of the Republican Party. From Matalin's perspective, this doomed the Republican campaign in 1992. The real issue for voters, she believed, was the economy. Republican positions on the economy were lost in the emphasis on family values.

Campaign themes are important for shaping the educational policies of a political party. As I will discuss in Chapter 2 regarding the current ideological positions of the Republican Party, there is little room for support of national standards and testing. The Republican emphasis on family values resulted in stressing family control over education and not national standards created by the federal government. For Republicans, family control in the 1992 election meant giving parents the power to choose their children's education.

On the other hand, a campaign emphasizing the economy can make room for national standards and testing through claims that they will raise school achievement and as a result cause economic growth. This is what happened in the 1994 Democratic campaign when Clinton boasted of his record as an "education governor." Similar to advisors to the Republicans, James Carville and his staff had a difficult time arriving at a central theme for the Clinton campaign. They also believed the economy, particularly unemployment and jobs lost to corporate restructuring, were central concerns in the minds of the voters. After three months of strategic planning—that's right, three months—they created the key media sound bite and image, "Putting People First." Carville wrote, "Ask five people who came up with it, they'll all say they did. I believe it was me, but I could be wrong."[21]

Under the banner "Putting People First" were placed many issues regarding the economy including education. The campaign book, *Putting People First,* stressed the importance of Goals 2000.[22] Clinton's acceptance speech at the 1992 Democratic convention was laced with the importance of creating jobs to meet the needs of an expanding global economy. Within the framework of what Clinton called the "New Covenant," educational reform would become part of a general global economic strategy and education would solve the problem of unemployment by training workers for high-skilled jobs. In his speech, Clinton said, that one thing the Covenant was about was, "An America in which the doors of college are thrown open once again to the sons and daughters of stenographers and steelworkers."[23]

Again in 1996, Bill Clinton was off and running as the "education president." Continuing to link success in the global economy to education, Clinton announced a voluntary program, 21st Century Teachers, that would instruct 500,000 teachers in the classroom use of computers. The National Education Association agreed to cooperate with the program and encourage volunteers at its 1996 national meeting. Delivering the commencement address at Princeton University on June 4, 1996, he proposed a $1,500 tax credit for the first two years of college with the goal of providing 14 years of education to all American youth.[24]

Trying to steal the Republican thunder over family values and probably trying to protect his image as a family man in the face of charges of extramarital affairs, Clinton, in May 1996, recommended that cities enact curfews to keep youths under 17 off the streets after 8 P.M. on school nights. During the same period, he attacked tobacco companies for advertisements aimed at children and teenagers and supported the idea of uniforms for public school students.[25]

On June 23, 1996, Congressional Democrats announced their fall campaign theme to be "Family First" under which they placed their educational promises of tax deductions for educational expenses and expanded child-care credits. With talk of "good fathers like Bill Clinton and Al Gore," the Clinton's reelection campaign picked up the same theme on June 24 at Al Gore's annual conference on family and work. At the conference, Bill Clinton called for an expansion of the 1993 Family and Medical Leave Act to provide 24 hours of unpaid leave for family events, such as parent-teacher meetings.[26]

According to *The New York Times* political correspondent Alison Mitchell, the family theme was designed to appeal to a large segment of the population: families with children at home. "Within that group," Mitchell wrote, "are represented other groups of swing voters: independent-leaning suburban voters, working-class Reagan Democrats, and women. Analysts say the strategy has paid off in the polls."[27]

While Bill Clinton was supporting the tighter controls over the behavior of children and teenagers, Hillary Clinton campaigned for family and community responsibility for student behavior and school achievement.[28] Her book on these issues, *It Takes a Village*, was released early in 1996 to provide a background document for the campaign.[29]

In contrast, the Republican nominee for the 1996 presidential election, Bob Dole, felt squeezed between the moderate and right-wing factions of the party. By the time of Dole's nomination, the education platform of the Republican Party was mainly under right-wing control. Ironically, the product of the education summit called by Republican George Bush in 1989, Goals 2000, was now supported by the Democratic Party. In 1994, Republican nominees for Congress agreed to enact, if elected, the policies outlined in their *Contract With America*. The *Contract With America* supported greater family control of education by giving parents the ability to choose their children's schools and reducing federal interference in schooling. No support was given to the national standards and testing. The educational role of the federal government according to the *Contract With America* should be limited to protecting the power of the family over schooling.[30]

In preparation for the 1996 campaign, Haley Barbour, Chairman of the Republican National Committee and of the National Policy Reform, outlined Republican goals in *Agenda for America: A Republican Direction for the Future*. Adopting the tone of the *Contract With America*, Barbour denounced Goals 2000 as "a step further down the road of federal control of education."[31] After attacking the two teachers' unions for "schoolmarm rhetoric and strong-arm tactics,"[32] Barbour called for the abolishment of the Department of Education, parental choice of schools for their children, and more competition between schools. Clearly, the moderate Republican education agenda of national standards and testing was dead.[33]

Consequently, the Republican nominee in 1996, Bob Dole, who is considered a moderate in the Republican Party, was without—as Bush was in 1992—a clearly formulated educational policy. During the early stages of the campaign, Dole's remarks on education were largely negative in the sense that they called for elimination of the Department of Education, opposed national standards, and opposed the schooling of the children of illegal immigrants.[34]

Republican conservatives were aware that they were not creating a positive image regarding education. "The conservatives clearly lost the message war on education." worried Jim Herni, at the conservative think-tank, the Heritage Foundation, in April 1996. "Once he [Bob Dole] gets on top of the message war, then he can come out with some proposals."[35] Herni's comment reflected the growing Republican fear during the early stages of the election campaign that like George Bush in 1992 Bob Dole's media managers and spin doctors can create a clear, positive media image of their candidate.

Bill Clinton's political rise from "education governor" to "education president" highlights the important role educational issues can play in the life of a politician. Living in a society where education credentials are needed for income and job advancement, a politician needs to project a positive image regarding educational issues. Maybe Jeanne Allen, the president of the Center for Education Reform, is right. "Any candidate," she said, "has to convince the American people that they are truly concerned about education, that they understand the problems in education, and what they would do about it as president."[36]

ADMINISTRATIVE POLITICIANS

Working for elected politicians are what I call administrative politicians. I am defining as *administrative politicians* those education officials whose tenure depends on the favor of elected politicians or on voter support. At the federal level, examples include the secretary and assistant secretaries of education. At the state level, it includes state superintendents of education (some state superintendents are appointed and others are elected). In local districts, school boards appoint most superintendents. Administrative politicians retain their positions by serving the interests of those responsible for putting them in office, and, usually, they share the same ideological outlook as the interests they serve.

At the federal level, the Department of Education and the position of Secretary of Education were created in the late 1970s during Jimmy Carter's administration. Before then, a commissioner of education headed the administrative branch in the Department of Health, Education and Welfare. During the 1976 presidential campaign, Jimmy Carter promised the National Education Association (NEA), the larger of the two teachers' unions, to establish a Department of Education in return for support and campaign aid. The primary responsibility of the secretary of education is to represent the administration's viewpoint on educational matters before Congress and the public.

A variety of political forces impinge on the work of administrative politicians. After he left office, Terrel Bell, secretary of education during the first years of the Reagan administration, complained of constant pressure from what he called the "radical right" of the Republican party. "Among the members of the radical right," Bell wrote about his experience, "the thinking was that I and others like me were keeping Reagan from being Reagan." While in office, Bell campaigned for the conservative educational agenda of the Reagan administration, which included changing academic standards for graduation from high school and for teacher education. He resisted pressure from the Republican right to enact the more conservative part of the Reagan agenda, which included abolishing the Department of Education, infusing Christian morality into the schools, and expunging secular humanism from the curriculum.[37]

For illustrating the activities of administrative politicians, I am going to trace the career of Bell's successor as Secretary of Education, William Bennett, who became one of the most outspoken commentators on U.S. education and culture in the 1980s and 1990s, and an educational commentator for the right-wing section of the Republican Party.

In *De-Valuing of America: The Fight for Our Culture and Our Children,* William Bennett describes the political maneuvering required to gain appointment as an administrative politician. His first government appointment was in 1981 as chair of the National Endowment for the Humanities (NEH). At the time of the appointment, he was heading a small private think-tank for scholars in the humanities in South Carolina. Initially, there were three finalists, including Bennett, for the chairmanship of the NEH. A call from President Reagan's Director of Presidential Personnel, Helene von Damm, informed Bennett that while President Reagan supported his appointment, two guardians of the conservative movement, Senators Jesse Helms and John East, were opposed. His job, Helene von Damm stated, was to gain the support of the two Senators.[38]

One finalist was eliminated when *The New York Times* reported that a candidate for the job, Professor Melvin Bradford of the University of Dallas, had published scholarly criticisms of Abraham Lincoln—the first Republican president and a founder of the Republican Party. While conservatives, such as President Reagan, might have agreed with Bradford's criticisms, the potential political fallout for the Republican Party was too great to risk continued support of Bradford's nomination.[39]

With Bradford removed from the competition, Bennett tried to gain Senator East's support. Senator East asked Bennett if, as head of the NEH, he would evaluate the applications of conservative scholars with the same standard as those applied to liberal scholars. This question reflected the belief of conservatives that the NEH primarily funded the applications of liberal scholars. The question highlights the influence of political views on the type of research funded by the federal agencies. Of course, Bennett answered, "Yes."[40]

While Senator East seemed satisfied with Bennett, Senator Helms feared that Bennett was a liberal. To overcome this problem, Bennett met with Edwin J. Feulner, president of The Heritage Foundation, who was reported to have a great deal of influence on Senator Helms's conservative thinking. Since the 1980s, The Heritage Foundation played an important role in articulating the conservative agenda for education and for funding research reflecting conservative values.[41]

At first, Feulner was suspicious until Bennett mentioned that he was the coauthor of a popular Heritage Foundation article, "Moral Education in the Schools," which criticized moral relativism in public schools and the values clarification movement. After commenting, "You're that Bennett,"

Feulner picked up the phone and called Senator Helms. Bennett was appointed chair of the NEH on December 21, 1981.[42]

As chair of the NEH, Bennett pressed his conservative agenda by supporting traditional cultural values against what he called the values of the "liberal elite." In 1985, President Reagan appointed him Secretary of Education. As Secretary of Education, Bennett immediately established his agenda for what he called "the battle over American education." The day after his Senate confirmation, Mary Futrell, president of the National Education Association, came to his office. Bennett reports that Futrell wanted to begin a continuing exchange with him in which disagreements between the Reagan administration and the union would not become public. Bennett refused by calling for a public debate and informed Futrell that "the NEA was a big part of the problem."[43] For Bennett, American schools needed to be saved from the "education establishment—that wide array of professional organizations putatively representing teachers, administrators, and other educators."[44]

In the 1990s, William Bennett, as I will discuss in Chapter 2, remained a major spokesperson for conservative views regarding education and culture. Besides exemplifying an administrative politician whose political views and contacts played an important role in getting and maintaining his government appointments, Bennett's career illustrates the increasing role of political ideology in the politics of education. During the 1980s and 1990s, political attitudes would play an increasing role in the lives of local school boards and superintendents.

BOARDS OF EDUCATION

Held by Dallas school board security personnel in a choke hold, a member of the New Black Panthers Party was removed from the May 23, 1996 school board meeting for not sitting down. Two other New Black Panthers Party members who refused to sit were ordered arrested by the board's newly installed president Bill Keever. Members threatened to return armed, which is legal in Texas under a recently passed law allowing the carrying of concealed weapons.[45]

Spokespersons for the Dallas black community complained that Keever was made president because he was the only white male on the school board. While only 10 percent of the student population of the Dallas schools is white, five white board members dominate the school board as opposed to three black and one Hispanic member. Black and Hispanic members complained that white control of the school board is responsible for the academic failure of many black and Hispanic students. "The students have changed, but the institution is essentially Eurocentric," said Yvonne Ewell, a black school board member.[46]

The Dallas school board conflict highlights the increasingly contentiousness of school board elections and power struggles. The two major sources of school board conflict are the attacks by the religious right and multiculturalists on the content of textbooks and curriculum. Somewhat ironically, attacks by the religious right have resulted in confirming and strengthening the power of school boards over textbooks and curriculum.

Several court rulings upheld the power of local school boards to monitor the content of the school curriculum and textbooks beginning with the U.S. Supreme Court decision *Board of Island Union Free School District* v. *Steven A. Pico* (1982). Here, school board members ordered the removal from the school library a list of books found objectionable by a conservative political organization. The court ruled against the school board because of the use of a political agenda for selection of books. On the other hand, the court firmly upheld the right of elected representatives on school boards to select books for the school library. The selection had to be made solely on "educational suitability."[47] In 1987, the Sixth Circuit Court of Appeals decided complaints that a textbook series contained explicit messages supporting secular humanism. As I discuss in more detail in Chapter 2, many right-wing religious groups consider secular humanism a religion. The Appeals Court rejected the idea that the books taught a religion but emphasized the right of school boards to select textbooks and determine the curriculum of the school.[48]

Therefore, the very issues that have contributed to the political contentiousness of school board elections and politics resulted in strengthening the role of the school board. In her study of the effect of the religious right on the censorship of textbooks, Joan Delfattore writes, "School boards have the authority to decide curriculums, and their decisions cannot be successfully challenged in court unless the materials they select are chosen for primarily religious reasons or have a primarily religious effect."[49]

An example of school board power over textbooks and the content of instruction occurred in June 1996 when the Hudson, Ohio school board turned down the recommendation of teachers and administrators to use an American history textbook, *The American People,* in a high school honor course. The school board objected to the book's presentation of the history of women, minorities, and slaves. School board member Kenneth Claypoole complained that the book was too multicultural. A local leader of the Hudson Chapter of Christians for Excellence in Education, Robert Lattimer, said, "There is an overabundant supply of material on women, African-Americans and Native Americans . . . [and there were too many] details on the difficulties experienced by slaves, indentured servants, immigrants, farmers and industrial workers."[50]

Given this power over textbooks and the curriculum, it is little wonder that school board elections are now characterized by struggles between liberal and right-wing religious groups, and between advocates and opponents of a multicultural curriculum. Although school board members cannot decide to use an explicitly religious or political agenda, they can make decisions that appear to be based on "educational suitability." Consequently, school board politics increasingly centers on such issues as sex education, evolution and creationism, interpretations of U.S. history, feminism, environmentalism, and multiculturalism.

The Dallas conflict also illustrates the transition occurring in the 1990s from elite-dominated school boards to school boards that are reflecting the social and racial composition of their communities. Traditionally, a group of powerful business leaders the Dallas Citizens Council, determined membership on the Dallas school board. The control of school boards by local business groups has been typical of school board elections from the beginning of the century.[51]

In the early twentieth century, school board elections were made nonpartisan and at-large, and school boards were reduced in size. These changes tended to favor the wealthier members of the community because nonpartisan elections eliminated the role of political parties from elections and at-large elections required campaigning throughout the school district rather than from a small district identified with a particular school. Consequently, it required money and an independent organization to campaign throughout a school district. Denied the use of political parties, these changes made it more difficult for the average citizen to be elected to school boards. In contrast, local business and professional organizations had the money and organizational ability to get their members on school boards.[52]

These changes in the early twentieth century were based on a concept of democratic elitism. In this context, elitism refers to control of the schools by local civic elites composed primarily of people who exercise power over local public policy without, usually, holding offices in government. They usually work through informal networks and civic organizations such as a local chamber of commerce or service club. The civic elites involved in school administration in the early twentieth century considered themselves enlightened leaders working for the good of the entire community. One recent study of the occupations of civic elites found that more than 50 percent were bankers, industrialists, and heads of local businesses, while the remainder included heads of local utilities, newspaper people, civic association executives, clergy, university administrators, and professionals (lawyers, doctors, and the like).

In the rhetoric of democratic elitism, only the "best"—the elite—should determine important public matters, because they have proven themselves successful and possess superior knowledge of public affairs. For instance, it was argued that a factory worker would have less ability than a banker to decide the public interest regarding schooling. Following this line of reasoning, reformers argued that the schools should be governed only by the "best" members of the community.

As a result, it has been difficult throughout the twentieth century for the poor and minority groups to gain membership on school boards. Since the civil rights movement of the 1950s and 1960s, the pattern of elite control has changed. This has resulted in major political conflicts over control of school boards. In the current situation in Dallas, the political conflict pits minority groups against the civic elite represented by the Dallas Citizens Council.

This type of political conflict will increase in the years ahead. The newly elected head of the National School Boards Association, Anne Bryant, announced in 1996 that one of her goals was to make local school boards more representative of their populations. "If you look across the nation," she said, "the percentage of African-American, Hispanic, Asian, and Native American individuals who are members of local school boards is not reflective of their percentage of the population."[53]

Similar to politicians and administrative politicians, school board members will increasingly be buffeted by the forces of liberal and conservative ideologies, and special interest groups representing religious, racial, and ethnic populations.

SPECIAL-INTEREST GROUPS

Special-interest groups play a major role in shaping the political agenda of U.S. schools. Politicians, administrative politicians, and school boards are constantly pressured by what I call "The Big Three" interest groups composed of teachers unions, the corporate sector, and private foundations, and by groups representing religious, racial, and ethnic populations.

Much of the U.S. political system is based on a symbiotic relationship between special-interest groups, politicians, and government administrators.[54] In this symbiotic relationship, a special-interest group will form around a particular administrative branch of government. For instance, the tobacco lobby has a major interest in continuing subsidies to its industry and works closely with the branch of the Department of Agriculture responsible for the program. In turn, the administrators of the tobacco program depend for their very jobs on the continuation of the subsidy. Therefore, the tobacco lobby and government administrators work together to insure continued congressional funding of the program. In addition, politicians from tobacco-growing areas depend on support from the tobacco lobby. The result is an alliance in which all members depend for their survival on the continuation of a particular government program.

David Stockman, the budget-cutting head of the Office of Management and Budget under President Reagan, complained that these symbiotic relationships made it impossible to cause significant changes in the U.S. government. For instance, while Stockman was working to cut the government budget, Senator Jesse Helms of North Carolina, who received strong support from the tobacco lobby, told him about budget cuts, "Now you go right to it, boy. But don't let them OMB bureaucrats down there confuse you. The tobacco program doesn't cost the taxpayers one red cent. And it never will as long as I'm chairman of the Agricultural Committee."[55]

TEACHERS' UNIONS

The teachers' unions—the National Education Associations (NEA) and the American Federation of Teachers (AFT)—have a similar symbiotic relationship with the Democratic Party as the tobacco lobby has with Jesse Helms. As noted earlier, while the fictitious Governor Jack Stanton wooed the teachers' unions, the Republican Secretary of Education William Bennett considered the larger of the two teachers' unions, the NEA, as the enemy and the source of many educational problems.

Well organized and politically active, the two teachers' unions try to protect their members' interests by supporting political candidates and pressuring officials in federal, state, and local governments. Since 1976, when the NEA first supported a presidential candidate, Jimmy Carter, both unions have supported national candidates from the Democratic Party. During the Bush and Reagan years from 1980 to 1992, the two unions complained about no longer having direct access to the White House.[56]

Highlighting the split between the Republican Party and the teachers' unions is the NEA contribution in 1994 of 98 percent of its $4 million Political Action Committee funds to Democratic candidates. In the same year, the NEA provided the following campaign funding primarily to democratic candidates: "political information and advocacy" ($53,000), "legislative and political activity" ($876,000), "national party participation" ($291,000), "Campaign Assistance to Affiliates" ($730,000), and "Education and Training Program" for political campaigns ($395,000).[57]

The broad political interests of teachers' unions are exemplified in a 1990 interview with the NEA's recently installed president, Keith Geiger. Geiger outlined the broad concerns of the union:

> All of the issues that I talked about are very critical to a teacher's union and to collective bargaining. As a union, we have to be in the forefront of the kinds of funding that are needed at the federal, state, and local levels. . . . The typical stereotype of teachers' unions in the past has changed considerably. We have to be an integral part of not only negotiating better working conditions, but also negotiating changes in schools. . . . [8]

When Geiger stepped down as president in 1996, he called upon the 10,000 delegates to the national convention to "retool collective bargaining as the great engine driving change and innovation in school districts across America."[59] He stressed the importance of a recent contract between the union and the New Albany-Floyd County Schools in Indiana. This contract gives the union control over three-fourths of the local school budget and the power to establish salaries, create new teaching positions, reduce class size, and provide more time for teacher planning.

Obviously, Geiger's speech represents a direct threat to the political power of local school boards and administrators. But Geiger sweetens the tone of the call for stronger contracts by giving the following political spin: "We are not talking here about sleeping with the enemy," Geiger assured the convention delegates. "We are talking about waking up school boards, administrators and association leaders to our shared interest in revitalizing public education."[60]

While the two teachers' unions often appeal to high educational ideals and the welfare of students, it is important to understand, as Bill Clinton did in Arkansas, that their primary concern is the welfare of teachers. In Arkansas, the union protested the report of Hillary Clinton's Education Standards Committee. Besides calling for testing of third-, sixth-, and eighth-grade students, Governor Bill Clinton decided to carry out the report's demand for greater teacher accountability by requesting basic skills testing of Arkansas's teachers. He also decided to tie the testing of teachers to the increasing taxes to raise teachers' salaries. "No test, no tax," he told the public.[61] As a result, the Arkansas Education Association withdrew support of Clinton's entire reform package and began to wage political war against him.

Governor Bill Clinton also received opposition to his educational reform plan from one of the other "big three" interest groups, the corporate sector. The corporate sector, which included public utilities and big business, objected to proposals for increasing corporate taxes to pay for raising teachers' salaries. As I will suggest frequently in this book, the corporate sector wants schools to educate better workers, but opposes increased corporate taxes to fund plans for educational improvements.

Faced with opposition from the Arkansas Education Association regarding testing teachers and the corporate sector over increasing taxes, Bill Clinton called a special session of the Arkansas state legislature and spent six weeks trying to convince legislators to tax and test.[62]

The result was that the corporate sector won and the teachers' union lost. Arkansas Representative Bill Foster said at the end of the special session, "I'm afraid this session will go down in history as the special session for the special interests and the wealthy people."[63] The legislature didn't increase corporate taxes but passed a regressive one-percent increase in the state's sales tax that had its major impact on the state's poor.

After passage of the teacher-testing legislation, they greeted Bill Clinton with absolute silence when giving the keynote at the 1983 annual meeting of the Arkansas Education Association. In the end, teacher testing didn't mean very much because anyone with an eighth-grade education could pass the test.[64]

After Clinton's experience in Arkansas, he learned the importance of winning the union to his side. At the July 1996 NEA convention, President Clinton received the endorsement of the 2.2 million-member organization. NEA president Geiger praised Clinton: "During the last four years, he [Clinton] has stood firm against daunting odds to protect children and strengthen public education in this nation."[65]

THE CORPORATE SECTOR

As both Bill Clinton and the teachers' union learned in Arkansas, the corporate sector often has more influence than teachers. As a special-interest group, the corporate sector is often interested in contradictory government policies—low taxes and schools that educate quality workers. Reflecting the extent of corporate power over the schools, a 1990 *New York Times* article states, "When it comes to reforming the nation's schools, these days the leading radicals are likely to be wearing pin-striped suits and come from oak-paneled boardrooms rather than the ivy-covered walls of academia."[66] After detailing business involvement in shaping the curriculum, managerial methods, and organization of the nation's schools, the article concludes, "The impetus behind the corporate embrace of education reform is concern about the quality of the American labor pool."[67] A year later, a *New York Times* article headlined "Brought to You by Exxon—School Reform." The article described the Bush administration's creation of the New American Schools Development Corporation. Reporting on the same development, *Education Week* proclaimed in its title that "Educators Watch With a Wary Eye As Business Gains Policy Muscle."[68] As Marc Tucker, president of the National Center on Education and the Economy, declared, "It is clear that business has an open door to the top policymakers, including the President, in a way that professional educators would envy."[69]

The corporate sector has tried to balance its desires to lower taxes and, simultaneously, improve the education of future workers by supporting the creation of higher academic standards. As I suggested in my discussion of Bill Clinton's career as an educational politician, the identification of low academic standards, as opposed to under-funded schools, as the reason for poorly educated students shifts the argument from increasing taxes to creating more stringent academic standards. Higher standards for graduation, competency tests, and statewide academic tests are a low-cost means, it is believed, of forcing students to learn more. Since the 1980s, the corporate sector has been leading advocates for establishing national academic standards.

The selection of IBM's conference center in Palisades, New York for the 1996 national education summit illustrates corporate interest and influence in education. Louis V. Gerstner, the chair and chief executive of IBM, cohosted the conference with Wisconsin Governor Tommy Thompson, chair of the National Governors Association. Interestingly, the 49 chief executives of corporations attending the conference outnumbered the attending 40 governors.[70]

The opening of the national summit's official policy statement emphasized corporate concern with schools training better workers. "The quality of our schools is one of the issues fundamental," the policy statement reads, "to America's future. . . . Business leaders understand that companies can be successful and the nation can be economically viable only if the United States has a world-class workforce."[71]

Reflecting his educational proposals as governor of Arkansas, President Clinton's speech called for state competency tests for promotion from elementary to middle school, from middle school to high school, and for graduation from high school. "You have to have," Clinton told the governors and business leaders, "an assessment system . . . that says no more social promotions, no more free passes."[72] Clinton's proposal for increased state testing was placed in the framework of his support of national standards in Goals 2000.

Business leaders threw their support behind the plan by saying that a state's high academic standards and student achievement levels would be a major factor in locating their businesses in a given state. In supporting standards and testing, the business leaders also said they would require job applicants to show academic achievement using school-based records.[73]

The desire of the corporate community for low taxes often, as in Arkansas, puts them in conflict with the teachers' unions. On the other hand, the work of the other member of the big three interest groups, private foundations, cuts across the political spectrum.

FOUNDATIONS

According to tax laws, foundations are private organizations that fund politically nonpartisan policy research, public projects, and basic research. The major sources of funds for foundations are outside contributions and earnings on previous contributions. For instance, the Ford and Rockefeller foundations draw a major source of their income from previous family contributions. In practice, most foundations reflect a particular political bias. For instance, in the example of administrative politician William Bennett, the conservative Heritage Foundation played an important role in his appointment as chair of the NEH.

Many larger foundations have traditionally supported social programs that help maintain a welfare state. Foundations such as the Carnegie Corporation, the Ford Foundation, and the Rockefeller Foundation have promoted welfare capitalism. The basic tenet of welfare capitalism is to avoid serious social discontent in a capitalist society by giving aid to those in dire economic and social need.[74]

Alan Pifer best expresses the general attitude of large U.S. foundations. In his last report issued in 1982, after serving eighteen years as president of the Carnegie Corporation, Pifer warns that without welfare capitalism,

> "there lies nothing but increasing hardship for ever-growing numbers, a mounting possibility of severe social unrest, and the consequent development among the upper classes and the business community of sufficient fear for the survival of our capitalist economic system to bring about an abrupt change of course. Just as we built the general welfare state in the 1930s and expanded it in the 1960s as a safety valve for the easing of social tension, so will we do it again in the 1980s. Any other path is simply too risky."[75]

A good example of the power of foundations is the role of the Carnegie Corporation, a private foundation, in creating national teacher certification. In 1986, the Carnegie Corporation sponsored the Task Force on Teaching as a Profession that issued the report *A Nation Prepared: Teachers for the 21st Century*.[76] In the early 1980s, the Carnegie Corporation was concerned with the faltering American educational system that, according to the critics, was causing the U.S. economy to fall behind those of West Germany and Japan. Thus, the primary issue was to shore up a failing capitalist economy by producing a better-educated labor force in the schools. The report on teaching reflected these economic issues.

The opening statement of the Carnegie report on teaching stresses the basic needs of welfare capitalism. First, it recognizes that poor and minority groups will continue to have economic problems in a rapidly changing technological world. The report states, "As the world economy changes shape, it would be fatal to assume that America can succeed if only a portion of our school children succeed."[77] The report emphasizes that by the year 2000 one out of every three Americans will be a member of a minority group and that currently one out of every four children is born in a state of poverty. Stressing the consequences of this situation, the report warns, "it is increasingly difficult for the poorly educated to find jobs. A growing number of permanently unemployed people seriously strains our social fabric."[78]

In addition, the report voices concern about the supply of well-trained workers: "A heavily technology-based economy will be unable to invest vast sums to maintain people who cannot contribute to the nation's productivity. American business already spends billions of dollars a year retraining people who arrive at the workplace with inadequate education."[79]

Therefore, for welfare capitalism, improving the quality of teachers— which is the intention of the report—will result in better-trained workers. Better-trained workers, in turn, can find jobs, thus reducing the social tensions caused by unemployment and saving the corporations millions of dollars in training-program costs.

An important feature of the report was its plan to influence state and local educational policies. The sponsoring foundation, the Carnegie Corporation of New York, proposed a two-fold strategy. First, by organizing and supporting a prestigious panel and paying for the distribution of its report, the foundation hoped to influence thinking about educational policy. Second, the foundation hoped to alter educational practices by changing government policies.

In 1987, based on *A Nation Prepared: Teachers for the 21st Century*, the Carnegie Corporation developed and funded the National Board of Professional Standards for improving the status and skills of teachers through a system of national certification. Organized in 1987, the National Board of Professional Standards is currently creating national standards for teacher skills and certification examinations. As part of its plan for continued funding of the organization and to gain the support of the federal government, the Carnegie Corporation lobbied for federal financial support. At first, the Bush administration was reluctant to seek funding for the organization, but, in July 1991, Secretary of Education Lamar Alexander showed the administration's willingness to support federal funding. Funding would closely link government and foundation policies.[80]

The establishment of the National Board for Professional Teaching Standards exemplifies how foundations can affect educational policies. *A Nation Prepared: Teachers for the 21st Century* was issued with full media coverage. Cooperation and funding were sought and received from the federal government for the support of the national Board for Professional Teaching Standards. Eventually, the report hoped, local school districts would be persuaded to hire teachers certified by the national board. The report recommends that "state authorities should begin drafting plans to offer districts incentives to engage such teachers in appropriate roles and at higher rates of pay than teachers without board certification."[81] In addition, the National Board for Professional Teaching Standards recommended that states take steps to ensure the equitable distribution of board-certified teachers.

The influence of foundations is evidenced by the result of the Carnegie Corporation's sponsorship of *A Nation Prepared: Teachers for the 21st Century* and the National Board for Professional Teaching Standards. In the 1993–94 school year, the National Board for Professional Teaching Standards conducted assessments for certification of teachers of English–language arts to children in early adolescence.

Since the National Board for Professional Teaching Standards lacks the legal power to enforce any requirement that teachers apply for national certification, it must depend on the actions of state and local governments. Subsequently, in 1994, five state legislatures passed laws about national certification. Iowa and Oklahoma legislatures passed laws that teachers with national certification would automatically receive an Iowa or Oklahoma state license if officials in those states decide the standards meet the standards of their states. The Mississippi legislature provided a $3,000 bonus and the North Carolina legislature provided a 4-percent salary increase to teachers attaining national certification. In addition, the North Carolina legislature provided money to pay the $975 testing fee. The New Mexico state legislature provided money to support and prepare teachers for the national test.[82]

Besides the major influence of teachers' unions, the corporate sector, and foundations on educational politics, other interest groups are concerned about educational policies, and the content of textbooks and school curricula. At the end of the millennium, these interest groups were engaged in a religious war over U.S. public schools.

OTHER INTEREST GROUPS

"Dear Friend," opened a letter I recently received soliciting financial support for an interest group called People for the American Way.

> Seldom in our history has so powerful an organizing network served so extreme an agenda.
>   Founded by televangelist Pat Robertson and his tough-minded political strategist, Ralph Reed, the *Christian Coalition* has developed a grassroots political operation unparalleled in its sophistication.[83]

The sponsor of this widely distributed letter, People for the American Way, was organized in the early 1980s as a liberal group to combat the influence of the religious right on textbooks and school curricula. By 1996, People for the American Way had organized an Internet rapid response network for "mobilizing our supporters to take political action," an "intensive national training program for grassroots organizers facing local challenges from right-wing political groups," a "clergy network, as one way to refute the religious right's claim that they represent all people of faith," and a national resource center for information on the "Religious Right."[84]

While the People for the American Way originally organized to counter the religious right's influence on textbooks and school curricula, and promotion of school prayer, they increased their political activities in the early 1990s when the Christian Coalition was formed and began supporting candidates for local school boards, and local and national political offices. The People for the American Way criticizes the Christian Coalition for the following:

1. "Strident opposition to educational efforts to prevent AIDS and cut teen pregnancies"
2. Support of "government-sponsored organized prayer in the schools"
3. Support of teaching creationism alongside evolution in science classrooms
4. Support of "government sponsored censorship of public broadcasting and the arts"
5. Support of "new curbs on reproductive freedom"
6. Support of "elimination of Head Start and other pre-school programs"
7. "The vilification of gays, lesbians and other minorities."[85]

On the other hand, leaders of the Christian Coalition believe they are counteracting the work of liberal organizations, such as the National Education Association and other labor unions. Ralph Reed, the organizer along with Pat Robertson, of the Christian Coalition, stated, "I see the Christian Coalition as more of an analog to the labor unions or the National Education Association."[86] While organizing the Christian Coalition, Reed said he met many organizers for the National Education Association, "and that's when I really began to understand that they were doing what we were doing, only they were mobilizing the base liberal vote."[87]

The Christian Coalition's position on censorship causes national magazines, such as *Playboy*, to respond with critical editorials. Based on the philosophy of sexual freedom espoused by founder Hugh Hefner, *Playboy* symbolizes the very values that the Christian Coalition believes are undermining America. On the other hand, *Playboy* editors worry about the potential threat of government censorship and the undermining of their libertine views. Writing in the *Playboy* "Forum," David Friedman warns of the attempt by the Christian Coalition to stop sex-education courses and ban books with sexual content. Paraphrasing Roger Evans, litigation director for the Planned Parenthood Federation of America, Friedman states that all attacks on sex education and abortion, and support for school vouchers can be linked to the Christian Coalition. Friedman quotes Evans, "You can trace a direct line back to organized extremists of the religious right. There's a monster out there, and its head is the Christian Coalition."[88]

Friedman warns that the Christian Coalition-backed Parental Rights Act would force local school boards to design specific curricula to meet the desires of the religious right. Friedman quotes Michael Simpson, an attorney for the National Education Association, "Why must school boards kow-tow to parents who belong to fringe groups? That isn't democracy. That's chaos."[89]

While *Playboy* is a profit-making organization, People for the American Way and the Christian Coalition are interest groups with a definite political persuasion that claim tax exemption as nonprofit and nonpartisan interest groups. Larry J. Sabato and Glenn R. Simpson in *Dirty Little Secrets: The Persistence of Corruption in American Politics* document how organizations similar to the Christian Coalition can organize and operate a political campaign while claiming to be nonpartisan. In fact, the Christian Coalition claims that in the 1994 Congressional campaign they were responsible for replacing twenty-five Democrats in the House of Representatives with Republicans. An exit poll taken during the 1994 election found that 33 percent identified themselves as "religious conservatives" who in overwhelming numbers voted for Republicans (70 percent). It was estimated that 40 percent of the votes received by Republicans in 1994 were cast by evangelical Christians and their allies in the Catholic Church.[90]

The effectiveness of the Christian Coalition is a result of its emphasis on grass-roots organizing which during the mid-1990s exerted a tremendous influence on local boards of education. The Christian Coalition inherited a religious-right political base originally organized by Jerry Falwell whose Moral Majority claimed 400,000 members in 1980. Falwell's Moral Majority played an important role in the election of President Ronald Reagan in 1980. In the 1984 election, President Reagan received four-fifths of the votes of the religious right. But scandals associated with Falwell and other evangelical leaders, such as Jim Bakker, destroyed the Moral Majority. The Moral Majority eventually folded in 1989.[91]

Television evangelist Pat Robertson stepped into the political vacuum left by the collapse of the Moral Majority. After a brief excursion into Virginia state politics in the 1970s, Pat Robertson focused his efforts on building a media empire with the creation of the Christian Broadcasting Network and the Family Channel. In 1988, Robertson returned to politics with an unsuccessful bid for the presidency. In 1989, Pat Robertson met conservative activist Ralph Reed and together they organized the Christian Coalition.[92]

Though the Christian Coalition received an initial $67,000 in seed money from the Republican National Committee, it was organized under the internal revenue laws as a tax-exempt "social welfare organization." The articles of incorporation state its goals as "education, the publication and distribution of literature, citizenship mobilization . . . and representation before public bodies."[93]

Under Ralph Reed's leadership, the Christian Coalition established the goals of chartering local affiliates in forty-eight states, selecting precinct captains for 10,000 precincts, and organizing a media program to reach ten million people.[94] While the Christian Coalition supported George Bush in the 1992 presidential election, most of the group's efforts were devoted to support of local candidates, particularly candidates for school boards. Describing the results of the 1992 election, Reed wrote, "Pro-family [Christian Coalition] candidates had won school board elections, religious conservatives had made inroads into the political parties, and our membership was already surging as the Clinton era dawned."[95]

While the Christian Coalition openly gives support to primarily Republican candidates, they continue to claim tax exemption as a nonpartisan organization. They achieve this by relying on the distribution of supposedly nonpartisan voter guides. On October 30, 1994, shortly before the election, evangelical churches across the nation distributed 20 million of the Christian Coalition's voter guides to their parishioners. In addition, voter guides were mailed to Christian Coalition's membership with instructions to reproduce the guide for distribution at polling places.[96]

The voter guides appear nonpartisan by simply listing the voting record of candidates. Of course, these voting records are designed to support Republican candidates and highlight themes important to Christian evangelicals. For instance, Democratic candidate Dan Rostenkowski was listed as "Promoting Homosexuality to Schoolchildren." Obviously, this claim would keep many voters, besides evangelicals, from casting their ballots for Rostenkowski. The guide distorted Rostenkowski's vote for legislation denying the use of federal funds to *promote* homosexuality in school programs. The Christian Coalition based its claim of Rostenkowski supporting the teaching of homosexuality on his lack of support of the Christian Coalition's backed legislation denying federal money to any educational program that *taught about* homosexuality. Similar distortions of Democratic voting records were found throughout the voting guides examined by Larry Sabato and Glenn Simpson.[97]

The bipartisan Federal Election Committee sued Christian Coalition in July 1996 for supporting the election of particular Republican candidates. The group's executive director, Ralph Reed, confidently responded that "the courts will affirm that people of faith have every right to be involved as citizens and voters."[98] The Federal Election Committee accused the Christian Coalition of supporting the 1992 Bush reelection campaign by identifying voters and getting them to the polls, and for distributing 28 million voter guides biased in favor of Bush's reelection. Similar efforts, the Committee charged, were made for Senator Jesse Helms, Oliver North, and Congressman Newt Gingrich. The president of People for the American Way, Carol Shields, applauded the actions of the Federal Election Committee and said, "The F.E.C. is recognizing the obvious: the Christian Coalition's deceptive voter guides and aggressive campaigns are designed to help elect right-wing Republicans to public office."[99]

In 1993, the Christian Coalition made national headlines for organizing a protest against the Rainbow curriculum being introduced into the New York City Public Schools. Much to the outrage of evangelical Christians, a section of the Rainbow curriculum dealt with lesbian and gay families. The New York *Daily News* warned of the "Christian Right's Battle Plan to Seize Control of City."[100] One result was that the media printed versions of the Christian Coalition's local voter guide giving free publicity to its candidates. According to Ralph Reed, the result was victory for 60 percent of the 130 candidates backed by the Christian Coalition and majorities on about ten of the local school boards in the thirty-two school districts of the New York City system.[101]

In 1994, the Christian Coalition began holding seminars for school board members and candidates on how to deal with the teachers' unions and reform local curricula. They encouraged their state organizations to distribute local voters guides for school board elections. The result of the seminars and the distribution of voting guides was, Ralph Reed claimed, widespread victories for Christian Coalition-backed school board candidates. In Reed's words, "The days when school boards were elected solely by labor unions and liberal pressure groups are over forever, and the pro-family community has leveled the playing field."[102]

The Christian Coalition and the People for the American Way are just two examples of many groups interested in influencing voters and educational policies. Along with teachers' unions, the corporate sector, and foundations, these groups exert a tremendous influence on the politics of education and the development of educational policy in the United States.

CONCLUSION: THE DOCTORS OF SPIN

A newspaper headline reads "Lower Test Scores in City Schools." A religious-right group might give a spin that "Lower scores exemplify the lack of instruction in traditional moral values." Another group might spin an interpretation that "Lower scores are the result of low academic standards." Or another interested party might respond: "Poorly qualified teachers are causing test scores to decline." A spokesperson for a teachers' union might put the following spin on the story: "Low teacher salaries make it impossible to keep good teachers, causing test scores to fall." And a union spokesperson might blame: "Inadequate school funding causes a decline in test scores." A spokesperson for a group representing a cultural minority might provide the following spin: "Culturally biased curriculum causes low test scores."

It could be that all or none of the above reasons explain the declining scores. What is important to understand is that each spin is designed to support a particular ideological position in educational politics. I do not want to leave you with a cynical view of political attitudes about education. I do believe that across the political spectrum, from the President to the Christian Coalition, people have sincere beliefs about what should be the content and goals of U.S. public schools.

NOTES

1. Anonymous, *Primary Colors: A Novel of Politics* (New York: Random House, 1996), p. 15.
2. "By Joe Anonymous," *The New York Times* (18 July 1996), p. A1.
3. Ibid., p. 189.
4. Mary Matalin and James Carville with Peter Knobler, *All's Fair: Love, War, and Running for President* (New York: Random House, 1994), p. 431.
5. Ibid., pp. 399–401.

6. Lynn Olsen and Julie Miller, "The 'Education President' at Midterm: Mismatch between Rhetoric, Results?" *Education Week* (9 January 1991), pp. 1, 30.

7. Mark Pitsch, "Polls Confirm Political Role for Education," *Education Week* (19 June 1996), p. 30.

8. Ibid., p. 1.

9. Meredith L. Oakley, *On the Make: The Rise of Bill Clinton* (Washington, D.C.: Regnery Publishing, 1994), p. 275.

10. Ibid., pp. 313, 328, 406.

11. Hillary Rodham Clinton, *It Takes a Village: And Other Lessons Children Teach Us* (New York: Simon and Schuster, 1996). Among other things, this book recounts her involvement in educational and children's issues.

12. Oakley, p. 277.

13. Ibid., p. 291.

14. John E. Yang, "Bush Unveils Education Plan: States, Communities Would Play Major Role in Proposed Innovations," *Compuserve Executive News Service, Washington Post* (19 April 1991). Kenneth J. Cooper, "National Standards at Core of Proposal: Model Schools Envisioned," *Compuserve Executive News Service, Washington Post* (19 April 1991). "Members of Board of New-Schools Corporation, *Education Week* (31 July 1991), p. 24. Lynn Olson and Julie Miller, "The 'Education President' at Midterm: Mismatch between Rhetoric, Results?" *Education Week* (9 January 1991), pp. 1, 30.

15. Governor Bill Clinton and Senator Al Gore, *Putting People First: How We Can All Change America* (New York: Times Books, 1992), p. 84.

16. Ibid., pp. 84–87.

17. Matalin and Carville, p. 201.

18. Ibid.

19. Ibid., pp. 202–203.

20. Ibid., p. 204.

21. Ibid., p. 175.

22. See Clinton and Gore.

23. "Gov. Bill Clinton, Democratic National Convention, New York City, July 16, 1992, Ibid., p. 227.

24. See "Clinton Highlights Schools, Technology," *Compuserve Executive News Service, United Press International* (5/29/96) and Sonya Ross, "Clinton at Princeton," *Compuserve Executive News Service, Associated Press* (6/4/96).

25. See Lawrence Knutson, "Clinton," *Compuserve Executive News Service, Associated Press* (5/8/96), and Sonya Ross, "Clinton-Curfews," *Compuserve Executive News Service, Associated Press* (5/29/96).

26. "Democrats in Congress Introduce 'Families First' Campaign Theme," *The New York Times* (24 June 1996), p. A3, and Alison Mitchell, "Banking on Family Issues, Clinton Seeks Parents' Votes," *The New York Times* (25 June 1996), p. A19.

27. Mitchell, p. A19.

28. Sean Davis, "First Lady Touts Education in Visit," *Compuserve Executive News Service, United Press International* (4/25/96).

29. Hillary Rodham Clinton, *It Takes a Village: And Other Lessons Children Teach Us* (New York: Simon and Schuster, 1996).

30. Ed Gillespie and Bob Schellhas, eds., *Contract With America: The Bold Plan by Rep. Newt Gingrich, Rep. Dick Armey and the House Republicans to Change the Nation* (New York: Random House, 1994).

31. Haley Barbour, *Agenda for America: A Republican Direction for the Future* (Washington, D.C.: Regnery Publishing Inc., 1996), pp. 128-129.
32. Ibid., p. 130.
33. Ibid., pp. 130–145.
34. See Mark Pitsch, "Dole Campaign Weighs Options On Education," *Education Week* (1 May 1996), pp. 1, 18, and Katharine Q. Seelye, "Dole Opposes Spending Billions in Tax Dollars for Education of Illegal Aliens, *The New York Times* (20 June 1996), p. A16.
35. Pitsch, p. 18.
36. Ibid., pp. 1, 18.
37. Terrel Bell, "Educational Policy Development in the Reagan Administration," *Phi Delta Kappan* (March, 1986), pp. 487-493.
38. William J. Bennett, *De-Valuing of America: The Fight for Our Culture and Our Children* (New York: Simon & Schuster, 1992), pp. 19-20.
39. Ibid., p. 23.
40. Ibid., p. 24.
41. Ibid., p. 24.
42. Ibid., p. 26.
43. Ibid., p. 45.
44. Ibid., p. 43.
45. Peter Applebome, "Racial Split On a Board Roils Dallas," *The New York Times* (27 June 1996), p. A14.
46. Ibid., p. A14.
47. See Joel Spring, *American Education, Seventh Edition* (New York: McGraw-Hill, 1996), p. 227.
48. Joan Delfattore, *What Johnny Shouldn't Read: Textbook Censorship in America* (New Haven: Yale University Press, 1992), pp. 61–75.
49. Ibid., p. 90.
50. "Rejected Textbook," *Compuserve Executive News Service, Associated Press* (6/26/96).
51. Applebome, p. A14.
52. A discussion of this early history of school boards can be found in Joel Spring, *The American School 1642-1993, Third Edition* (New York: McGraw-Hill, 1994), pp. 250–260.
53. Ann Bradley, "With Bryant at Helm, NSBA Eyes New Role: Activist Agenda Seeks To Strengthen Boards," *Education Week* (5 June 1996), p. 11.
54. For the classic description of this symbiotic relationship, see Theodore J. Lowi, *The End of Liberalism: The Second Republic of the United States* (New York: Norton, 1979), pp. 22–42.
55. David Stockman, *Triumph of Politic* (New York: Harper & Row, 1988), p. 12.
56. See Maurice Berube, *Teacher Politics: The Influence of Unions* (Westport, Conn.: Greenwood Press, 1988).
57. These figures are provided by Larry J. Sabato and Glenn R. Simpson in *Dirty Little Secrets: The Persistence of Corruption in American Politics* (New York: Times Books, 1996), p. 52. They were originally taken from the National Education Association, *Budget: Fiscal Year 1994-95* (Washington, D.C.: National Education Association, 1995).
58. Carolyn Herrington, "NEA's New President: Perspectives on the Union's Role for the Nineties," *Politics of Education Bulletin* (Winter 1990-91), Vol. 17, No. 2, p. 2.
59. "NEA President," *Compuserve Executive News Service, Associated Press* (7/31/96).
60. Ibid.

61. Oakley, p. 287.
62. Ibid., p. 291.
63. Ibid., p. 290.
64. Ibid., p. 292.
65. "Teachers-Clinton Endorsement," *Compuserve Executive News Service, Associated Press* (7/5/96).
66. Steven Holmes, "School Reform: Business Moves In," *The New York Times* (1 February 1990), p. D2.
67. Ibid., p. D8.
68. Karen DeWitt, "Brought to You by Exxon—School Reform," *The New York Times* (21 July 1991), p. 4E, and Jonathan Weisman, "Educators Watch With a Wary Eye As Business Gains Policy Muscle," *Education Week* (31 July 1991), p. 1.
69. Weisman, p. 1.
70. Millicent Lawton, "Summit Accord Calls for Focus On Standards," *Education Week* (3 April 1996), pp. 1, 14-15.
71. "Text of Policy Statement Issued at National Summit," *Education Week* (3 April 1996), p. 13.
72. Lawton, p. 15.
73. Ibid., p. 14.
74. See Waldemar Nielsen, *The Big Foundations* (New York: Columbia University Press, 1972).
75. Alan Pifer, "When Fashionable Rhetoric Fails," *Education Week* (23 February 1983), p. 24.
76. Task Force on Teaching as a Profession, *A Nation Prepared: Teachers for the 21st Century* (New York: Carnegie Corporation of New York, 1986).
77. Ibid., p. 14.
78. Ibid., p. 14.
79. Ibid., p. 20.
80. Julie Miller and Karen Diegmuller, "Bush Shift Seen On Federal Aid to Teacher Board," *Education Week* (31 July 1991), pp. 1, 22.
81. Ibid., p. 13.
82. For descriptions of the early work of the National Board for Teaching Standards, see Ann Bardley, "Pilot Test Offers a Glimpse of Board's Teacher Assessment," *Education Week* (16 September 1992), pp. 1, 16, and "Pioneers in Professionalism," *Education Week* (20 April 1994), pp. 19–20, 24.
83. I received this letter on June 20, 1996 from the People for the American Way, 2000 M Street, Suite 400, Washington, D.C. 20036. The letter was signed by the organization's president, Carole Shields.
84. Ibid.
85. Ibid.
86. Quoted in Sabato and Simpson, p. 140.
87. Ibid., p. 141.
88. David Friedman, "Forum: Congressional Sex Cops—Washington Hates Sex," *Playboy* (August 1996), p. 39.
89. Ibid., p. 39.
90. Sabato and Simpson, p. 139, and Ralph Reed, *Active Faith: How Christians Are Changing the Soul of American Politics* (New York: The Free Press, 1996), p. 187.
91. Sabato and Simpson, pp. 105–106.
92. Ibid., p. 109.
93. Quoted in Ibid., p. 111.

94. Ibid., pp. 113–115.
95. Reed, p. 154.
96. Sabato and Simpson, p. 128.
97. Ibid., pp. 136–141.
98. Richard Berke, "Lawsuit Says Christian Coalition Gave Illegal Help to Candidates," *The New York Times* (31 July 1996), p. A1.
99. Ibid., p. A13.
100. Ibid., p. 172.
101. Reed, pp. 172–173.
102. Reed, p. 157. Quote is from p. 173.

CHAPTER 2

Sources of Conflict: Power and Knowledge

"You'll be flying in a jet maintained by Tommy," headlined a full page ad in *The New York Times* sponsored by The Business Roundtable, U.S. Department of Education, National Governors' Association, The American Federation of Teachers, and The National Alliance of Business. Promoting higher standards in education, the ad shows a young boy standing on a box gripping a large wrench and staring quizzically into a jet engine.[1] Possibly intended to panic readers about the future safety of flying, the ad warns that aircraft mechanics will "require an advanced knowledge of chemistry, physics, and trigonometry. Unfortunately, very few American children are being prepared to master such sophisticated subjects."[2]

A critical reader should wonder who is really going to benefit from Tommy learning advanced sciences and mathematics, and whether or not future aircraft mechanics will need to know these subjects. The government and business leaders warning of unstated consequences from Tommy not studying science and mathematics have a stake in building a global economy. However, what are the consequences of the global economy to the quality of life and human happiness?

Why would the Business Roundtable and The National Alliance of Business be interested in giving Tommy a technocratic education for a global economy? Economist Paul Krugman stresses that despite recent attempts to change methods for measuring the Consumer Price Index and inflation, "We can't change history with a happy new statistical formula. Whatever the measure, workers are still losing out."[3] Krugman points out that between 1970 and 1994 the percentage of total income of families in the bottom fifth declined from 5.4 percent to 4.2 percent while the share of the top 5 percent increased from 15.6 to 20.[4] The members of the Business Roundtable and The National Alliance of Business were major beneficiaries of the new global economy with, in Krugman's words, "corporate C.E.O.'s, who used to make about 35 times as much as their employees, now mak[ing] 120 times as much or more."[5]

Other comments on the effect of the global economy stress the phenomenon of the rich getting richer and poor getting poorer. Economist David M.

29

Gordon reports that the bottom 80 percent of all U.S. workers between 1979 and 1993 suffered a real decline in hourly wages of 3.8 percent. In contrast, the top 20 percent gained 10.04 percent in hourly wages. During this period blacks and Hispanics suffered a decline in wages of 3.6 percent and 7.9 percent respectively.[6] Michael Lind presents figures that show a 18-percent decline in real wages for production and nonsupervisory workers between 1973 and 1995. During the same period, the real annual income of corporate chief executives increased by 19 percent. Between 1977 and 1990, 1 percent of American families received 79 percent of all income generated in the United States.[7]

Besides growing economic inequalities, there are quality-of-life issues. As multinational corporations leap around the globe in search of cheap labor, they are also looking for governments that will ignore the use of child labor and the destruction of the environment. Rivers, oceans, forests, savannahs, and lakes lay in waste because of global greed.

Similar to others who want to influence education, I would like public schools to prepare students to tackle the following types of questions.

- How do we decrease economic inequalities?
- How do we increase human happiness?
- How do we save the environment from corporate greed?
- What is the best education for making people happy?

CONFLICTS OVER KNOWLEDGE AND POWER

Controlling the flow of ideas and information is a major source of power. What students learn in school could affect their future decisions regarding politics, economics, consumption, and social and moral issues. One example is the way that most governments of the world use their school systems to build loyalty to state policies among their citizens. If the school is effective in building loyalty and patriotism, then citizens will make choices that are congruent with the needs of their particular government. While teaching in Singapore in the 1970s, the writer Paul Theroux recalls criticizing to a businessperson the educational policies of the Singapore government. The businessperson was benefitting from the dictatorial methods of the government. Theroux complained, "Recently the government took all [my students'] scholarships away because studying English literature isn't part of nationbuilding. That was the expression. The government wants economists and scientists. Poetry's an aberration."[8]

A more mundane example is corporate attempts to influence the future consumer decisions by students. In *Giving Kids the Business: The Commercialization of America's Schools,* Alex Molnar devotes a chapter to corporate advertising in schools. This advertising ranges from Campbell's Labels for Education, which offers a film strip and projectors to schools collecting more than 20,000 Campbell soup labels, to Pizza Hut's BOOK IT program which rewards students with free Pizza Hut pizzas for attaining reading goals.[9]

As major disseminators of knowledge, public schools are targets for a variety of groups trying to influence the values, ideas, and information distributed to students. The history of public schooling in the United States is filled with religious objections to teaching evolution, sex education, and secular humanism, and with demands that schools teach a morality based on religious values. Traditionally, unions and businesses have wanted schools to teach ideas that support their respective economic interests. Political leaders want the schools to teach political values that support their positions, while social crusaders want the schools to solve problems ranging from alcoholism to death on the nation's highways by instilling particular values and information in students.

On the other side of the coin, consumers of education want schools to serve their particular needs. Students and parents might want public schools to provide an education that will enhance their ability to protect their political and economic rights, and give them equality of opportunity in the labor market. A major part of the recent history of public schooling involves struggles by dominated racial groups to have schools serve their particular interests. The recent history of the South involves a clash between the white establishment wanting the schools to serve its interests by maintaining a segregated social order and African-Americans seeking to end that social order by gaining equal educational opportunities.

Therefore, the politics of education involves several arenas of conflict. One arena includes those competing to have their ideas distributed through the schools. Another arena involves those wanting schools to teach their children particular values and ideas. Obviously, as with the civil rights movement, these arenas often overlap. The civil rights movement included those wanting schools to teach all children the values of integration and racial tolerance, and those wanting their children to receive an education equal to that received by white students.

The goal of this chapter is to analyze the relationship between power and knowledge, and the sources of conflict in education. I am defining power as the ability to control the actions of other people and the ability to escape from the control of others. Included in this concept of control is the attempt to gain economic advantages. For instance, workers might try to improve their economic advantages by organizing a union for the purposes of bargaining for higher wages, while businesses might try to reduce labor costs by fighting against unionism. In both situations, groups are seeking economic advantages by trying to influence the actions of others.

This definition provides two dimensions to the connection between knowledge and power. In one dimension, the distribution of knowledge (or schooling) is used to control others. In the second dimension, knowledge gives the individual the ability to gain freedom from the control of others.

Conflict over the type of knowledge distributed represents one dimension of the political struggle over schooling. Another, often a related dimension, is conflict over the control of the operations of educational institutions. Sometimes the struggle for control of school operations is directly related to control over the type of knowledge distributed by schools. Currently, the best example is the business community's extension of control over school operations through attempts to dominate local school boards, create local business and school compacts, establish adopt-a-school programs, and influence state and national policy statements. This attempt to control school operations is directly related to the business community's desire for the schools to disseminate knowledge that will give workers skills and attitudes needed by employers, and create a pro-business attitude in the United States. Obviously, most businesses are not interested in the schools disseminating ideas that will foster unionism and demands for better working conditions and wages.

This type of struggle, however, may have little to do with the type of knowledge distributed by schools. For instance, in recent years, teachers' unions and administrative organizations have struggled for control of educational organizations. At the school level, many teachers' committees and school councils are taking over part of the power traditionally exercised by principals. In large educational bureaucracies, particularly in urban areas, conflicts frequently occur for position and power.

Economic struggles are a third type of conflict. Issues involving who will pay and how much will be paid for schooling are obvious causes of friction. Often, the business community wants schools to serve its needs, but it also wants to shift the tax burden from itself to others. People without children frequently want to keep down the costs of schooling, while those with children often want more money for schools without having to pay increased taxes. Of course, the inequitable distribution of educational monies generates political battles. Many citizens and educators are concerned about rich school districts existing side-by-side poor school districts.

Economic issues involve more than funding and taxes. Education is big business. Educators want higher incomes and more money for pet projects. The knowledge industry, which includes publishers of textbooks and tests, wants to maximize its profits. Although nothing currently approaches the textbook scandals of the 1920s when publishers manipulated local school boards to assure adoption of their textbooks, publishers still attempt to influence decisions regarding textbook purchases. In turn, the textbook market influences the content of textbooks and the knowledge distributed in the schools. Of course, publishers of tests have a major economic stake in an educational system that judges its products by performance on standardized tests.

The remainder of this chapter will discuss the relationship between knowledge and power, and the conflicts generated by that relationship. Chapter 3 will discuss conflicts generated by economic issues related to education.

KNOWLEDGE AND POWER

Schools can be used to control others by distributing knowledge that builds allegiance to ruling elites and convincing individuals to accept their subordinate position in society and in existing power relations. Also, as often happened, knowledge can be presented for getting a job and building a career, while, at the same time, denying individuals an education that would increase their ability to raise critical questions about power relationships. In addition, institutional relations can be used to support power relationships. For instance, segregated education in the South was used to keep African-Americans "in their place." On the other side of the coin, knowledge, and the institutional mechanisms for its distribution, can be a means for understanding how to free oneself from control and protect oneself from economic exploitation.

The following hypothetical situation depicts the possible use of schooling to gain advantages for religious and cultural groups. Imagine a totalitarian nation composed of several cultural, linguistic, and religious groups. Although diversity exists in the nation, the ruling elite share a common culture, language, and religion. The ruling elite tries to perpetuate its political power by allowing only its culture, religion, and language to be taught in government-operated schools. Schoolchildren are left with the impression that the elite culture, language, and religion are superior to all others in the nation.

In addition, children of the elite are more successful in school because their home culture and language are the same as the school's. To further the sense of superiority among elite children, the schools claim to give everyone equal access to either a vocational curriculum or a college preparatory curriculum. Because their language and culture differ from that of the schools, non-elite groups do poorly and, as a result, are tracked into the vocational curriculum. Children of non-elite groups believe they are intellectually inferior to elite children because they are in vocational studies and, consequently, condemned to spend their lives in the lower levels of the economic system.

In this totalitarian state, the political content of the curriculum includes patriotic exercises, a national history, and national literature that emphasize the role of the elite. In addition, the curriculum touts the superiority of the country's economic and political systems and proclaims the inferiority of other political and economic systems.

This state of affairs might be difficult to maintain because knowledge carries with it the seeds of rebellion. In fact, one could argue that the best way to maintain political control is to deny schooling to all children except those of the elite. Today, this would be difficult because industry requires educated workers. A modern totalitarian state cannot maintain its economic system if it excludes large sections of the population from the educational system.

Any attempts to maintain political control through schooling carries with it the potential for rebellion. Increased knowledge and mental ability breed resistance to control. As Henry Giroux argues, pockets of resistance severely hinder attempts to dominate.[10]

The educational practices of our hypothetical totalitarian state contain many forms of control that, when exercised in real situations, spark conflict around the world. For instance, educational conflict often occurs when several ethnic or religious groups exist within a political system. Elite groups will impose their culture and religion in the schools to establish their cultural superiority and, more important, to destroy the cohesiveness of other cultural groups. Cultural groups that lack cohesiveness are unable to form organizations opposing the ruling elite.

KNOWLEDGE AND ECONOMIC POWER

Some people will use knowledge to improve their economic situation; others will attempt to control people for economic exploitation. This is an important issue when considering the education of children from poor families and from dominated racial and ethnic groups. For instance, economic issues for the poor include problems of employment and distribution of national income.

Education for employment can occur in an economy where the real wage for workers is declining and their percentage of the economic pie is remaining the same or declining. Obviously, these conditions are advantageous for businesses that want to maintain or increase profits by reducing labor costs. Under these conditions, the questions can legitimately be asked,

- Is the public school system teaching the knowledge and skills needed to help workers stop the erosion of their share of the economic pie?
- Is the school system helping people both to gain employment and to protect themselves from economic exploitation?
- Is the public school system teaching African-American students the knowledge and skills needed to end the disparity between white and African-American family income and wealth?

These questions are directly related to the historical debate over the education of children from poor families. One position in this debate is that poverty is a product of social and economic conditions; therefore, the elimination of poverty depends on educating active citizens who will work to change those conditions. In differing forms, Workingmen's Parties during the common school movement made this argument, labor unions during the nineteenth and early twentieth centuries, progressive educators led by John Dewey, social reconstructionists during the 1930s, and most recently by educational philosopher Paulo Freire.[11]

In sharp contrast, many members of the business community and conservative educational leaders in the nineteenth and twentieth centuries argued, and continue to argue, that poverty can be eliminated by giving the children of the poor an education that will help them to fit into existing economic and political relationships. This argument has persisted from the common-school movement in the 1830s to the current development of compacts between urban school systems and private industry councils. The emphasis in this argument is on giving students the knowledge and social habits to meet the needs of the business community.

The debate about the role of schooling in ending poverty reflects differing concepts about what schools should be teaching and how students should be treated. For instance, the argument for political activism stresses (a) the imparting of knowledge that will help individuals protect their political and economic rights and (b) the socialization of students for political participation. During the common-school movement, the Workingmen's Parties campaigned for public schools so that future workers could gain the knowledge necessary for protecting themselves from exploitation by the rich. Today, Paulo Freire argues that what students learn and how they learn makes a difference whether or not they are economically exploited and politically disenfranchised. On the other side of the coin, during the common-school movement the advocates of the Lancasterian system argued that drill and routine in schooling were important in shaping the behavior of students to meet the needs of the workplace.[12] Advocates of closer business–school relationships are currently making similar arguments. In these arguments, stress is placed on the need for the workplace to decide the curriculum and the socialization.

Another economic aspect of using education as an instrument of power is the attempt to control entrance into the labor market by a differentiated curriculum that sorts students according to their future destination in it. Often, the separation of students into various curriculum tracks reinforces and perpetuates social-class and cultural differences.

Throughout the twentieth century in the United States and other countries, students from lower income families have been channeled into vocational and technical curricula, while they have channeled students from upper income families into college-preparatory curricula. If a relationship exists between social class and political power, such differentiation does not give lower income students the knowledge required to exercise political power. For upper-class students, differentiation guarantees continued position in the political elite. In addition, educational credentials dispensed by a school system with a differentiated curriculum sort lower income students into the bottom rungs of the labor market and higher income students into the top rungs.

The debate over differentiated curricula has continued through the twentieth century. In the 1980s Mortimer Adler attacked the idea, arguing that separate curricula were undemocratic because they deny equal access to knowledge for all students. He argued that students channeled into vocational studies receive an education that has less political and economic value than that received by students preparing for college. According to Adler, a truly democratic education gives everyone the same fund of knowledge and intellectual skills.[13]

In contrast to Adler's call for a truly democratic education, Oregon's Governor Barbara Roberts signed a bill in July 1991 to end the traditional high school education at the tenth grade. The Oregon legislation even rejects the concept of the comprehensive high school, which was designed to provide students in separate curriculum tracks with a common social experience. Under the Oregon legislation, students receive a certificate of initial master at the conclusion of the tenth grade. Students are then separated into entirely different education programs, in which one group receives vocational training under influence of business organizations and the other group is sent to a college-preparatory school. Concerning the power of private foundations, it should be noted that Oregon's legislation is based directly on the recommendations of the Carnegie Corporation-sponsored National Center on Education and the Economy.[14]

In short, to maximize profits, businesses try to influence school systems to assure that they socialize students to be compliant workers, receive the skills needed for the workplace, are sorted according to the needs of the labor market, and adopt a pro-business attitude. Still, students can learn how to resist economic exploitation, develop the ability to analyze the actions of business critically, and gain skills to rise in the labor market.

POWER AND CULTURE

Besides the struggle over economic advantages, issues of knowledge and power are related to conflicts over culture. As I am using the term, *culture* includes both historical traditions, religion, literature, and art, and a group's beliefs regarding acceptable behaviors, manners, styles of dress, accents, and patterns of speech.

For instance, consider the use of education for creating cultural differences that are directly related to the exercise of one group's power over another. Historically, the collegiate education of "gentlemen" was often used to distinguish one social class from another. In the eighteenth and nineteenth centuries, the liberal education provided by elite schools such as Harvard, Yale, and Princeton was rooted in the study of Greek, Latin, and classical literature. Except certain professions such as theology and law, the study of classical languages and literature was of little practical value. Nevertheless, knowledge of these areas did serve an important social function: dividing social classes. Those possessing an elite college education, no matter how impractical, were considered "gentlemen" and socially superior to those who did not possess this body of knowledge.

An important dimension of creating a sense of social superiority is how others internalize a belief in their own inferiority. Consider this issue in the framework of the previous discussion about the study of Greek and Latin in the eighteenth and nineteenth centuries. A person who was taught that a collegiate education creates a superior human but who was never able to achieve that level of learning would tend to believe that she or he is inferior to the college-educated.

The same feelings of superiority and inferiority extend to manners, accents, dress, and patterns of speech. A working-class person who a wealthy Park Avenue family invites to a dinner might feel uncomfortable because of a lack of knowledge about what the Park Avenue crowd might consider proper dress and table manners. This lack of knowledge can easily slip into a feeling of social inferiority.

Furthermore, this working-class person might worry about carrying on conversation with dinner companions who probably do not share the same set of experiences to serve as reference points. A feeling of social inferiority might be caused by the difficulty of understanding references to these shared experiences. In addition, this working-class person might feel inferior because of his or her accent and speech patterns.

In the United States, the children of the very wealthy share a similar set of educational experiences that gives them common manners, conversational points of reference, accents, and speech patterns. The most important part of this shared educational experience is attendance at secondary boarding schools, the most prestigious of which are in New England and associated with the Episcopal Church. At the top of the list of secondary boarding schools are Saint Paul's, Saint Mark's, Groton, Middlesex, Saint George's, Phillips Exeter, and Phillip Academy. A major emphasis in these schools is on building character through a shared set of experiences. The focus on character training results in graduates who have the same set of cultural attributes. Domhoff quotes one upper-class woman: "Where I went to boarding school, there were girls from all over the country, so I know people from all over. It's helpful when you move to a new city and want to get invited into the local social clubs."[15]

Graduates of these elite boarding schools usually attend prestigious private universities and colleges such as Harvard, Princeton, Yale, and smaller Ivy League schools. At these institutions, graduates of boarding schools tend to create their own social world that is separate from that of other students. Sociologist C. Wright Mills wrote,

> "That is why in the upper social classes, it does not by itself mean much merely to have a degree from an Ivy League college. That is assumed: the point is not Harvard, but which Harvard? By Harvard, one means Porcelain, Fly, or A.D.: by Yale, one means Zeta Psi or Fence or Delta Kappa Epsilon: by Princeton, Cottage, Tifer, Cap and Gown or Ivy."[16]

Of course, this shared educational experience and common culture carries over to the workplace. Employment in the upper echelons of leading banking, investment, legal, and corporate firms is made much easier for those with the correct cultural background and friends.

Those who attempt to change their cultural patterns to gain advantages in the employment market are faced with the psychological dilemma of possibly branding their cultural heritage as inferior. Traditionally in the United States, this has been a problem for immigrant groups and for dominated groups, such as African-Americans, Native Americans, and Hispanics.

POWER AND LANGUAGE

In late 1996 a raging debate broke out when the Oakland, California school system announced that it was going to apply for federal bilingual education funds to teach Ebonics. The term *Ebonics* was used to identify what had been traditionally called *black English* as a separate language rather than as a dialect of English. At one level, the action could be seen simply as a method to get extra federal support for the financially strapped Oakland schools. On the other hand, the action could be considered a legitimate attempt to help African-American students make the transition from black English to standard English.

The immediate reaction of many white politicians and some African-American academics was to consider the move as an attempt to legitimize black English and, consequently, hurt the future economic opportunities of African-American students. The Clinton administration refused to recognize Ebonics as a separate language. This created the interesting situation of politicians defining what is a language and what is a dialect.

The incident over Ebonics highlights the political and social issues of language. Writing in the ARTS section of *The New York Times,* Margo Jefferson asks, "Why . . . are we treating a cultural controversy that has everything to do with class and social status as if it had only to do with race?"[17] As she shows, no one objects to black English when a speaker of standard English uses it as a form of chic slang or when musical performers use it. In fact, when used as a clearly calculated style, it can earn a great deal of money for artistic innovators.

However, Jefferson writes, the issues change when talking about poor black students wanting to achieve social mobility. "How you talk," she argues, "is either a dead giveaway or a flawless disguise. Grammar, syntax and accent allow or forbid people to patronize and penalize you on the ground of where you came from."[18] She claims that schools have always been important for changing lower class dialects. Nevertheless, now the real problem, she argues, is how financially underfunded school systems are going to achieve this goal. "Speaking practically," she writes, "the middle and upper classes of all races will always look down on those who speech reads as strictly lower or working class."[19]

In another example, consider the community turmoil caused by the 1990 creation of a bidialectical program for African-American children in the suburban Washington school system of Silver Springs, Maryland. A letter from the school urged parents of elementary school-age students to send their children to an after-school program to learn to move between black English and standard English and speak them both successfully. The intention of the program was to prepare African-American children for college and good jobs. Trying to avoid any implication that the program would demean black dialect, parents were assured that the school was not in the business of cultural eradication.[20]

This assurance did not stop an outburst of protest from some African-American community members. If anything, one African-American mother criticized, "they could have done something for the white kids, geared toward their slang when they say 'That's awesome,' or 'That's radical.'" Another parent called the program insulting because it singled out particular students.

MULTICULTURAL, BICULTURAL, AND ETHNOCENTRIC EDUCATION

There are two important aspects to the discussion of multicultural, bicultural, and ethnocentric education. One aspect, which will be dealt within later chapters, is the political action that was required to put these issues on the agenda of public schools. The second aspect, which I will deal within this section, is how these educational movements can be understood in the framework of the relationship between culture and power.

I am defining multicultural education as the effort to teach children about a variety of cultures for maintaining social harmony and integrating immigrant groups into American society. Bicultural education, as I am using the term, means teaching children their cultural background and the culture of white society. The term is most often applied to educational programs in which Hispanic, African-American, and Native American children are taught their cultural heritage and simultaneously are taught the cultural attributes required by the mainstream economy. The general purpose of these programs is to strengthen the self-esteem of children, while giving them tools for advancing in American society. Ethnocentric education focuses on instruction in a particular culture. The most talked-about ethnocentric educational programs are the Afrocentric ones. The general goal of ethnocentric programs is improving educational achievement, empowering students, and maintaining cultural traditions.

Multicultural education originated from concerns with the integration of American society and the social problems caused by increased immigration. As an extension of the integrationist thrust of the civil rights movement of the 1950s and 1960s, the purpose of multicultural education is to provide equality of opportunity in the existing economic system by reducing racial and cultural prejudice. Cynics might argue that multicultural education is a method of maintaining the power of socially dominant groups by curbing the animosity against upper-class groups often generated by prejudice and intolerance. In addition, cynics might argue, multicultural education perpetuates the myth that everyone has a fair chance to rise to the top of the socioeconomic structure. In other words, multicultural education maintains existing social relationships by reducing the threat of social conflict caused by racial and cultural tensions.

Multicultural education is also promoted for integrating immigrants into mainstream society and the economic system. Beginning in the 1960s, immigration laws were changed to favor (a) those with skills needed by the American economy, (b) political refugees, and (c) those with families already in the United States. During the 1990s, it is predicted, 5 million children of immigrants are expected to enter American public schools. In 1991, it was estimated that there were 3.5 million children from homes where English was not the first language and that more than 150 languages were represented in public schools across the country.[21] In this climate, multicultural education maintains existing social and economic arrangements and eases the transition for immigrant workers.

The problem of immigrant labor is not peculiar to the United States. Currently, multicultural education is gaining importance in many countries with the development of an international labor force. Throughout the world, people are migrating in search of employment. Guest workers in Europe, the migration of workers to the oil-producing parts of the Middle East, and the large migration of foreign workers to the United States and Canada are part of this pattern. Economist Robert Reich argues that just as international corporations search for manufacturing sites with the lowest labor costs, many workers are moving to areas with higher wages.[22]

Because of concerns about the internationalization of the labor force, multicultural education is evolving in conflicting directions. First, multicultural education is being considered part of job training. The recent report of the Secretary of Labor's Commission on Achieving Necessary Skills defines the work skills that should be taught in the schools. For example, the report states the following as a skill for the food-service industry: "Interpersonal. Participate in a staff meeting with a multicultural group of workers."[23]

Of course, immigrant labor threatens the status of some groups already in the United States. In the late nineteenth and early twentieth centuries, African-Americans, Hispanics, and Native Americans watched from the sidelines as immigrant labor from southern and eastern Europe was used in building industrial America. In the 1990s, these same groups may be forced to wait on the sidelines as new waves of immigrants move into the labor force.

From this perspective, easing the transition of immigrant workers might not be in the interest of African-Americans, Hispanics, and Native Americans. The use of immigrant labor at this point might draw attention away from educational and social programs designed to improve the conditions of dominated groups in the United States. In other words, immigration policies might result in the perpetuation of existing economic conditions among dominated groups. Rather than benefitting dominated groups, multicultural education, at least in this argument, might be a mechanism for keeping dominated groups in their existing places in the social and economic structure.

Bicultural education, on the other hand, is conceived of as a method for empowering dominated groups.[24] Originating in bilingual education programs for Hispanic children, bicultural education is designed to help children succeed in the mainstream economy while also affirming and teaching about their cultural heritage. In trying to achieve a balance between cultural preservation and achieving equality of opportunity, bicultural programs attempt to have the best of both worlds.

In bicultural programs, students such as Mexican-Americans learn about their cultural heritage while being taught other subjects in their native language. In transitional bilingual programs, the use of Spanish (for Mexican-American students) in the classroom serves as a bridge to learning English and is decreased as students improve their skills in English. In maintenance bilingual programs, a continuing emphasis is placed on learning Spanish even after proficiency increases in English.

The purpose of maintaining instruction in Spanish and emphasizing students' cultural background is to overcome a feeling of cultural inferiority. It is hoped that student self-esteem and achievement will improve because of bicultural instruction, and that students will feel less hostile toward public schools. Ideally, the decline in feelings of hostility about public schools will result in undercutting the culture of resistance. In other words, Hispanic students will no longer feel that school is a hostile environment and will not develop a culture to resist its demands.

As I discuss in more detail in the next section on language, some people feel that bicultural and bilingual education threaten the dominant English-speaking culture of the United States. For those whose background is in the dominant English-speaking culture, promotion and recognition of another culture threaten their advantages in the labor market. Since the English-speaking culture is dominant in the economic system, people raised in an English-speaking culture have clear advantages over people from other cultures. In addition, recognition that another culture might have equal value with the dominant English-speaking culture threatens the myths of cultural inferiority used to justify economic exploitation. For example, if Mexican-American culture is given equal value when compared with the dominant English culture, then it is difficult to perpetuate myths such as Mexican Americans are basically lazy, and the only type of work they are fit for is migrant farm labor.

Ethnocentric education takes the arguments made for bicultural education one step further. Advocates of ethnocentric education argue that empowering students and curtailing of a resistance culture can only be achieved through a curriculum focused on the students' cultural heritage. In 1990, similar proposals in Detroit, Minneapolis, and New York quickly followed a proposal for the establishment of an Afrocentric school for black males in Milwaukee. In February 1991, a Hispanic-centered school was proposed for the Denver public school system.

The advocacy group Latin American Research and Service Agency advanced the proposal for a Hispanic school. The executive director of the organization, Audrey Alvardo, argues, "What our children need is a school that works, and they need it now." In Denver, Hispanic students are the fastest-growing part of the school population, with nearly 40 percent of the students. Hispanic students have the highest dropout rate of any ethnic student population and are among the lowest-scoring students on college entrance examinations. "Not only do Hispanic youths enter school slightly behind their white counterparts," says Alvardo, "but they continue to fall further and further behind as they go through school."[25]

The proposals for Hispanic and Afrocentric schools are designed to redirect resistance cultures and build student self-esteem. The inspiration for ethnocentric schools comes from the work of Jawanza Kunjufu, president of the Chicago-based African American Images. African American Images serves as a publishing house for Kunjufu's books, and other books and videos focused on the teaching of African-American culture. Also offered by African American Images is a model curriculum called Self-Esteem through Culture Leads to Academic Excellence (SETCLAE). The stated goals of the curriculum are to "improve academic achievement," "improve discipline and school atmosphere," and "transmit racial pride and enhance the students' knowledge of culture and history and its significance to contemporary living."[26]

Kunjufu argues that for most African-American students, being successful in school means acting white. Kunjufu exemplifies this situation with an exchange within a group of African-American students about two other academically successful African-American students:

> "Girl, she thinks she's something, making the honor roll."
>   "I know, she's beginning to act like Darryl. They both think they're white, joining the National Honor Society."[27]

One effect of American slavery, Kunjufu argues, was the public characterization of Africans as intellectually inferior. The expectation of intellectual inferiority eroded the confidence in academic success among black youth. In addition, having been stripped of their cultural heritage, slaves internalized white ideals about beauty and culture. Consequently, later black resistance to domination involved the creation of a culture that opposed certain white ideals. Kunjufu found that when black teenagers are asked, How do you act black? They respond with cultural issues. From their perspective, being black is speaking black English, listening to rap and rhythm and blues, and attending parties; and being white is speaking standard English, listening to rock and classical music, and going to museums.

Kunjufu found the same pattern among black college students. Recalling his own years in college, Kunjufu felt almost ostracized by his fellow black students when he joined the college debate society. What saved him from cultural exclusion was being an athlete, liking to dance, and "talking the talk." On the other hand, white students made comments such as, "You're different," and "You're not like the rest of them." Out of the 1,000 African-Americans in his entering class, only 254 graduated. In Kunjufu's words, "Many of them flunked out while pledging, roller skating, partying, talking in the cafeteria or dormitories, playing ball or records, and getting high."[28]

In this concern about the development of a self-destructive resistance culture among African-American students, Kunjufu advocates the teaching of an Afrocentric curriculum for breaking cultural stereotypes. He wants African-American students to know that Africans have a long history of learning and creativity. He wants them to understand that within African cultural traditions, it is all right to be black and to be an intellectual. He wants them to realize that studying hard and learning is not being "white," but follows the best traditions of African culture.

In addition, he wants African-American students to understand that there is an Afrocentric way of viewing the world that is different from a Eurocentric view. Molefi Kete Asante, chairperson of the Department of African American Studies at Temple University and a proponent of an Afrocentric curriculum, argues that Afrocentricity is a transforming power involving five levels of awareness. During the first four levels of this transforming experience, individuals come to understand that African people around the world share their personality, interests, and concerns. Afrocentricity is achieved in the fifth level, when people struggle against foreign cultures that dominate their minds. At this stage, "An imperative of will powerful, incessant, alive, and vital, moves to eradicate every trace of powerlessness. Afrocentricity is like rhythms; it dictates the beat of your life."[29]

By purging white-culture images of African-Americans as stupid and pow-
erless, African-American students can, according to the arguments of those
advocating Afrocentricity, gain a new image of themselves as a people of ability
and power. In this sense, Afrocentricity is considered a curriculum of empowerment. With it, students lose the lenses that filter the world through a white,
Eurocentric perspective and replace it with a set of Afrocentric lenses.

Therefore, ethnocentric curricula in the United States creates a cultural
battle at two levels. At the first level, ethnocentric curriculum is an attempt to
give equal value to different cultural traditions. At the second level, it means
purging a Eurocentric view of the world from Hispanic and Afrocentric children's minds and replacing it with a view of the world that is Hispanic or
African-American. The purpose of this cultural battle is to empower Hispanic
and African-American children to believe that they can succeed in the world.
From this perspective, getting ahead in the economic and social system is not a
matter of being white, but rather learning to believe in oneself and one's cultural traditions.

An important aspect of culture is language. In countries with diverse
language groups, language policies are a common means of maintaining
political power. The events of June 16, 1976, in the township of Soweto, South
Africa, provide an example of how language policies in the schools can lead
to political violence. The South African government, as part of its general
policy of dominating blacks, decreed the use of the white Afrikaans language
in black schools. Following the decree, thousands of black students protested
in the streets. In response, South African police shot a 13-year-old black boy,
causing an uprising and motivating an entire generation of black students to
become radical.[30]

Language policies, particularly as pertain to the issue of bilingual education, are also a source of conflict in the United States. The major conflict is
between the Hispanic community, which believes that bilingual education
strengthens its cultural identity, and groups wanting to make English the official language of the United States. Hispanic leaders believe a strong ethnic
identity will increase their political power. Furthermore, it is believed that bilingual education linked to bicultural education will achieve the goals of empowerment discussed in the previous section.

The two major U.S. political parties are divided over bilingual education.
Traditionally, organized ethnic groups, including Hispanics, have been a strong
force in the Democratic Party. In contrast, Republicans have felt threatened by
some organized ethnic groups. Consequently, bilingual education became a
major target of attack during the Republican administrations of the 1980s and
1990s. In fact, some members of the Republican Party joined a movement
opposing bilingual education and supporting the adoption of English as the
official language of the United States. Making English the official language
would weaken organized ethnic politics and ensure the continued domination
of the majority culture. The organization U.S. English led the movement for
making English the official language, founded in 1983 by S. I. Hayakawa, a
former Republican senator.

In 1986, in reaction to the Reagan administration, the National Association of Bilingual Education increased its political activities and intensified its public relations efforts. Concerning Hayakawa and U.S. English, Gene T. Chavez, the president of the Association of Bilingual Education, warned, "Those who think this country can only tolerate one language" were motivated more by political concerns than by educational concerns. At the same meeting, the incoming president of the organization, Chicago school administrator Jose Gonzalez, attacked the Reagan administration and the Department of Education for entering an "unholy alliance with right-wing groups opposing bilingual education groups such as U.S. English, Save Our Schools, and the Heritage Foundation."[31]

Within the Reagan administration, Secretary of Education William Bennett attempted to reduce support for bilingual education by appointing opponents of it to the government's National Advisory and Coordinating Council on Bilingual Education. The new appointees preferred immersing non-English-speaking children in the English language, rather than teaching them in a bilingual context. In addition, the new appointees favored giving more power to local officials to decide programs. Of course, such a policy would undercut the power that the Hispanic community gained by working with the federal government. Originally, Hispanics turned to the federal government for assistance because they lacked power in local politics.[32]

One of Bennett's appointees to the National Advisory and Coordinating Council on Bilingual Education, Rosalie Pedalino Porter, director of Bilingual and English as a Second Language programs in Newton, Massachusetts, wrote a book on the controversy with the descriptive title, *Forked Tongue: The Politics of Bilingual Education*. For Porter, the politics of bilingual education involves political struggles within the educational establishment and the broader issue of cultural politics. Like other Bennett appointees, Porter rejects bilingual education that is also bicultural. She believes that language training should be geared toward giving the student the language tools necessary for equal opportunity within the mainstream economy. But, unlike the more conservative of Bennett's appointees, she does not support attempts to make English the official language of the United States.

Porter's conclusions regarding bilingualism are a reflection of her broader views on cultural politics. She argues against bilingualism that is also bicultural because it segregates minority communities with the least power. In her words, "The critical question is whether education policies that further the cultural identity of minority groups at the same time enable minority children to get the knowledge and skills to attain social and economic equality."[33] Her argument represents the position of those who want a multicultural society integrated into the dominant U.S. socioeconomic system. Porter does not consider arguments regarding the necessity of overcoming resistance cultures among students or to arguments that empowerment involves recapturing cultural traditions that are different from those of the dominant white culture. Consequently, her support of language instruction designed for integration into mainstream society reflects an acceptance of existing social relationships.

Critics of Porter's position might charge her with not understanding the plight of dominated groups such as African-Americans, Native Americans, and Hispanics. They might argue that an immigrant child from China or Vietnam comes from cultural traditions that do not reject formal education because it represents white domination. These immigrant children might enter programs focused on teaching English and mainstream American culture, and graduate with the ability to compete in the economic system.

On the other hand, dominated groups such as African-Americans, Native Americans, and Hispanics know that educational success does not necessarily mean economic success because racism plays a role in the distribution of economic rewards. In the 1980s, black men with four years of college earned on average only 72.6 percent of what white males with four years of college earned. In addition, black and white men were unevenly distributed through the labor market. The distribution of white men with at least four years of high school was 53 percent in white-collar jobs, 37.6 percent in blue-collar jobs, and 6.5 percent in service jobs; meanwhile, for black men with the same level of education, the distribution was 32.6 percent, 51.9 percent, and 14.6 percent, respectively.[34]

Therefore, critics of Porter might claim that she can maintain her argument against bicultural bilingualism because she does not consider arguments about the potential inherent racism of white American culture, the difficulty children from dominated groups have identifying with institutions considered "white," the low level of self-esteem created by the dominant culture, and the resistance to institutions and programs considered being based on "white" culture.

On the other hand, Porter opposes the efforts of U.S. English because they are provocative, based on anti-immigrant attitudes, and threaten special programs for language minority groups. She quotes a statement by Richard Rodriguez as representing her position on attempts to amend the Constitution to make English the official language:

> What bothers me most about defenders of English comes down to a matter of tone. Too shrill. Too hostile. Too frightened. They seem to want to settle the issue of America's language, once and for all. But America must risk uncertainty if it is to remain true to its immigrant character. . . . We must remind the immigrant that there is an America already here. But we must never forget that we are an immigrant country, open to change.[35]

Despite opposition from civil rights organizations and professional organizations including the National Association of Bilingual Education, the National Council of Teachers of English, the Linguistics Society of America, and the Modern Language Association, efforts to make English the official language continue at state and national levels. Nebraska made English its official state language in 1923, followed by Illinois in 1969. In 1978, Hawaii made English and Hawaiian its official state languages. Indicative of the concerns of the 1980s, between 1984 and 1988 fourteen other states made English their official language.[36]

The major target of those supporting English as the official language is the ballot. Extensions to the 1965 Voting Rights Act grant citizens the right to voting information in their native languages. In communities where 5 percent or more of the population speak languages other than English, voting material must be provided in those languages. Supporters of English-language amendments argue that voters should be fluent in English and that naturalization procedures require passing a test given in English. Therefore, from their standpoint, ballots and election material should be kept in English. On the other hand, opponents argue that election materials should be presented in native languages so that all groups will be on equal footing. And, as I suggested before, the issue of voter participation is directly related to the strengths of both Republicans and Democrats.

Besides the issue of political power, language is a cultural issue. One's cultural perspective is directly related to one's attitudes regarding making English the official language. This connection is exemplified by Humberto Garza's comment regarding a requirement that Los Altos, California city employees speak only English on the job: "Those council people from Los Altos should be made to understand that they are advocating their law in occupied Mexico. . . . They should move back to England or learn how to speak the language of Native Americans."[37]

RELIGION

Religion is often part of attempts at cultural domination through schooling. Even in countries with a single religion, differing sects will attempt to impose their point of view in the schools. For instance, a historic struggle continues in Israel between Orthodox and liberal Jews. At the heart of this struggle is the effort to gain political control of the Israeli government. Orthodox Jews, in contrast to liberal Jews, wish to impose stricter standards of morality. In 1986 Orthodox Jews burned bus stops to protest a revealing bathing-suit advertisement. In response, liberal Jews attacked Orthodox houses of worship. Some Jews complained that the intolerance of Orthodox Jews was causing many liberal Jews to emigrate to the United States.

In response to charges that they were responsible for driving young Jews out of the country, Orthodox Jews claimed that the real problem was the lack of moral teaching in the elementary and high school curriculum. In a letter to *The New York Times Magazine*, R. Ben-Chaim of the Orthodox KACH movement in Israel blamed secular Jews for creating a school curriculum lacking traditional Jewish values. He linked the migration of young Jews to the United States to the teaching of materialistic values in schools. The answer to this religious and political struggle, he wrote, "is to infuse the Israeli educational system with a hearty dose of traditional Judaism."[38]

Religion is a major source of political conflict in the United States as well. Problems regarding culture and religion date to the beginning of the common-school movement in the nineteenth century. Carl Kaestle argues that a primary reason for establishing the common-school system was to ensure that the Protestant republican culture would prevail over the Catholic immigrant culture. Resisting this attempt at religious and cultural domination, Catholics organized a system of schools that more closely reflected the cultural values of new immigrant groups.[39] Throughout the nineteenth century and into the twentieth, both Catholics and Protestants often called U.S. public schools "Protestant schools."

By the middle of the twentieth century, political elites were no longer primarily Protestant but included a mixture of religious groups. Consequently, there was a growing movement to remove all religious content from the schools and achieve religious neutrality. In part, these changes in attitude resulted in the school prayer and Bible decisions by the U.S. Supreme Court in the 1960s. These decisions declared it unconstitutional to read the Bible in schools for religious purposes and to conduct school prayers.[40]

The Supreme Court decisions infuriated some religious groups. Historically correct, these religious groups argued that American public schools had always emphasized Christian morality. But the Court's decisions symbolized that Protestant ideology dominated the ruling culture of America. The election of President John F. Kennedy in 1960 showed not only that Catholics had joined the ranks of the political elite, but also that public statements on morality were losing their religious tone and becoming increasingly secular.

The result was a sharp political reaction from Protestant fundamentalist groups, who saw themselves displaced from the dominant American culture. These groups attacked the public schools in the 1970s for teaching secular humanism. According to Protestant fundamentalists, secular humanism taught individuals to rely on their own ability to interpret human events and make decisions, as opposed to relying on the authority of God.

While some Protestant groups abandoned the public schools in the 1970s, others joined a political campaign to restore traditional Christian values in the schools. The Protestants who abandoned the public schools established private Christian schools, which in the 1970s became the fastest-growing private-school system in America.[41]

The political goals of the campaign to restore traditional Christian values in the public schools included increasing parental control of schooling, amending the Constitution to allow school prayer, and expelling all signs of secular humanism from the public school curriculum. Eventually, these groups supported the Republican Party because President Reagan promised to restore school prayer and support tuition tax-credit legislation that would provide funding for private Christian schools.

Religious groups have also campaigned to expunge immorality from textbooks. With claims that public schools are teaching an anti-religious philosophy of secular humanism, Christian fundamentalists have attacked textbook publishers and school officials. Exemplifying the tensions over charges of secular humanism in textbooks, a group of parents in West Virginia's Hawkins

County School System charged the 1983 edition of the Holt, Rinehart & Winston reading series with creating the possibility that after reading the books, "a child might adopt the views of a feminist, a humanist, a pacifist, an anti-Christian, a vegetarian, or an advocate of a 'one-world government.'" The protest resulted in violence and a series of court cases.[42]

In 1990, Holt, Rinehart & Winston was attacked for its 4-year-old reading series entitled *Impressions*. The books in the series contain stories by outstanding writers, including Lewis Carroll, A. A. Milne, Laura Ingalls Wilder, and C. S. Lewis. Leading the attack were the religious-right organizations Focus on Family, Christians for Educational Excellence, the National Association of Christian Educators, and the Western Center for Law and Religious Freedom. These groups object to both the realism and the fantasy in the stories: the realism for being depressing and violent, and the fantasy for satanic references.[43]

Controversy over the series erupted in late September 1990, when *Citizen*, a publication of Focus on Family, issued a list of objections to the series. The controversy spread to North Carolina and Georgia, where state textbook-advisory committees advised against adopting the series. Karen LaBarr, a parent, testified about the series before the Georgia textbook-advisory committee, "The issue is a pervasive negativeness and pervasive weirdness that just doesn't need to be there." On the other side, Donald Fowler, issues director for People for the American Way, warned that controversies would increase when you give "real literature that might expose them to potentially controversial topics in contrast to the pablum of 'See Spot run.'"[44]

In summary, religion, like other aspects of culture, is often related to struggles over power. These struggles extend into the educational system as various groups compete for dominance by trying to control the ideas distributed through the schools. Therefore, knowledge, manners, behavior, accent, language, and religion are focal points in educational controversies.

EQUALITY OF EDUCATIONAL OPPORTUNITY

With the increasing economic and social importance of education in contemporary society, many groups struggle for equal access to schooling. These struggles are directly related to concerns about power. Traditionally, four major positions have been taken regarding the expansion of educational opportunities to the general population.

1. The most conservative position opposes the expansion of educational opportunities because it might undermine the obedience of lower income groups to upper income groups and make lower income groups unwilling to work at menial occupations.
2. Another position, which also protects the interests of the upper income groups, seeks expanded opportunities for the lower income groups so that they can be educated for obedience and for their place in society.

3. The third position justifies expanded educational opportunities because they supply citizens with the knowledge to protect their political and economic interests.

4. The final position argues that if the government provides schools, then justice requires that schools should be provided equally to all citizens.

The history of education in the South illustrates some of these positions. Many white, southern planters did not want educational opportunities provided for the freed black population out of a fear that educated blacks would be dissatisfied with menial work and therefore difficult to control. On the other hand, whites interested in industrial expansion of the South during the late nineteenth century believed that expanded educational opportunities were necessary to build an industrial workforce.[45]

Also, divisions existed between African-Americans themselves. Under the leadership of Booker T. Washington, many blacks agreed that expanded educational opportunities for blacks would occur only if they accepted segregated schools and industrial education. Opposing Booker T. Washington, W.E.B. DuBois argued that education should prepare blacks to protect their political, social, and economic rights.[46]

Although Washington's ideas triumphed in the nineteenth century, DuBois went on to help found the National Association for the Advancement of Colored People (NAACP), which struggled throughout the twentieth century to end segregated schooling. The conflict over segregated education became the most intense struggle for expanded educational opportunities in the United States in the twentieth century.

In recent years in the United States, the legal struggle over equal educational opportunity has become a major factor in expanding educational opportunities for the disabled, special learners, women, and racial and linguistic minorities. The heart of the legal issue is the Fourteenth Amendment, which provides equal protection before the law. As interpreted by the Supreme Court, the Fourteenth Amendment guarantees that if a state provides a service such as education, then all citizens must have equal access to the service.

For years, disabled people complained that they were denied equal access to education because school buildings had not been constructed to meet their physical needs and to accommodate wheelchairs. In addition, they argued that the particular problems faced by the physically disabled and those with learning problems were not being considered in school programs. Also, those children for whom English was a second language required special programs if they were to receive equal educational opportunities in U.S. schools. Using the same legal reasoning, it was argued that women were being excluded from educational programs and opportunities.

From the 1950s to the 1980s, the struggle to end segregation in the United States and to meet the needs of groups requiring special attention involved a major expansion of educational opportunities. In fact, it was a primary source of political conflict during this period. All parts of the political structure of American schooling were forced to deal with the issues raised in these conflicts.

CONCLUSION

The use of knowledge as an instrument of power usually provokes political confrontation. Adding fuel to these confrontations are disagreements about moral values, religious doctrines, political ideas, and cultural beliefs. In the end, the common-school ideal of eliminating economic and cultural conflicts proved unworkable because of political disagreements over the values and beliefs that were to form the public school consensus.

Using education to enhance economic opportunities and increase political power also generates conflict. Waiting in the wings is a revolt against the global economy. As conservative educators and businesspeople press for schools to adopt standards that will provide workers for the global economy, some political thinkers are warning of the consequences of corporate globalization. Ethan Kapstein, director of studies at the Council of Foreign Affairs, warned in the summer of 1996, "The global economy is leaving millions of disaffected workers in its train. Inequality, unemployment and endemic poverty have become its handmaiden."[47]

Also, schools supply an arena for conflict between politicians. Differing political groups struggle to have their ideas emphasized in schools. Politicians attempt to win votes by claiming that their educational policies will improve schools and society. Ethnic politicians demand language and cultural policies in schools that will maintain the cohesiveness of their particular constituencies. And a long-standing conflict exists between business interests and workers over the content of education. Many workers want schools to be avenues of economic mobility for their children, while many businesspeople want the schools to focus on job training to meet corporate needs.

The next chapter provides a framework for analyzing educational conflicts generated from economic concerns. The economics of schooling is an important part of the consideration of the relationship between education and power. A great deal of educational conflict is a result of economic struggles over education.

NOTES

1. Advertisement appearing in *The New York Times* (5 January 1997), p. 14E.
2. Ibid.
3. Paul R. Krugman, "New Math, Same Story," *The New York Times Magazine* (5 January 1997), p. 32.
4. Ibid.
5. Ibid., p. 33.
6. David M. Gordon, *Fat and Mean: The Corporate Squeeze of Working Americans and the Myth of Managerial "Downsizing"* (New York: The Free Press, 1996), pp. 12, 25.
7. Michael Lind, *Up From Conservatism: Why the Right is Wrong for America* (New York: Free Press, 1996), p. 247.
8. Paul Theroux, *My Other Life* (New York: Houghton Mifflin Company, 1996), p. 102.

9. Alex Molnar, *Giving Kids the Business: The Commercialization of America's Schools* (Boulder, Co.: Westview Press, 1996), pp. 21–53.

10. Stanley Aronowitz and Henry Giroux, *Education under Siege: The Conservative, Liberal, and Radical Debate over Schooling* (South Hadley, Mass.: Bergin & Garvey, 1985), p. 69.

11. Paulo Freire, *Pedagogy of the Oppressed* (New York: Continuum, 1970), and Joel Spring, *The American School 1642-1990, Second Edition* (White Plains, N.Y.: Longman, 1990).

12. Spring, *American School*, pp. 73-115.

13. Mortimer J. Adler, *The Paideia Proposal* (New York: Macmillan, 1982).

14. Brad Cain, "School Overhaul," *Compuserve Executive News Service, Associated Press,* no. 2356 (7/16/91), Ethan Rarick, "Oregon Moves to End High School at 10th Grade," *Compuserve Executive News Service, Associated Press,* no. 1540 (7/31/91).

15. G. William Domhoff, *Who Rules America Now? A View from the '80s* (New York: Simon & Schuster, 1983), p. 25.

16. C. Wright Mills, *The Power Elite* (New York: Oxford University Press, 1956), p. 67.

17. Margo Jefferson, "The 2 Faces of Ebonics: Disguise and Giveaway," *The New York Times* (7 January 1997), p. C11.

18. Ibid.

19. Ibid., p. C14.

20. Teresa Simons, "Black Dialect Class Draws Parent Complaints," *Compuserve Executive News Service, United Press,* no. 1441 (1/31/91).

21. Connie Leslie, Daniel Glick, and Jeanne Gordon, "Classrooms of Babel," *Newsweek* (11 February 1991), pp. 56-57.

22. Robert B. Reich, *The Work of Nations: Preparing Ourselves for 21st Century Capitalism* (New York: Alfred A. Knopf, 1991), pp. 81-171.

23. Lonnie Harp, "Schools Urged to Revamp Instruction to Stress Workforce Skills," *Education Week* (31 July 1991), p. 11.

24. A discussion of bicultural education from a critical point of view can be found in Rosalie Pedalino Porter's *Forked Tongue: The Politics of Bilingual Education* (New York: Basic Books, 1990), pp. 159–193.

25. "Hispanic School," *Compuserve Executive News Service, Associated Press,* no. 1442 (2/8/91).

26. SETCLAE: Self-Esteem through Culture Leads to Academic Excellence, *Model Curriculum for Educators, Youth, Workers and Parents* (Chicago: African American Images, 1991), advertising brochure.

27. Jawanza Kunjufu, *To Be Popular or Smart* (Chicago: African American Images, 1988), p. 11.

28. Ibid., pp. 22–23.

29. Molefi Kete Asante, *Afrocentricity* (Trenton, N.J.: Africa World Press, 1988).

30. Richard Manning, "Soweto—The Spirit of '76: Three Black Leaders Recall a Day of Glory and a Decade of Disunity," *Newsweek* (23 June 1986), pp. 40, 42.

31. James Crawford, "Bilingual Educators Seeking Strategies to Counter Attacks," *Education Week* (9 April 1986), pp. 1, 9.

32. James Crawford, "Administration Panel Praises Bennett's Bilingual-Education Stance," *Education Week* (9 April 1986), p. 9.

33. Porter, *Forked Tongue*, p. 188.

34. Christine E. Sleeter and Carl A. Grant, "A Rationale for Integrating Race, Gender, and Social Class," in Lois Weis, *Class, Race, and Gender in American Education* (Albany: State University of New York Press, 1988), pp. 144–160.

35. Quoted in Porter, *Forked Tongue*, pp. 219–220.
36. Ibid., pp. 210–211.
37. As quoted by Porter, *Forked Tongue*, p. 216.
38. R. Ben-Chaim, "America in the Mind of Israel," *The New York Times Magazine* (29 June 1986), p. 58.
39. Carl Kaestle, *Pillars of the Republic: Common Schools and American Society* (New York: Hill & Wang, 1983).
40. For a discussion of the Supreme Court rulings regarding education and religion, see Joel Spring, *American Education, Fifth Edition* (White Plains, N.Y.: Longman, 1991), pp. 233–239.
41. William J. Reese, "Soldiers for Christ in the Army of God: The Christian School Movement in America," *Educational Theory*, vol. 35, no. 2 (Spring 1985), 175-194.
42. "The Ruling in *Mozert* v. *Hawkins County Public Schools*," *Education Week* (5 November 1986), p. 18.
43. Debar Viadero, "Panels in Ga., N.C. Reject Controversial Textbooks," *Education Week* (10 October 1990), pp. 13-14.
44. Ibid., p. 13.
45. See Henry Allen Bullock, *A History of Negro Education in the South: From 1619 to the Present* (New York: Praeger, 1970).
46. Booker T. Washington, *Up from Slavery*, and W.E.B. DuBois, "The Souls of Black Folk," in John Hope Franklin, ed., *Three Negro Classics* (New York: Avon Books, 1965).
47. Quoted by Michael Elliot, "International Globalization: Going Home," *Newsweek* (30 December 1996), p. 41.

CHAPTER 3

Sources of Conflict:
The Economics of Education

This chapter builds on the assumption that all people want to maximize their benefits from education while reducing their personal costs. In this assumption, the ideal situation for an individual would be an educational system that increased the individual's political power and economic benefits at a cost being paid by other people.

For members of the educational community, however, increasing the costs of education often gains economic benefits. Teachers, administrators, educational bureaucrats, and knowledge brokers can maximize their personal incomes by gaining increased financial support for the educational system. Unlike other groups, educational workers do not necessarily seek to reduce their personal expenditures on education. For example, educators will often support tax increases (though the increases affect the taxes they themselves pay) because the money will eventually be returned in their paychecks.

Consider the recent decreases in corporate taxes and taxes on the wealthy, which occurred while corporations were demanding better schools to meet the rigors of international economic competition. Harvard economist Robert Reich argues that corporate donations to schools are a smoke screen for decreasing corporate support of schools through taxation. "It's a great irony that business is saying it is supporting education in the front door," Reich said in a 1991 interview for *Education Week,* "but [is] taking away money through the back door." Reich notes that the decline in corporate tax support of schools is occurring while corporations are demanding that schools provide an education to meet their labor needs. According to Reich, corporate donations increased by 1.7 percent in 1987 and 2.4 percent in 1988, while the corporate share of local property-tax measures declined from 45 percent to 16 percent between 1957 and 1987. "Corporate munificence is a high-profile affair," Reich says. "Lobbying for huge tax breaks is conveniently, far less so."[1]

Reich's analysis is tied to a general theory of the internationalization of capital and labor. In his book *The Work of Nations,* he argues that the withdrawal of corporate support of public schools in the United States is part of a general withdrawal of support from the infrastructure of the country.[2] International corporations no longer feel an allegiance to a particular country, according to Reich and, consequently, are primarily seeking production sites with the lowest taxes and labor costs. On the other hand, corporations do need an educated labor force. As I will discuss later in this chapter, Reich's analysis of the tension between reducing taxes and labor costs and having an educated workforce provides an important explanation for current trends in education, including the development of multicultural education.

Economist E. G. West provides an example of the economic self-interest of educators. West is concerned with the provision of free public education to all social classes, including the upper middle class and the rich. On the surface, there may be no reason to provide free education to those who can afford direct costs. West examines the development of free public schools in New York state during the nineteenth century. Originally, common schools were not free to all children. They were funded in part by the government and in part by parents, who paid rate bills according to the number of days attended. They provided children whose parents were too poor to pay the rate bills a free education. Therefore, public schools were supported partially through taxes and partially through user costs.

West found that this method of funding disturbed educators' schools. Educators faced the problem of collecting the rate bills and gaining support of the middle class. Rate bills provided the opportunity for the middle class to decide to spend their money on public or private schools. These issues led to a campaign by public school administrators and teachers for free public schooling.

The actions of the teachers and administrators fit into what West calls the "economic theory of democracy." This theory suggests that people working in a government service can afford to bring more influence on a government policy related to that service because their incomes depend on the policy. The average citizen has interests spread over most government services and cannot devote so much time to a single government issue such as education. Those in the service of government tend to try to maximize their benefits on policies regarding their incomes. In West's words, the educator "may be prompted by the desire to help others and by the desire to help himself and his family. . . . And what people do is a better guide than what they say."[3]

West believes that the interests of teachers and administrators in government service were enhanced by reducing the problem of salaries dependent on the collection of rate bills and the creation of a monopoly situation. The creation of free public schools made it more difficult for private schools to continue to exist. With rate bills there was still some option available to parents to choose private schooling, but with compulsory taxation providing free schools, it became more difficult for private schools to compete for students.

In fact, West found that the provision for free public schools resulted in a decline in the number of private schools. Few parents wanted to pay taxes to support free public schools and then pay again to send their children to private schools. West's figures from the office of the New York State superintendent show an increase in the number of students in private schools from 48,451 in 1863 to 68,105 in 1867, when legislation was passed abolishing rate bills. In

1871, four years after the provision of free public schools in New York, private-school enrollment decreased to 49,691.[4]

Admittedly, the assumption that individuals want to maximize their gains from schooling while reducing their costs adds a cynical edge to an economic analysis of education. It suggests that educational rhetoric depends on economic interests. West argues that educators campaigned for free public schools on platforms that promised reduced crime and poverty and increased political stability. There was no proof that these benefits would result from free schools. West states, "The suppliers of educational services to the government, the teachers and administrators, as we have seen, had produced their own organized platforms by the late 1840s; it was they indeed who were the leading instigators of the free school campaign."[5]

Therefore, the assumption of this chapter includes the desire to maximize benefits and reduce costs and the consideration of educational rhetoric as a function of economic interests. The next section of the chapter will examine economic theories of education in the framework of this assumption, and the final section will analyze the effects of the internationalization of capital and labor.

ECONOMIC THEORIES OF EDUCATION

There are several basic questions in the economics of education.

- Who should pay?
- Should all people, even those without children, pay for public schools?
- Should only users pay?
- How should educational monies be distributed?
- Should all education monies be given directly to public schools?
- Should vouchers be given to parents to purchase an education for their children?
- How should money for education be collected?
- Should educational costs be paid by regressive or progressive taxes?
- Should they be paid by tuition or a combination of tuition and government subsidy?
- How much money should be spent on education?
- Should the government spend enough money on education to maximize the life chances of all children?
- Should the government spend only the money required to educate children according to their demonstrated abilities?

WHO SHOULD PAY?

Answers to the first question are most often argued concerning public benefits. If there are no public benefits, then arguing that all people including those without children should support public schools is difficult. Economists make a distinction between private and public benefits. Private benefits from education include increased personal income, personal satisfaction gained through learning new skills and acquiring new knowledge, and increased political and social power. Private benefits can be used as a justification for personal investment in education. In other words, one could argue that all people should pay directly for education because it is an investment that yields an economic return as higher lifetime wages. Public benefits include economic growth, political stability, efficient use of labor, and reduction in crime. These benefits can be used to justify public investment in schooling.

To understand the role of public benefits in the debate about the financial support of schooling, consider the arguments of two individuals widely separated in time and economic perspective: nineteenth-century common-school crusader Horace Mann and twentieth-century economist Milton Friedman. Both individuals are important with respect to current debates about schooling. Mann provided the basic justification for public support of schools in the United States. Friedman gave the original arguments for the introduction of choice in the public school system.

In campaigning for public support of the common-school ideal, Mann needed to convince all adults that they should support public schools even if they had no children or sent their children to private schools. If schooling provided only private benefits, such as increased income or personal satisfaction, there may be little justification for all members of the community to pay for the support of a common school. Purely private benefits from schooling would support the argument that users should bear the expenses of public schools.

Mann made economic benefits the center of his argument that all adults should support public schooling. He argued that property values depended on the quality of the surrounding community and on improvements made in that community. In addition, a present owner of property was merely a trustee of wealth inherited from a previous owner. This meant that personal wealth was dependent on the wealth of the community and the wealth of previous generations.

If schooling increased the skills and abilities of one individual, Mann argues, then all individuals in the community would benefit and all future generations would benefit. According to this reasoning, even if an individual had no children or sent his or her children to private schools, he or she still benefited economically from common schools because an educated generation increased the value of the individual's property. Therefore, the public benefits of schooling justified taxing all members of the community to provide financial support for schools. Mann wrote, about successive generations of citizens of Massachusetts, "The property of this Commonwealth is pledged for the education of all its youth, up to such point as will save them from poverty and vice and prepare them for the adequate performance of their social and civil duties."[6]

Mann's arguments remain the major justification for general support of public schooling. In this argument, the wealth of a community depends on how much crime and poverty, the fulfillment of political obligations by its citizens, and the skills and knowledge of its workers.

While efforts have been made to use education to eliminate crime and poverty, there is still no proof that education can effectively limit crime and poverty. Despite this lack of documentation, educators continue to claim these as public benefits from education. In the twentieth century, the major public benefit claimed for public schooling has been the improvement of the workforce or, in the language of the twentieth century, the development of human capital.

Working within the tradition of Mann, twentieth-century economist Theodore Schultz elaborated on the theory of human capital as a major public benefit of education. Schultz defined human capital as that form of capital that is an integral part of a person and enhances the capabilities of individuals to produce. As a form of capital, human capital lends itself to investment. These potential investments include health facilities and services, the migration of individuals to adjust to changing job opportunities, study programs for adults, on-the-job training, and formally organized education.[7]

Schultz admitted, however, that deciding the amount each factor contributes to the improvement of human capital is difficult. Despite this difficulty, Schultz tried to decide the relationship between education and economic growth. He argued that if one compared increases in labor and capital invested in the U.S. economy between 1919 and 1957 with the 2.1 percent per annum economic growth during that period, then the economic growth could not be explained by inputs from the quantity of labor and capital. In other words, whereas the number of hours of labor and capital increased each year by 1 percent, the output of the system increased by 3.1 percent. For Schultz, part of the unexplained 2.1 percent annual increase was the result of improvement in human capital, which in turn was a consequence of increased education levels.[8]

Regarding the public-benefits issue, Schultz was concerned about the economic payoff of investment in education. Using three different estimates, he concluded, "The increase in the education per person of the labor force that occurred between 1929 and 1957 explains between 36 and 70 percent of the otherwise unexplained increase in earnings per laborer, depending on which of the estimates of the rate of return that is applied."[9] Even at the lower figure of 36 percent, education made a significant contribution to increasing national income.

In the tradition of Horace Mann, Schultz concluded that the modern state had nothing to lose and everything to gain by pouring money into education. Schultz's optimism about the importance of education in economic development continued after the 1960s: "Education has become a major source of economic growth in winning the abundance that is to be had by developing a modern agriculture and industry. Having this abundance simply would not be possible if people were predominantly illiterate and unskilled."[10] Other studies seemed to confirm Schultz's optimism about the economic benefits of education. Economist Edward Denison concluded that education accounted for one-fifth of the increase in national income in the United States between 1929 and 1957, and studies of underdeveloped countries seemed to confirm that investment in education resulted in economic growth.[11]

An important thing to note about the economic returns on investment in education is that they vary according to race and gender. One study, using the value of the dollar in 1967, found the lifetime income associated with four years of high school to be $478,280 for white males, $125,428 for white females, $309,765 for nonwhite males, and $139,863 for nonwhite females.[12]

Considering these rates of return on investment in education, it is reasonable to argue that certain groups might see greater economic advantage from investment in education than other groups would. The benefitting groups might actively support increased investment in education and, of course, seek to reduce their personal expenditures.

HOW SHOULD EDUCATIONAL MONIES BE DISTRIBUTED?

A major political issue in education is public financing of private schools. Since the nineteenth century, many religious schools, particularly Catholic schools, have sought some form of government aid, arguing that private schools produce public benefits similar to public schools and that private school parents pay taxes to support education. Private school parents often argue that they must pay twice to support the educational system: First, they pay taxes to support schools, and, second, they pay tuition to send their children to private schools. In addition, private school parents argue that by paying tuition for private schools they reduce public school expenditures.

On the other hand, common-school advocates argue, as Mann did, for the importance of all children attending a public school. Part of the public benefits of attendance at a common school were to be the creation of common moral and political values.[13] In addition, government financial support of private schools continues to raise the issue of separation of church and state.

Besides the issue of government support of privately controlled education, there is the explosive political issue of inequality of educational funding. Dividing the educational system into separate districts allows the wealthy to live in districts that spend more per student than areas containing many poor people.

In recent years, the issues of government aid to private schools and inequality of educational funding have been linked to proposals for vouchers and tuition tax credits. Under a voucher system, a voucher worth a particular sum of money would be given to parents to spend on their child's education. Tuition tax credit plans, alternatively, would allow parents to credit educational expenses to their income taxes. Both plans offer the possibilities of government funding of private schools and erasing differences in educational expenditures. For instance, vouchers or tax credits could be given to parents sending their children to private schools, and an equivalent amount of money could be provided to all children.

Economist Milton Friedman was one of the first to make the link between vouchers and ending inequality in educational expenditures. His arguments for the use of vouchers provided an early justification for the choice plans supported by the Reagan and Bush administrations. Government support of education, he argues, can be justified by the necessity of maintaining a stable and democratic society, and the maintenance of these public benefits requires that each person receive "a minimum amount of schooling of a specified kind."[14]

Unlike Mann, Friedman believes that public benefits justify government financing of education, but they do not justify "the actual administration of educational institutions by the government, the 'nationalization,' as it were, of the bulk of the 'education industry.' " He proposes government subsidization of education by giving parents vouchers "redeemable for a specified maximum sum per child per year if spent on 'approved' educational services."[15] Through a system of vouchers, parents would purchase education for their children from private institutions. Public benefits would be guaranteed by the government regulating private schools to assure that schools met certain minimum standards and had certain minimum content.

An important reason Friedman gives for a voucher system is the inequality in financing public schools. Although Mann dreamed of the rich and poor being mixed in the same school buildings, the reality is that the district system resulted in the creation of rich school districts and poor ones. One major source of inequality of educational opportunity is the existence of the district system. The district system allows the wealthy and middle class to live in school districts where more money is spent per pupil than in districts with lower income families. The option to move into school districts that spend more per pupil is not usually available to low-income families because they cannot afford housing in the wealthier district.

Friedman argues that these disparities result in schools that create social class divisions in education: "Under present arrangements, stratification of residential areas effectively restricts the intermingling of children from decidedly different backgrounds."[16] Further, parents can still send their children to private schools. Except for parochial education, Friedman argues, only a few can afford private schooling, which results in further stratification.

Friedman gives the example of a low-income African-American family in an inner city trying to obtain a high-quality education for their gifted child. The district system makes it almost impossible for the family to send the child to a school outside the inner city. Friedman argues that because good schools are in high-income neighborhoods, it is difficult for a poor family to save extra money for a child's education and afford the expense of moving to a wealthy suburb.

The first major court case dealing with inequality of educational funding sparked another proposal for a voucher system. In *Serrano v. Priest* (1971), the California Supreme Court found that California's method of financing schools was contributing to inequality of educational opportunity. The case involved the two sons of John Serrano, who lived in a poor, mainly Mexican-American community in Los Angeles. The local school experienced increasing class sizes and a resulting shortage of textbooks and supplies. Local school authorities told Serrano that the financial situation in the school would not improve, and the only option for the Serrano family was to move to another school district. The California Supreme Court decision states, "Plaintiff contends that the school financing system classifies on the basis of wealth. We find this proposition irrefutable. . . ."[17]

John Coons and Stephen Sugarman, the lawyers involved in the *Serrano* case, argue that the only means of overcoming inequality of educational funding is through some form of voucher system in which the family is allowed to exercise educational choice. Under one type of voucher proposal, intended to overcome problems associated with different educational needs, all children receive a voucher of equal value. In addition, grants based on needs are made to each family. Larger grants then go to the poorest families, with a progressive reduction in the grant to zero for families of average income.[18]

During the Republican administrations of the 1980s and early 1990s, voucher and tuition tax credit proposals have often been associated with providing choices between public and private schools. Religious groups have lobbied heavily for choice plans that would allow government support of religious education, and the growth of private Afrocentric schools have provided another source of support for choice plans.

In 1991, a variety of choice plans appeared at the local, state, and national levels. In February 1991, President George Bush unveiled a plan to reward districts that developed choice plans that allowed parents to enroll their children in public or private schools. During the same month, the Detroit board of education considered a plan that would allow private schools to be publicly funded. As of December 1990, the government of Epsom, New Hampshire, allows tax abatements for property owners who send their children to private schools. In September 1990, the Milwaukee school system adopted a voucher plan that allows low-income families to send their children to nonsectarian schools.[19]

Although arguments for vouchers and tuition tax credits shifted their focus to choice between public and private systems, problems in inequality of funding continued. In *Rodriguez* v. *San Antonio School District* (1973), the U.S. Supreme Court refused to consider the issue of school finance, declaring, "The consideration and initiation of fundamental reforms with respect to state taxation and education are matters reserved for the legislative processes of the various states."[20] This meant that changes in educational financing would have to be the work of state courts and legislatures. Consequently, by the early 1990s many states had made little progress in equalizing funding between school districts.

Examples continue to abound of disparities in educational finance. Highland Park, Texas, a wealthy suburb of Dallas, spends twice as much per pupil as two other area school systems. Teachers' salaries are 50 percent higher in New Trier High School, in Winnetka, Illinois, than in the Du Sable, Illinois, school system. The average teacher in the Belmont, Massachusetts, school system earns $36,100, while the average teacher in Chelsea earns $26,200.[21] Table 3-1 indicates the relationship between household income and the school revenue per student.

TABLE 3-1. Total Revenue Per Student by Wealth of Community 1989-90

Median household income of school district	Percentage of enrollment	Revenue per student
Less than $20,000	10.1	$4,297
20,000-24,999	21.3	4,622
25,000-29,999	25.4	5,107
30,000-34,999	15.9	5,015
35,000 or more	27.2	5,862

Source: National Center for Education Statistics, "Public School District Funding Differences," http://www.ed.gov/NCES.

The continued disparities in spending between school districts highlight the magnitude of the problem. Of course, the major difficulty in resolving these differences is the resistance of privileged school districts. The logical solution is for state governments to increase their role in financing schools. Nevertheless, increased state involvement resulting from school finance reforms during the 1970s and 1980s did not eliminate the differences between rich and poor school districts. For economists such as Friedman and lawyers such as Coons and Sugarman, the best answer for providing equality of financing is state or federal funding of a voucher system.

HOW SHOULD MONEY FOR EDUCATION BE COLLECTED?

As mentioned at the beginning of this chapter, the ideal situation for most taxpayers is to pay a minimum of taxes, while having a maximum amount spent on the education of their children. The traditional reliance on local property taxes for the support of schooling provided this type of opportunity. As the California Supreme Court found in *Serrano* v. *Priest*, property taxes are often regressive forms of taxation. In other words, property taxes can be a greater burden for middle- and low-income families than for wealthy families. When a regressive property tax is combined with the process of school districting, extreme inequalities result in both the payment of taxes and the distribution of revenues to schools. Low-income families pay higher rates and receive less revenue for their efforts. In the *Serrano* case, the California Supreme Court gave an example of this situation: "Baldwin Park citizens, who paid a school tax of $5.48 per $100 of assessed valuation, can spend less than half as much on education as Beverly Hills residents, whom they taxed at a rate of $2.38 per $100."[22]

Because of the *Serrano* case, state legislatures in the 1970s were embroiled in school-finance reform. One result of this involvement was to strengthen the role of state legislatures in education. In addition, the issue of who should pay for public schooling became a major problem at the state level of government and an issue among various interest groups. For instance, most corporations resist increased corporate taxes to support education and favor reliance on lotteries and sales taxes.

Corporate resistance to taxation for schools is described in Ira Shor's book *Culture Wars: School and Society in the Conservative Restoration, 1969-1984*. Shor argues that business leaders in the early 1980s, while campaigning for state school reform, saw to it that increased taxes resulting from reforms would fall primarily on the shoulders of the poor and the lower middle class. "Once public acceptance of the crisis and of official solutions emerged," Shor writes, "it was time to present the bill. Regressive taxes were identified as the source of funds to finance school excellence."

Shor argues that strong resistance to increased taxes was overcome by claims that the failure of the public schools was a major cause of economic decline. Because of this argument, tax-increase plans have spread from state to state. However, most of these plans avoid increasing corporate taxes and rely instead on regressive funding, particularly sales taxes and lotteries, that primarily affect the poor and lower middle class. In Shor's words, "This strategy generated new revenues from the bottom in hard times, while protecting key constituencies at the top military-industrial complex, high-tech corporate profits, the rich and their tax loopholes, tax abatements for corporate construction in local areas, the oil depletion allowance, etc."[23]

One could conclude from Shor's argument that because of school finance reforms in the 1970s, corporations dominated school-funding issues at the state level. Of course, whether or not this is true for a particular state depends on the power of other interest groups to affect the decisions of legislators and governors. Obviously, business groups favor regressive taxes, while politicians avoid unpopular increases in state income taxes. The tendency, because it often represents the path of least resistance, is to rely increasingly on regressive taxation. This can place a disproportionate amount of the tax burden for supporting public schools on the poor and lower middle class.

Like Reich, Shor accuses business interests of having adopted a Machiavellian attitude in the early 1980s, when, rather than pay increased taxes, business interests gave their support directly to schools through grants, partnerships, and direct aid. Shor writes, "Businesses in the third-phase plan were called upon to 'do their part,' by getting more involved in schools, adopting poor districts like orphans, donating over-age equipment, offering excess supplies and furniture, and by lending experts to short-staffed departments. All this generosity was tax-deductible."[24]

The problems associated with the use of property taxes were exacerbated in the 1980s with the practice of granting tax abatements to corporations. This became a major issue in the 1990s as school districts faced major financial problems. During the spring of 1991, state teachers' unions launched major campaigns in Kansas, Texas, Minnesota, Washington, Ohio, and other states to increase corporate contributions to school funding. Professor of Education Michael Apple commented, "Companies are caught in a contradictory situation. They want more spent on education but prefer that it not come out of their own pockets."[25]

Examples of the effect of tax abatements exist across the country. The following instances were reported in May 1991 by *The New York Times*:

1. Corpus Christi, Texas, lost $900,000 in tax support because of breaks given to local companies. On the other hand, local companies donated $250,000 to the school system. Consequently, corporations reduced their support of the schools by $650,000, while projecting an image of increasing financial support.
2. In Wichita, Kansas, local companies reduced their tax support of schools through concessions by $1.6 million, while donating $1.1 million.[26]

Tax concessions at the state level proved the biggest aid to business. The issue of state-tax concessions will increase as state governments assume a greater role in school-finance issues. *The New York Times* reported the following examples for 1991:

1. Florida granted $500 million in concessions to businesses through breaks in state sales taxes, fuel costs, and machinery. These concessions overshadowed the $32 million given to schools.
2. In Washington, tax concessions to businesses have come under increasing attacks by the state teachers' unions. A particular concern to the unions are the concessions given to the Boeing Corporation, which received breaks on sales taxes from 1989 to 1990 totaling $900 million.[27]

Businesses can win these tax concessions by threatening to leave a local area or state or by demanding breaks before locating in a given area. They defend their tax exemptions as necessary for remaining competitive. Nevertheless, in compensating for these tax reductions by contributions to the schools, they can exert greater control over education. Corporate contributions can be made for specific educational programs and, therefore, shape local school practices.

Tax concessions to businesses represent only one part of the current protest over collection of taxes to support schools. During the 1980s, changes in local, state, and federal taxes resulted in a major redistribution of the tax burden. According to economist Robert Reich, the federal tax burden for the top fifth of taxpayers dropped from 27.3 percent to 25.8 percent, while the rate for the bottom fifth increased from 8.4 percent to 9.7 percent. Reich found that the combined federal, state, and local taxes on the top 1 percent of American earners declined from 39.6 percent in 1966 to 26.8 percent at the end of the 1980s.[28]

Those objecting to decreases in taxes on businesses and the wealthy, and who are concerned about equalizing school financing, face major problems in political organization. Obviously, workers in the educational system have the greatest interest in increasing taxes on businesses and the wealthy. Teachers' unions now play an active role in trying to cause these changes in the tax structure. On the other hand, school board members and administrators in wealthy school districts resist any changes that might threaten their privileged positions. Consequently, educators from these districts are often at odds with educators who advocate equalization of funding. Those who have the most to gain—taxpayers and parents in low-wealth school districts—are poorly organized to deal with complex tax and school-finance issues in state legislatures.[29]

Clearly, two of the major educational issues of the 1990s will be the method of collecting taxes for the schools and equalization of funding. The conflict generated by these two issues will frequently pit business against teachers' unions and the poor against the wealthy. All will be seeking to maximize their educational and economic advantages.

HOW MUCH MONEY SHOULD BE SPENT ON EDUCATION?

One event sparking the 1990 strike by the West Virginia Education Association was the decision of the state legislature to grant raises of 5 percent to 25 percent per year to the division of highways engineers and $7,000 per year to state troopers, while deciding that no money would be available for increases in teachers' salaries.[30] The conflict in West Virginia highlights the problem of deciding how much money should be spent on education. Any society will have some limit on its resources; therefore, no society can provide maximum amounts for all of its government agencies. Obviously, most government agencies would like to maximize their revenues. Under political pressure, Congress and state legislatures must decide how to distribute money among human services, defense, law enforcement, and many other government functions.

Political philosopher Amy Gutmann has provided some guidelines for considering this problem. Concerned about the amount of resources that a democratic state should devote to schooling as opposed to other social ends, she argues there are four possible guiding principles. The first principle, *maximization*, would result in the government spending as much money on education as necessary for maximizing the life chances of all children. The second principle, *equalization*, involves the government spending enough money to raise the life chances of the disadvantaged child to those of the most advantaged child. *Meritocracy*, the third principle, would distribute educational money according to ability and desire to learn. Gutmann adopts the fourth principle, *the democratic threshold principle*, only after rejecting the other three principles.[31]

Gutmann argues that the principle of maximization holds a moral ransom over society. In fact, it suggests that citizens should give up everything they value for the sake of education. The problem is that some claims for improving life chances might be trivial. In fact, it would be difficult operating under this principle to establish any criteria for denying educational expenses. Consequently, it is difficult, if not impossible, to fund schools according to this principle.

Gutmann also rejects the principle of equalizing the chances of less advantaged children with more advantaged children because of the possible increase of government intrusion in daily lives: "To equalize educational opportunity, the state would have to intrude so far into family life as to violate the equally important liberal ideal of family autonomy."[32] In addition, she argues that equalization requires eliminating all differences in cultural, intellectual, and emotional dispositions—something that she believes is neither possible nor desirable.

Gutmann finds the argument for meritocracy completely undemocratic because it does not provide average and below-average students with an education adequate for democratic citizenship. Overall, Gutmann finds it difficult to dismiss the meritocratic principle. Nevertheless, as she points out, enough money to provide an adequate training in citizenship could be spent on all children while extra money is being spent on children with greater intellectual ability. Still, Gutmann argues that the principle must be tempered by democratic principles. In other words, within a democratic framework, a meritocracy should not mean that more money should be distributed to those with greater intellectual abilities, but that the population may decide to make that type of distribution.

The democratic threshold principle, according to Gutmann, allows for this type of flexibility: It allows for unequal distribution of educational money but only after enough money is provided to educate all children for democratic citizenship. Following in the tradition of Horace Mann, Gutmann believes that the major public benefit from education is the training of democratic citizens. Recognizing the difficulty of determining this standard for the distribution of money, she nevertheless feels that it should be the principle. Working under this principle, citizens or their elected representatives would decide how much money to appropriate for education.

Of course, citizens and elected representatives might not function according to the democratic threshold principle. Gutmann sees the principle as a moral guide for decision making. Her principles take on a different meaning when cast into the real world of educational politics. For instance, let us consider each of her principles according to the assumption that people want to maximize their educational benefits while reducing their costs.

Within the framework of these assumptions, one could argue that the maximization principle might be supported by all people with children. Nevertheless, of course, this would mean that they would have to sacrifice other social goods for maximum spending on education. The only group that might favor the maximization principle would be educators, who would greatly benefit from maximum spending on education.

The equalization principle might be supported by a variety of groups. Parents of disabled and mentally retarded children would be interested in schools giving their children an equal chance. Dominated racial and ethnic groups would also be concerned about maximizing their children's life chances. Of course, low-income families would have an important stake in any equalization plan.

Obviously, parents with intellectually talented children would tend to support plans for distributing money according to a principle of a meritocracy. Because of a variety of factors, including the cultural environment of the family, role of peer groups, and biases within the school and in standardized tests, students identified as academically talented tend to come from upper income families. Consequently, it is these families, as opposed to low-income families, that would tend to support the meritocracy principle.

Identifying groups that might support the democratic threshold principle would be difficult. It could be argued that all people support the idea of schools preparing all children for democratic citizenship. Nevertheless, the idea of democratic citizenship is vague. Unions might want schools to prepare children for an industrial democracy, while conservatives might have a more law-and-order idea of citizenship. I would argue that because of the difficulty in defining good citizenship (Gutmann has her own definition), the democratic threshold principle is unworkable.

The most important of Gutmann's principles for understanding the distribution of money for education are equalization and meritocracy. When social concerns about the poor are at the top of the agenda, as they were in the 1960s, the equalization principle becomes most important. When the emphasis is on educating more engineers and scientists, as in the 1950s and 1980s, the meritocracy principle becomes important.

THE ECONOMICS OF SCHOOLING IN THE NEW WORLD ORDER

A chief characteristic of the emerging new world order in the 1990s is the internationalization of the labor force. Workers, corporate leaders, and companies increasingly move from country to country in search of higher wages or, for companies, in search of a cheap labor supply. As companies move, their management, and spouses and children, also move.

The internationalization of the labor force is affecting education in many ways. First, the upper strata of the new international force, a group Reich labels the 'symbolic analysts,' are losing allegiance to any particular nation and are withdrawing support from national infrastructures, including public schools. Second, symbolic analysts require an education that emphasizes higher order thinking and technical skills. Third, the international quality of the labor force is resulting in demands for multicultural forms of education in most developed nations of the world.

The internationalization of the labor force affects the distribution of jobs in the U.S. economy. Many companies moved their manufacturing facilities to other countries in search of cheap labor, resulting in a decline in traditionally well-paying jobs in steel and other forms of industrial production. As this occurred, immigration laws changed, allowing many immigrants to enter the United States and compete for jobs. The combination of these factors along with changes in the tax laws contributed to a decline in after-tax income for the lowest 60 percent of wage earners and an increase for the top 20 percent. The most dramatic changes were between the top 20 percent and the bottom 20 percent. Between 1977 and 1992, the top fifth of American families earned 27 percent more, while the bottom fifth earned 13 percent less. The incomes of the top 1 percent of American families doubled during the same period.[33] As a proportion of national income in 1990, the poorest fifth of U.S. population received 3.7 percent and the richest fifth received 50 percent. The top 5 percent received 26 percent of the nation's income.[34]

These increased differences between wage levels parallel the new occupational structure in the United States. The top 20 percent of the labor force is made up of symbolic analysts, who, as the name implies, include managers and analysts of information and ideas. Specifically, occupations that are typical of symbolic analysts are lawyers, investment bankers, computer experts, corporate managers, engineers, scientists, software developers, advertising executives, media experts, writers, journalists, and college professors. It is this group of occupations that is benefiting from the redistribution of incomes.[35] The remaining occupations are classified by Reich in the following manner:

1.25 percent production,

2.30 percent service,

3.50 percent farmers and miners, and

4.20 percent misc., including government workers and teachers.[36]

Wielding the most economic power and seeking to maximize educational benefits, the education of symbolic analysts topped the educational reform agenda of the 1980s. This was reflected in calls for more academic requirements for high school graduation and a stress on "higher order thinking skills." Reich states, "The formal education of an incipient symbolic analyst thus entails refining four basic skills: abstraction, system thinking, experimentation, and collaboration."[37] Usually, these reforms are designed to educate more symbolic analysts to help U.S. corporations compete in a world market.

Of course, symbolic analysts, who understand the wage structure of the present international economy, want their children to enter similar occupations. The key, of course, to entering these occupations is the right education. Nevertheless, while symbolic analysts are seeking a good education for their children, they are attempting to withdraw financial support from the nation's infrastructure. As mentioned previously, support of the infrastructure through paying taxes declined significantly for upper income groups. As their tax contributions decline, symbolic analysts demand more educational benefits for their children.

Several options exist for educating the children of symbolic analysts. One option is for symbolic analysts to abandon public schooling completely by sending their children to private schools and reducing the taxes they pay for the support of public schools. Certainly, any form of voucher and tuition tax credit that would help this process would be welcomed by symbolic analysts.

Another option is for symbolic analysts to live in privileged suburban communities, where public schools are clearly designed to provide the best education necessary for entering upper income occupations. If the symbolic analyst cannot live in a privileged suburban community, then the next option is a choice plan. By being able to select from a wide variety of offerings, a choice plan would allow symbolic analysts to send their children to the best schools in their area.

Many symbolic analysts are transferred by their companies to foreign countries. Of course, this creates a problem for the education of their children. For instance, many Japanese transferred to the New York metropolitan area chose to live in the suburban Westchester County community of Scarsdale because of the reputation of its school system. The increase in Japanese students in the Scarsdale schools resulted in the implementation of multicultural education programs. Concerned about the enrollment of their children in Japanese universities, the Japanese corporate community in the New York area established, in cooperation with a Japanese university, a private Japanese high school for Westchester County.

In reality, many countries are adopting multicultural education programs because of the internationalization of the labor force. In the United States, multicultural education can be analyzed from the standpoint of the economics of education. The internationalization of the labor force in the United States is marked not only by the movement of symbolic analysts, but also by the immigration of service and production workers particularly from South America, Central America, and Asia.

One result of the immigration of service and production workers, and the movement of corporations out of the United States in search of cheap labor, is a growing resentment between native-born American workers and the new immigrants. Wages and the number of production jobs have fallen dramatically for American workers.[38] Viewed in this context, multicultural education in public schools is a method of reducing the friction between native-born and immigrant labor.

Of course, reduced friction is not the only reason for the growth of multicultural education. Multicultural education has its roots in attempts by dominated groups in the United States to gain cultural recognition in the public schools. In the 1960s and 1970s, African-American, Native American, Mexican-American, and Puerto Rican groups struggled for a place for their cultures in the school curriculum. In part, this struggle was economic, because equal treatment of cultures was to give these groups greater equality of economic opportunity. Multicultural education originating from these sources places emphasis on liberation and political struggle.

On the other hand, multicultural education that originates in corporate concerns about friction in the American labor force places emphasis on what could best be described as getting along well with others. This form of multicultural education has parallels in many European countries that have relied on foreign labor. Sweden adopted multicultural education programs in 1973 because its foreign-born made up one-eighth of its population. Beginning in the 1960s, West Germany brought in many 'guest workers' to fuel its economic expansion. By the 1980s, these guest workers totaled 5 million out of a population of 61 million. West Germany adopted several models of multicultural education to handle the education of the children of these guest workers. Similar experiences occurred in France as the result of the use of foreign labor.[39]

Conflicts over the goals of multicultural education will probably continue. The major tension will be between those who see multicultural education as a

form of liberation for dominated groups and those who see it for building cooperation in the labor force.

In summary, the new world order has resulted in several economic issues
concerning education. The internationalization of the labor force is resulting in
many symbolic analysts wanting to withdraw their financial support from
national public school systems, while seeking the best education for their children in either privileged suburban public schools or private schools. The key
concerns for these groups are choice plans for public and private schooling, a
stress on education for higher order thinking, and protection of privileged
school systems. In addition, the internationalization of the labor force places a
new focus on the issue of multicultural education.

CONCLUSION

The economics of schooling adds an important perspective to the politics of
education. It is an analytical tool that raises important questions about who
benefits and who pays. Because of the economic importance of education in
determining a person's place in the labor market, any educational proposal
needs to be scrutinized to decide public and private benefits. Throughout the
1980s and the early 1990s, the major direction of school reform may be for the
benefit of those entering upper income occupations.

Every educational proposal needs to be scrutinized according to who pays.
As discussed in this chapter, the pattern in the 1980s and early 1990s is for the
wealthy and corporations to pay less for the support of schools, and for middle
and lower income groups to pay more for the support of public schools. In
addition, every educational proposal needs to be examined according to the
economic benefits that might be gained by educational workers. Admittedly,
this type of examination places the actions of educators in a cynical light, but
one must remember that educators are people, and, like many people, they
want to increase their economic benefits.

NOTES

1. Quoted in Jonathan Weisman, "Business's Words, Actions to Improve Education at
   Odds, Economist Argues," *Education Week* (13 March 1991), pp. 1, 26.
2. Robert Reich, *The Work of Nations: Preparing Ourselves for 21st Century Capitalism*
   (New York: Alfred A. Knopf, 1991).
3. E. G. West, "The Political Economy of Public School Legislation," in *Studies in Education,* no. 4 (Menlo Park, Calif.: Institute of Humane Studies, 1977), p. 19. This
   article was originally published under the same title in the October 1967 issue of the
   Journal of Law and Economics.
4. Ibid., p. 25.
5. Ibid., p. 20.
6. Horace Mann, "Tenth Annual Report," in Lawrence Cremin, ed., *The Republic and the
   School* (1846; reprint, New York: Teachers College Press, 1957), p. 77.

7. Theodore W. Schultz, "Investment in Human Capital," in M. Blaug, ed., *Economics of Education* (Middlesex, England: Penguin, 1968), pp. 22–24.

8. Theodore W. Schultz, "Education and Economic Growth," in Nelson Henry, ed., *Social Forces Influencing American Education* (Chicago: University of Chicago Press, 1961), pp. 48–51.

9. Ibid., p. 82.

10. Theodore W. Schultz, *Investment in Human Capital: The Role of Education and of Research* (New York: Free Press, 1971), p. 56.

11. Ibid., p. 69.

12. Walter Garms, James Guthrie, and Lawrence Pierce, *School Finance: The Economics and Politics of Public Education* (Englewood Cliffs, N.J.: Prentice-Hall, 1978), p. 57.

13. See Joel Spring, *The American School 1642-1990*, Second Edition (White Plains, N.Y.: Longman, 1990), pp. 73–115.

14. Milton Friedman, *Capitalism and Freedom* (Chicago: University of Chicago Press, 1962), p. 86.

15. Ibid., p. 89.

16. Ibid., p. 92.

17. Joel Spring, *American Education: An Introduction to Social and Political Aspects* (White Plains, N.Y.: Longman, 1978), p. 227.

18. John E. Coons and Stephen D. Sugarman, *Education by Choice: The Case for Family Control* (Berkeley: University of California Press, 1978).

19. Lynn Olson, "Proposals for Private-School Choice Reviving at All Levels of Government," *Education Week* (20 February 1991), pp. 1, 10.

20. Spring, *American Education*, p. 228.

21. Reich, *Work of Nations*, pp. 275-276.

22. "Poorer New York School Districts Seek More Aid," *The New York Times*, 6 May 1991, pp. A1, B4.

23. Ira Shor, *Culture Wars: School and Society in the Conservative Restoration, 1969-1984* (Boston: Routledge & Kegan Paul, 1986), p. 152.

24. Ibid., p. 152.

25. William Celis III, "Educators Complain Business Tax Breaks Are Costing Schools," *The New York Times* (22 May 1991), p. A1.

26. Ibid., p. A23.

27. Ibid., p. A23.

28. Reich, *Work of Nations*, pp. 199-200.

29. Garms, Guthrie, and Pierce, *School Finance*, p. 343.

30. Kelly Kissel, "Teacher Strike," *Compuserve Executive News Service, Associated Press* (3/17/90).

31. Amy Gutmann, *Democratic Education* (Princeton, N.J.: Princeton University Press, 1987), pp. 127–171.

32. Ibid., p. 132.

33. Jason DeParle, "Richer Rich, Poorer Poor, and a Fatter Green Book," *The New York Times*, (26 May 1991), p. E2.

34. Reich, *Work of Nations*, p. 197.

35. Ibid., pp. 177–179.

36. Ibid., pp. 175–180.

37. Ibid., p. 229.

38. Ibid., pp. 208–226.

39. Rosalie Pedalino Porter, *Forked Tongue: The Politics of Bilingual Education* (New York: Basic Books, 1990), pp. 85–121.

CHAPTER 4

Sources of Conflict: The Educational Establishment

Power issues in education have two sides. On one hand, outside individuals and groups attempt to use education as an instrument of power. In other words, they try to exert power over the educational system. On the other hand, people within educational institutions strive for more power and money.

In fact, power and money are at the heart of most conflicts within the educational establishment. Educational administrators struggle to protect or improve their position within the educational bureaucracy; teachers struggle against administrators to gain money and power; and the knowledge industries compete for profits. In this intricate interweaving of conflicts, members of the educational establishment reach out to make alliances with politicians, interest groups, and the public.

THE REVOLT AGAINST BUREAUCRACY

Why is there a tendency to blame the supposed failure of the schools on a bureaucracy composed of educational administrators, supervisors, curriculum planners, research specialists, and subject matter experts? At the beginning of the century, the bureaucracy was considered the salvation for politically corrupt school systems. Politicians were assumed to serve the interests of those wanting to exploit the school system. On the other hand, educational bureaucrats were public servants who primarily served the interests of students. Using the rhetoric of reform, educators built a bureaucratic shield around the schools to protect them from avarice politicians, greedy book sellers, and corrupt contractors.

Beginning in the 1950s, conservative political thinkers reversed the reform rhetoric and called the bureaucracy the enemy of high academic standards and the source of most school problems. The revolt against bureaucracy was spearheaded by Austrian economist Friedrich Hayek who taught at the University of Chicago from 1950 to 1962. Writing in an era of anti-Communism, Hayek attacked all forms of government intervention in the economy and society. His ideas influenced the Reagan-style Republicanism of the 1980s and 1990s.

In *The Road to Serfdom,* Hayek attacked government bureaucracies for being self-serving and damaging. Believing in the importance of self-interest in determining human action, Hayek argued that bureaucratic decisions most often promote the personal advantage of members of the bureaucracy. In addition, he maintained, bureaucrats and intellectuals supported by a bureaucracy will advance social theories that vindicate the continued existence and expansion of the bureaucracy.[1]

Hayek's argument reversed the image of educational bureaucracies as the savior of schools to an image of bureaucrats neglecting students while pursuing their own self-interests. What were these interests? One was hiring professors from colleges of education who created educational theories justifying the existence of educational bureaucrats. Who were these educational professors? For conservatives they were, and they still are, liberals wanting to impose a child-centered progressive education on the schools. Beginning in the 1950s, conservatives campaigned for a return to academic standards and a rejection of progressive educational methods. For conservatives, the enemy became educational bureaucrats and their liberal educational consultants.

Hayek's enduring legacy is defining the enemy as the bureaucracy. Now, many critics complain that the problem with public schools is the educational bureaucracy. A frequently heard statement is, "The problem's not money! The problem's bureaucratic waste!" By placing the blame on the educational bureaucracy, school reformers avoid the issue of equal funding between school districts. Some public school students receive the benefits of living in well-financed suburban school districts while others languish in overcrowded classrooms in poorly-funded school districts lacking adequate textbooks and educational materials. Blaming the bureaucracy became an easy method for avoiding increased educational funding.

In the rest of this chapter, I will explore some major criticisms of educational bureaucracies.

POWER

In traditional school administrations, the struggle for power takes place within the corporate model adopted by educators in the early twentieth century. For example, the superintendent of a school district occupies the top position in the hierarchy, and orders flow from top to bottom. Positioned between the superintendent and the schools is a central office staff, which supervises and monitors the flow of incoming and outgoing information.

Administrators in the central office are often in conflict with those in the field, each claiming that the others do not understand their problems. Field administrators, usually principals and assistant principals, feel that administrators in the central office, often called "downtown," are out of touch with the real world of the schools and make demands that disrupt the enterprise of educating students. In response, central-office staffers claim that they have to deal with the broad educational picture, which field administrators do not understand. The split between field and downtown administrators occurs in similar form among local, state, and federal education officials. Local school administrators accuse state authorities of being unaware of the real problems of the schools and of pursuing political objectives. On the other hand, state school officials are suspicious of local educators. Often, state officials believe that local school administrators sabotage state programs out of lack of understanding and narrowness of vision.

Historically, the split between federal school authorities and local school districts has shaped the direction of federal aid to local schools. During the 1950s, school critics accused local educators of making the schools anti-intellectual, and, because of this, of putting the country at a disadvantage in the Cold War with the Soviet Union. School critics opposed general aid to public schools because they believed local educators would misuse the funds. Consequently, the federal government adopted a policy of categorical aid, to force local schools to abide by federal educational policies. One result was that local school officials complained that politicians in Washington did not understand the real educational problems of those in the field.

Accompanying the tension between field administrators and central-office personnel are turf battles and attempts to extend power. In a bureaucracy, the more responsibility a person has, the higher his or her status, power, and sometimes income. Bureaucrats resist surrendering functions to other parts of the organization and seek to increase the importance of their role in the organization. Therefore, educational policies are often caught in the crossfire that occurs in territorial battles between field and downtown administrators, state and local administrators, and federal and state officials.

One method used by bureaucrats at all levels of government to deal with perceived incompetence or lack of understanding from another part of the bureaucracy is to engage in *discretionary insubordination*. The phenomenon of discretionary insubordination is highlighted in a study of Chicago school principals. The authors of the study argue that as educational bureaucracies become larger, their members must often ignore the chain of command by disobeying or changing orders. Without discretionary insubordination, the researchers believe, the educational bureaucracy can adapt to human needs. They state that the object of discretionary disobedience "is to obey so the disobedient behavior produces the maximum effect locally—that is, within the school—but with minimum impact on one's superiors."[2]

One example of discretionary insubordination is the principal who must decide whether to meet a deadline for submitting paperwork to the central office. From the perspective of the school principal, the administrators downtown generate paperwork in their quest for something to do. Because much of the work is without immediate educational value and school principals risk being swamped in paperwork from the central office, the viability of the system depends on lower level administrators determining which paperwork is urgent and worthwhile.

Although hierarchical organization, turf battles, splits between headquarters and field administrators, and discretionary insubordination characterizes power politics within the educational bureaucracy, the desire to control defines the relationship between the educational bureaucracy and the community. In his book *School Politics Chicago Style*, Paul Peterson describes how Chicago school administrators resist attempts to share power with the local community. In one situation described by Peterson, school administrators could not avoid meeting some demands for greater community participation in decision making in the school system. They responded by placing community advisory groups in the schools and turning over responsibility for their operation to school principals, by that preserving their power. Peterson writes about the unwillingness of the bureaucracy to share power, "Organizational resistance to sharing power with outsiders was increasingly successful the closer proposed changes approached real centers of power with the organization."[3]

Joseph McGivney and James Haught wrote the classic study that found the major desire by educational bureaucracies is to maintain control and that actions by the central office staff could be best explained and predicted by the desire to control a situation.[4] This most often occurs in relationships between the central office staff and the community. Central office administrators are often hostile to any public input into the school system that is not under the control of the informal network of the school bureaucracy. The general view held by administrators is that most outsiders who want to make changes in the school system are troublemakers. In part, according to McGivney and Haught, the desire to control is a result of the desire to avoid any public criticism of central-office staff members.

McGivney and Haught found that the organizational methods for maintaining control included control over the flow of information, the hiring of new personnel, and promotion from within the organization. The researchers found that informal networks within the central office staff must be satisfied in the decision-making process. Approval by these informal networks is required before the school system can give any proposal originating outside the school bureaucracy serious consideration.

They also found that the effort to control public input depends on public criticism. The greater the public criticism of the school, the greater the desire of the central office to maintain control. In other words, the more the public demands control of the schools, the more the bureaucracy protects its power.

TEACHER POWER

Educational administrators resist sharing power with the public and with teachers. Within the corporate-like school hierarchy, teachers are at the bottom of the chain of command and the objects of power from above. Teachers' unions have attempted to provide an antidote to the corporate model of school organization, and beginning in the 1970s, the teacher-power movement has become an important element in the politics of education.

Two aspects of teacher power can be identified. The first is the direct involvement by teachers in politics for ensuring the passage of state and national laws that support their educational interests. A symbolic step in this direction was the 1976 endorsement of Jimmy Carter for the presidency by the National Education Association (NEA). This was the first time the larger of the teachers' unions had endorsed a presidential candidate. Since the 1970s, both teachers' unions (the NEA and the American Federation of Teachers [AFT]) have flexed their political muscle by supporting and campaigning for candidates for local, state, and national offices.

The second aspect of teacher power is the relationship of teachers to the rest of the educational bureaucracy. Currently, teachers find themselves in direct competition with administrators for control of educational policy. Teachers have strengthened their position within the educational system through contract agreements achieved by collective bargaining. One issue in contract negotiations is control of working conditions. Teachers' unions, with varying success, have attempted to gain contract agreements on class size, the length of the working day, the number of meetings that can be called by the building principal, extracurricular assignments, and the teaching schedule. In addition, unions have sought control of teacher evaluations, textbook selections, and general educational policies.

Administrators and teachers' unions will continue to compete for power over the educational system. Their battle will take place against a background of community attempts to participate in the control of school systems. Thus educational administrators will struggle to protect their power from other members of the bureaucracy, from the public, and from teachers' unions. It is also possible, given the nature of organizations, that as teachers gain power they will unite with administrators to resist public involvement in school governance.

In recent years, the introduction of site-based management has increased tensions between administrators and teachers. Site-based management involves some sharing of power between a building administrator and a school council composed of teachers, community members, or both. Politically, site-based management threatens the power of school administrators and makes school management more difficult. Consequently, many school administrators object to the use of site-based management.

This position is exemplified by an advertisement placed in the April 3, 1991, issue of *Education Week* by the American Federation of School Administrators. Written by the president of the administrators' union, Ted Elsberg, the advertisement reviews a report on the effect of site-based management in the Dade County, Florida, school system. Dade County is a pioneer in the use of site-based management. One major conclusion of the report was that academic achievement did not increase because of site-based management.

Regarding attitudes of school administrators about site-based management, the report found that only 17 percent of the principals involved in the project believed that the process made their jobs easier, and 90 percent wanted to end site-based management. Writing for the union, Elsberg asks, "Are these results good enough to warrant the planned expansion of the program to every school in the district or as some request to every school in the nation? Why not place our limited resources into programs with records of success?"[5]

POWER AND MONEY

The struggle for power within the school system is often related to issues of income, and the pursuit of money is a major element in the internal politics of education. Administrators, teachers, and members of the knowledge industry vie for greater shares of the money spent on education. In his study of the central office staff of the Chicago public schools, Peterson found that educational bureaucrats are interested primarily in policies that increase the economic benefits of the members of their organization; policies in five major areas were found to enhance the position of bureaucrats:

1. salaries;
2. increasing the number of jobs within the bureaucracy;
3. promotion from within the organization;
4. protecting the organization from outside interests; and
5. increasing the prestige of the organization.[6]

Increasing the number of jobs in the educational bureaucracy and promoting from within the organization give administrators more opportunities to increase their salaries. Obviously, the greater number of jobs increases the chances for promotion to a higher paying position. Limiting promotion to people within the organization decreases competition for higher paying jobs.

Items four and five reflect the desire of administrators to maintain control over outside influences and to increase the money flowing into the educational enterprise. Obviously, the more money the school receives, the more likely it is that administrators' salaries will rise. Efforts to protect the organization and maintain its prestige can make the public more willing to spend money on schools.

Such policies often conflict with the economic goals of teachers. Teachers, like administrators, want higher salaries. From the perspective of teachers' unions, any increase in the size of the educational bureaucracy means a decrease in the money available for teachers' salaries. Therefore, besides their efforts to increase teacher power and control, the unions resist attempts to expand the educational bureaucracy. On the other hand, teachers join administrators in trying to win greater financial support for the schools. Teachers and administrators are quick to defend the public school enterprise against outside criticism, but they disagree over how the money should be spent.

Over the past several decades, salary issues have been the primary cause of teachers' strikes in the United States. In the 1960s, when teachers' unions conducted their first major strikes, wage issues involved a demand for a simple salary schedule that guaranteed annual pay increases and pay increases for earning additional college credits.

In the 1980s and early 1990s, the introduction of career ladders and merit pay has complicated negotiations over teachers' salaries. First, unless the state mandates career ladders or merit pay, local unions must decide whether to accept or reject these new pay proposals. Second, if the unions accept either proposal, then they have to bargain over the conditions surrounding each proposal. For instance, if a local teachers' union agrees to merit pay, then it must negotiate the percentage of the salary increase that will be devoted to merit pay and the methods to be used for determining merit. If there is agreement over career ladders, then the methods of promotion, the number of steps in the career ladder, and the salary increases attached to each step must be determined through collective bargaining. If state legislatures mandate career ladders, then teachers' unions must work at the state level to influence legislation regarding salaries and promotions.

While each change in the political climate of education provides new opportunities for profits by private companies, it also creates the possibility of political battles over limited educational funds. With all levels of government providing limited amounts of money for education, the potential always exists for conflict over the percentage of the economic pie to be received by different sectors of the education world. If the money for education is fixed, then any increase in spending for teachers' salaries, administrative salaries, or textbooks would result in reduced spending in other areas.

The same situation exists among educational programs at different levels of government. For example, in 1986 the federal government proposed shifting funds from major educational programs to a new anti-drug campaign in the public schools. Because of the wide publicity given in 1986 to the cocaine-related deaths of two major sports stars, both political parties decided that a strong anti-drug stance was good politics. Nevertheless, the Republican administration wanted to launch an anti-drug program in the schools without increasing federal spending on education. The result, according to *The New York Times*, was that "Education Department officials . . . along with Republicans in Congress . . . said . . . they would agree to finance the plan through cuts in other areas." The primary federal programs available for major cuts were student aid for higher education and aid to disabled and disadvantaged children. On the other hand, Republicans admitted that they hoped to be relieved of the political burden of making cuts in education programs for the drug legislation by letting the Democrats vote money for the anti-drug campaign.[7]

Changes like those described above can result in major shifts in income within the education world. Obviously, a national anti-drug program would allow publishers to increase their profits by producing material on drug abuse for use in the public schools. Experts on substance abuse could collect more fees by conducting staff-development programs in the schools. University-based researchers could also find a new source of funds. In other words, changes in educational policies directly affect the distribution of money in the knowledge industry.

Even competition between differing research paradigms can affect the flow of money. During the 1960s and early 1970s, research money from the government and foundations went primarily to research projects that had a strong quantitative orientation. This trend changed in the late 1970s with the increasing popularity of qualitative, or ethnographic, research. The present result is competition between quantitative and qualitative researchers for limited educational funds.

CONCLUSION

Important political conflicts occur within the education establishment over the distribution of education funds. It could be hypothesized that conflict over money increases as the availability of education funds decreases. On the other hand, it could also be hypothesized that conflict over money exists even with a surplus of education funds, because educators and members of the knowledge industry can always find new ways to spend increasing amounts of money.

Increasingly, educators may find it difficult to raise money to support public schools. As I discussed in Chapter 3, the world economic conditions are changing so that certain groups are no longer interested in funding public schooling. These groups are interested in sending their children to private schools, and they have little interest in supporting an educational system in any particular country. Their primary concern is with reducing their economic support of public school systems. These new world conditions add a different perspective to the economics of education.

Is the problem educational bureaucracies? Will financial problems in education disappear with the disappearance of educational bureaucracies? Or is the criticism of educational bureaucracies a smokescreen for the imposition of a conservative agenda on schools? Are politicians more trustworthy than school administrators? Does increased parental control guarantee better schools? Does the influence of the business community guarantee a quality education? Who should control U.S. schools?

NOTES

1. Friedrich Hayek, *The Road to Serfdom* (Chicago: The University of Chicago, 1994).
2. Quoted in Kathryn Borman and Joel Spring, *Schools in Central Cities* (White Plains, N.Y.: Longman, 1984), p. 97.
3. Paul E. Peterson, *School Politics Chicago Style* (Chicago: University of Chicago Press, 1976), p. 93.
4. Joseph McGivney and James Haught, "The Politics of Education: A View from the Perspective of the Central Office Staff," *Educational Administration Quarterly,* Vol. 8 (Autumn 1972), 18.
5. Ted Elsberg, "In Our Opinion," *Education Week* (3 April 1991), p. 19.
6. Peterson, *School Politics,* p. 112.
7. *New York Times* (12 August 1986), p. A19.

CHAPTER 5

Political Organization and Student Achievement

Evaluation of different types of political organization can be done from the perspective of effects on student achievement, equality of educational opportunity, and curriculum content. This chapter begins with a review of research projects that argue there is a direct relationship between the political organization of schools, and student achievement and equality of educational opportunity. The last section of the chapter shows how the political organization of schools determines the political content of instruction.

STUDENT ACHIEVEMENT AND EQUALITY OF EDUCATIONAL OPPORTUNITY

Three important studies—John Chubb and Terry Moe, *Politics, Markets & America's Schools*; Kenneth Meier, Joseph Stewart, Jr., and Robert England, *Race, Class, and Education*; and Kenneth Meier and Joseph Stewart, Jr., *The Politics of Hispanic Education*—focus on the relationship between student achievement and the political organization of schools.[1] Chubb and Moe are concerned with student achievement as measured by standardized tests. Their central argument is that increased school autonomy will increase student achievement. Therefore, their suggested reforms in the political organization of education are designed to promote school autonomy by reducing outside controls over schools, particularly from bureaucratic structures.

The books by Meier, Stewart, and England, and by Meier and Stewart, on the other hand, are concerned with political organizations that promote segregative practices in schools and deny certain groups equality of educational opportunity. These researchers consider student achievement to be dependent on equal access to educational opportunities. Their central argument is that they reduce segregative practices in schools when representatives from affected groups, such as Hispanics and African-Americans, are present on boards of education and in educational bureaucracies. Therefore, these researchers suggest that reforms focus on ways to increase representation from dominated groups.

All three studies find the source of educational problems in the educational reforms of the latter nineteenth and early twentieth centuries. During this period, significant changes were made in the administration of schools and in the organization of school board elections. Administratively, public schools developed extensive bureaucratic structures on the argument that education should be controlled by professionally trained experts. These changes were adopted under the slogan of keeping politics out of education. It was assumed that politicians owed allegiance primarily to special interests that supported them in their campaigns for office. Therefore, politicians could never focus exclusively on the interests of students. Bureaucratic experts, it was argued, were free of outside influences and, therefore, could give most of their attention to the interests of students. Of course, these administrative structures tended to insulate schools from community pressures.[2]

Reforms in school board elections were designed to assure that only the "best" members of the community were elected. "Best" in this situation meant the most successful and best educated. The key elements in this reform were nonpartisan and at-large elections. In effect, these changes ensured the domination of school board elections by upper class groups and the exclusion of dominated groups such as Hispanics and African-Americans. An at-large election, as opposed to an election from a small, city district, requires that a candidate campaign throughout the urban area. Campaigning within a small district in an urban area requires minimal expense and organization. In many situations, the candidate can campaign simply by going door to door. At-large elections require more money and organization. Since nonpartisan elections remove the influence of political parties, the candidate must turn to other sources for financial and organizational support. Usually, these other sources are community business groups.[3]

Chubb and Moe argue that the winners in these progressive reforms were business, the middle class, and the educational professionals in charge of the bureaucratic system. The losers were "the lower classes, ethnic and religious minorities, and citizens of rural communities."[4] They argue that most reform movements after this period took this structure for granted. Even when civil rights groups in the 1960s and 1970s attacked the bureaucracy as racist, it maintained its power over public schools.

Meier and Stewart agree that these school reforms did not benefit lower classes and minority groups.[5] They are concerned that at-large elections resulted in the exclusion of Hispanic and African-American representatives from boards of education. In turn, this exclusion from school boards hindered the hiring of Hispanics and African-Americans in the educational bureaucracy. Without representation on school boards and in educational bureaucracies, say Meier, Stewart, and England, these groups can do little to stop educational practices that deny equal educational opportunity to Hispanic and African-American students.

Although both groups of researchers are concerned about the political organization of education and about the linkage between student achievement and the political structure, their methodologies are quite different. I will first analyze Chubb and Moe's arguments for eliminating the educational bureau-cracy and then turn my attention to Meier, Stewart, and England's arguments regarding the importance of political representation.

DEMOCRACY VERSUS THE MARKET

To establish a relationship between student achievement and the political orga-nization of education, Chubb and Moe use data collected in the "High School and Beyond" survey.[6] This data includes test scores in reading comprehension, vocabulary, writing, mathematics, and science. Chubb and Moe compare these test scores with the findings of the effective schools research. The goal of effec-tive schools research is to decide school characteristics that enhance learning, particularly among students from poor families and dominated cultures. Overall, effective schools research emphasizes the importance for students to comprehend clear educational goals, high academic standards, orderly school climate, homework, the principal acting as an instructional leader, teacher involvement in decision making, cooperation with the community and family, and high teacher expectations.

The major shortcoming of effective schools research, according to Chubb and Moe, is the lack of research on how the characteristics of an effective school can be nurtured and developed in individual schools. They approach this problem first by comparing student achievement scores from the "High School and Beyond" survey with the findings of the effective schools research. From this comparison, they conclude that organizational factors (clear goals, princi-pals as instructional leaders, cooperative teachers, orderly classrooms, and rigorous academic standards) do affect student achievement between one-third and one-half year of added achievement. Chubb and Moe determine that the major causes of student achievement are student ability followed in order of importance by school organization and family background. Next, they compare the existence of effective organizational characteristics to the degree of bureau-cratic constraint, and they conclude that autonomy is the strongest influence on creating an effective school organization.

From these findings, Chubb and Moe argue (a) that a major hindrance to student achievement is the existence of a large bureaucratic structure, and (b) that the best organizational condition for improving student achievement is the ability of schools to operate free of bureaucratic controls. They maintain that bureaucracies work against the basic requirements of effective school or-ganizations by imposing goals, structures, and requirements. According to Chubb and Moe, bureaucracies do not allow principals and teachers to exer-cise their professional expertise and judgment; rather, they deny them the flex-ibility needed to work effectively together to assure student achievement.

Democratic control of schools, Chubb and Moe contend, promotes bureau-cracy and therefore hinders student achievement. They reason that officials in democratically controlled institutions cannot be sure that employees will carry out their instructions. Consequently, bureaucratic structures are created to ensure that all members of the organization will comply with all orders. In addition, democratic control creates an uncertainty among leaders about their ability to remain in office and pursue their particular agendas. By making policies a part of the bureaucratic process, elected officials try to protect their favored policies against changes from opponents who might be elected in the future.

In contrast, Chubb and Moe argue, schools controlled by competition in a free market are not bureaucratic and consequently promote student achievement. The two conditions created by democratic control, the problem of authority and the uncertainty of the political future, do not exist in private schools competing in a free market. Under the conditions of private ownership, the owners of the school can make employees conform to their policies. They do not need a bureaucracy to ensure their power or the continuation of their policies. The owners and operators of private schools have the legal authority, according to Chubb and Moe, to decide the basic policies for operating their institutions. Therefore, they argue that competition in a free market promotes effective school organizations.

Free of bureaucratic controls, principals and teachers can work together to ensure policies and practices that promote student learning. On the other hand, pressure from competition with other schools forces educators to attend to the promotion of effective school practices. The resulting combination of autonomy and pressures from competition results, according to the authors, in higher student achievement.

This line of reasoning leads to the conclusion that public schools under democratic control are inherently flawed regarding their ability to improve student achievement. The major hope for basic reform of public schools, Chubb and Moe conclude, is a basic change in the method of political control. This can be accomplished, they argue, by transforming the political organization of public schools from a system controlled by democratic politics to a system controlled by the forces of the marketplace.

The system of governance proposed by Chubb and Moe is founded on the ability of parents to choose between public schools. In their proposal, students would be free to attend any school in their state, and every effort would be made to provide transportation for students to schools outside their immediate area. A parent information center would distribute information on schools, which would also collect applications for schools. While conforming to nondiscrimination requirements, each school would decide on admissions. Chubb and Moe argue that schools cannot define their own mission and establish programs if a student population is forced on them.

In Chubb and Moe's plan, schools would be funded through a system of state scholarships that would go directly to the schools. A choice office would determine the amount of the scholarship to be awarded to each student according to the student's needs. For instance, children with disabilities, learning problems, economic problems, and those identified as at-risk would receive higher scholarships to cover their more costly educational programs. The higher scholarships accompanying these students would provide an incentive for schools to provide programs that would attract them.

Each public school in this choice plan would be free to decide its own governing structure. For instance, a school could be run by a committee of teachers, a principal, or a combination of educators and members of the community. The state would not tell schools how to do their work. It would continue to certify teachers but would have only minimum requirements. This would allow schools greater flexibility in the selection of teachers.

In summary, Chubb and Moe believe that their choice plan would contribute to the improvement of student achievement in public schools. They believe that educational reformers cannot change other factors contributing to poor student achievement, such as family background and student ability. Consequently, reformers should focus on those things within their ability to change, namely, the political organization of public schools.

POLITICS AND SECOND-GENERATION SEGREGATION

Meier, Stewart, and England examine the impact of political organization on second-generation segregation.[7] They are not concerned with achievement scores, but with barriers to gaining an equal education. By second-generation segregation, they mean educational practices that still tend to separate racial and ethnic groups in schools despite the existence of court rulings declaring segregation unconstitutional. They argue that schools still practice segregation through academic grouping, such as placement in special education classes, ability grouping, curriculum tracking, and segregated bilingual education. In addition, they are concerned that discipline might be applied in different ways to different ethnic and racial groups (for instance, Hispanic and African-American students might be suspended or expelled from school at different rates than white students). Finally, they are interested in the effect of these factors on high school graduation rates.

Second-generation segregation results in inequality of educational opportunity. For instance, schools might segregate dominated groups from whites by placing them in special education classes, lower ability groups, vocational tracks, and segregated bilingual education programs. Hispanic and African-American students placed in these classes and tracks for segregation are denied access to higher levels of education available to higher ability groups and academic tracks. Obviously, students who are expelled or suspended are denied an education.

Meier, Stewart, and England use a concept of representation that centers on a socialization model. In this model, it is assumed that the representative and the represented share common political values when they share common social origins. Obviously, this type of model does not hold in all situations, but Meier, Stewart, and England cite research that it holds the most meaning for dominated groups in the United States. Hispanics, African-Americans, and Native American representatives tend to see their role as representing the desires of their particular groups.

Focusing on Hispanic-Americans, Meier and Stewart conclude that the larger the number of Hispanic representatives in an educational system, the less chance of second-generation segregation occurring among Hispanic students.[8] In their study, representation includes boards of education, educational bureaucracies, and teachers. In other words, there will be less second-generation segregation if there are more Hispanics on boards of education and working as school administrators and teachers.

In addition, Meier and Stewart found an interrelationship between representation on boards of education and representation in the bureaucracy and teaching ranks. The higher representation of Hispanics on boards of education, the higher representation of Hispanics in the school administration. In other words, Hispanic representation on boards of education creates a greater-than-normal possibility that the board will choose Hispanic administrators. In turn, they found the higher representation of Hispanics in the bureaucracy, the higher the number of Hispanic teachers.

Meier and Stewart's findings suggest a chain reaction. Hispanics are elected to the board of education and subsequently select more Hispanic administrators, who in turn select more Hispanic teachers, which results in a decline in second-generation segregation and greater equality of educational opportunity. Specifically, Meier and Stewart found that greater Hispanic representation is associated with proportionately fewer Hispanic students in special education classes and larger numbers of Hispanic students in gifted programs. Also, higher rates of Hispanic representation are related to less disparity in discipline. And, finally, a higher representation of Hispanics is related to a higher proportion of Hispanics graduating from high school.

The ability to gain seats on boards of education, Meier and Stewart found, depends on political resources (population and education), the electoral structure of the school district, and poverty among Anglos. They conclude that at-large elections are particularly detrimental to Hispanic candidates aspiring to boards of education. Some Hispanic groups have greater political resources than others. Cuban-Americans, for example, have the greatest political resources and, consequently, experience less second-generation segregation than other Hispanic groups do. The reverse is true for Puerto Ricans.

Policy recommendations follow logically from these conclusions. Meier and Stewart recommend the elimination of at-large elections because they discriminate in terms of representation against minority populations. They recommend greater federal scrutiny of second-generation forms of discrimination and increased hiring of Hispanic administrators and teachers within school districts. They recommend the elimination of most academic grouping. Although Meier and Stewart do not want to eliminate bilingual education, they do want to avoid its becoming a segregated academic track for Hispanics. Therefore, they argue for integrated bilingual programs in which both Anglos and Hispanics learn two languages. In addition, they want bicultural education to be multicultural education with an emphasis on exposing all children to a variety of cultures.

The most important message in this research is that political power is the key to serving a group's educational interests within a school system. And, for dominated groups, this political power is essential to ending forms of inequality in educational opportunity. Just as African-Americans in the South had to organize to stop segregation, other groups must exercise political muscle to stop second-generation forms of segregation.

POLITICAL CONTENT

Political organization is an important factor in determining the political content of the public school curriculum. Since the beginning of the common school in the nineteenth century, a variety of groups have competed to have their political ideas distributed through public schools. Ironically, in a society that prizes open political debate, fears of controversy over political teachings in the classroom, along with market forces that influence the publication of textbooks, created bland, uncontroversial social studies and history classes. An inherent problem for public schools in a democratic society is the necessity of accommodating many viewpoints. Concerning political issues, public schools open the door for attack from opposition groups when they present any one political viewpoint. Consequently, school administrators tend to take the safe route by not presenting anything that might provoke attacks by outside groups.

Horace Mann, often called the father of the American common school, feared that teaching any political content in the classroom might destroy the public schools; political factions would compete, each demanding that their interpretations dominate classroom teaching. On the other hand, Mann believed that political stability depended on the teaching of republican principles of government. His solution was to teach only noncontroversial aspects of the functioning of government and to avoid issues open to dispute.[9]

In the twentieth century, "patriotic" organizations, such as the American Legion and the Daughters of the American Revolution, are the most active in trying to influence the political content of schooling. Their primary goal is to weed out what they considered "un-American" ideas and to ensure the teaching of what they consider to be the basic values of Americanism. Their targets are the political content of the curriculum and textbooks and the political attitudes of teachers.

From the 1920s to the late 1980s, a primary concern of these organizations was with the possibility of communist influence on schools. The American Legion played a major role in attempting to purge what was considered the communist menace from public schools. The American Legion was organized in 1919 in the wake of World War I by U.S. Army officers who were fearful that members of the U.S. military forces in Europe were being exposed to radical political ideas, and worried about reports from the United States of the increasing spread of bolshevism. The organizational structure of the American Legion maximized opportunities for influencing both local and national education policy. Policy making was centralized, while membership was attached to local American Legion posts. An organizational goal of the American Legion was to present a united front.[10]

Within this organizational structure, its National Americanism Commission dictated the Legion's Americanism campaign to local posts. The resolution passed at the Legion's first convention in 1919 calling for the creation of the commission stated, "The establishment of a National Americanism Commission of the American Legion [is] to realize in the United States the basic ideal of this Legion of 100% Americanism through the planning, establishment and conduct of a continuous, constructive educational system." The resolution lists the following goals in the promotion of "100% Americanism":

1. Combat all anti-American tendencies, activities and propaganda;
2. Work for the education of immigrants, prospective American citizens and alien residents in the principles of Americanism;
3. Inculcate the ideals of an Americanism in the citizen population, particularly the basic American principle that the interests of all the people are above those of any special interest or any so-called class or section of the people;
4. Spread throughout the people of the nation information as to the real nature and principles of American government;
5. Foster the teaching of Americanism in all schools.[11]

The campaign for "100% Americanism" reinforced a traditional goal of using government schools for building patriotism. Most governments of the world, in varying degrees, use national educational systems for this purpose. Normally, the goal is to create a love of country or government. This is accomplished by having schoolchildren sing patriotic songs, recite a loyalty pledge or pledge of allegiance, study a highly patriotic form of the nation's history, participate in nationalistic ceremonies, and study the national literature. For some governments, the ideal is to instill in citizens such a strong love of their country that they are willing to die in war for its preservation.

As part of its Americanism campaign, local American Legion members were urged to help weed out subversives from local school systems. The 1921 Legion convention passed a resolution calling for state laws to cancel certificates of teachers "found guilty of disloyalty to the government." In addition, Legion members were asked to volunteer the names of subversive teachers to local school boards. In 1919, the National Americanism Commission warned, "We have those who believe that the red, white and blue presided over by the eagle shall be replaced by the red flag with the black vulture of disloyalty and international unrest perched upon its staff. Through the schools and through the churches the radicals are not seeking to put across their policies."[12]

American Legion pressure on the public schools continued through the 1930s. In 1934, Edward Hayes, national commander of the American Legion, told the delegates at the National Education Association (NEA) convention, "I pledge to you the tireless and loyal support of our 11,003 posts of the American Legion, in making of our schools the guardians of good citizenship...." The secretary of the NEA, J. W. Crabtree, responded to this pledge with a declaration of pride about "cementing the relationship" between the two organizations and declared, "The members of the Legion, if need be, will fight as hard to save the schools as they did to save a world."[13]

During the 1930s, the American Legion continued to advocate the firing of "disloyal" teachers. To that end, it supported requiring loyalty oaths of all teachers. The Legion considered any opposition to loyalty oaths to be the work of "subversive" elements in American society. In 1935, the National Americanism Commission reported that eight states had passed legislation requiring loyalty oaths of teachers. Other reports showed that by 1935, twenty states required loyalty oaths of teachers.[14]

After World War II, the American Legion joined many other patriotic organizations in attempts to weed subversion from schools. Suspected teachers and administrators were fired, and they purged textbooks of anything that sounded like liberalism or communism. The most famous firing of a school administrator—one that put most school administrators in a state of apprehension about attacks from patriotic groups—was that of Superintendent Willard Goslin of Pasadena, California, in 1950.

Goslin was a national figure in professional education circles. In 1948, the same year he accepted the superintendent's position in Pasadena, he was installed as president of the American Association of School Administrators. The problems for Goslin began when some parents read a pamphlet from the right-wing National Council of American Education, entitled, *Progressive Education Increases Juvenile Delinquency*. The author of the pamphlet, Allen Zoll, also wrote the widely read pamphlet *The Commies Are After Your Kids*. After reading this material, parents organized an investigation of written material used in the school system. To Goslin's amazement, the school system was charged with promoting un-American ideas in their handbook *Audio-Visual Education* because of a passing reference to Rome as a democracy and the supposed use of the "Star-Spangled Banner" as a warmongering song.[15] School administrators around the country watched in dismay while the president of their organization was dragged through the wringer of an anticommunist crusade.[16]

The anticommunist drive continued through the 1960s and into the 1980s. The efforts of the American Legion and other patriotic organizations are a model of the types of political pressure placed on the educational system to control the distribution of political ideas. Although the threat of communism declined in the 1980s, there remained the possibility of organizations attacking or promoting political ideas in the public schools.

As I discuss throughout this book, pressure from the patriotic organizations and the religious right played a major role in federal education politics in the Reagan years. Overall, pressures from patriotic organizations heightened the concern by school leaders about the presentation of controversial political opinions in the classroom, particularly ideas that might be "left wing" or "radical." Certainly, controversy about political ideas in textbooks and school curricula will be a persistent source of conflict in education.

CONCLUSION

The research by Chubb and Moe; Meier, Stewart, and England; and Meier and Stewart suggests that the political organization of schools can be changed to satisfy a variety of political viewpoints. For instance, Chubb and Moe's arguments for increasing school autonomy through a choice plan could be extended to include the accommodation of a variety of political ideologies. One characteristic of schools under a choice plan could be their political orientation.

In the framework of the research of Meier, Stewart, and England, and of Meier and Stewart, at-large elections tend to favor those within a community who have a conservative orientation. A key to gaining representation of other political viewpoints might be the elimination of at-large elections. A consequence of changing the political composition of school boards might be the hiring of school administrators with a variety of political perspectives, who in turn would hire teachers with differing politics.

An example of how these changes in political organization can affect the political content of schooling can be found in the rise of Afrocentric education. Afrocentricity represents the viewpoint that white politics is based on avarice and exploitation. Advocates of Afrocentricity want to create a common consciousness of African traditions and political orientations among African-Americans. The result of this common consciousness, according to Afrocentrists, will be the throwing off of the chains of white political domination.[17]

The introduction of an experimental voucher system in the Milwaukee public school system in 1990 made it possible for parents to have the choice of sending their children to private black academies. In addition, the system made available a public school with an Afrocentric curriculum that parents could choose for their children.[18]

Representation of African-Americans in the administration enabled the proposal of a 1991 plan to establish an Afrocentric school within the New York public school system. The proposal to establish the Afrocentric school came from an employee, Basier Mchawi, of the chancellor's office of the New York public school system. The proposal was part of a lifetime effort by Mchawi to improve the education of African-Americans.

Originally, Mchawi pursued his goals outside the public school system. In 1976, he became a teacher at the privately operated Uhuru Sasa, which a group of black nationalists started in New York City. The major goal of the school was the transmission of African culture to black students. When Uhuru Sasa closed in the mid-1980s because of a lack of financial support, Mchawi began to think about creating a similar school within the public school system and, in 1986, he began teaching in the New York public school system. At a series of community meetings in 1988, Mchawi was able to attract the attention of Chancellor Richard Green, who appointed him to be an assistant in his office.

While working within the chancellor's office, Mchawi became an outspoken critic of the New York public school system. At community forums, he announced, "I work for the Board of Mis-education, and I mean that." One parent quoted him: "Don't think that because there are two black men in the

Chancellor's office that the revolution has started. It hasn't. Nothing's changed."[19]

Obviously not interested in being promoted within the system, Mchawi continued his criticism, which resulted in a request for his resignation. In response, Mchawi proposed the establishment of the Ujamaa Institute, which, he explained, would synthesize traditional African values and the needs of African-Americans. To gain political momentum for his proposal, he sought the help of Roger Green, a Brooklyn assemblyman and former chairperson of the Black and Puerto Rican Caucus.

Green was interested in the problem of alienated black youth and had convened a series of workshops on "reclaiming and empowering" black youth. Green felt that Mchawi's proposal was a possible answer to the problem and he contacted the chancellor's office. The result was the chancellor's approval for Mchawi to develop the plan.

Mchawi's story illustrates the political power that representatives of minority political opinions can exert in the educational establishment. Minority representatives have the opportunity of institutionalizing their proposals. Because of his proposal, Mchawi was made an associate on the chief executive staff for instruction of the New York public school system. In the end, his pursuit of his lifelong dream of an African-American educational program resulted in his advancement in the public school bureaucracy.[20]

The political organization of public schools acts as an important filter for political ideas, and it affects student achievement and equality of opportunity. It mediates and shapes political conflict over educational issues. In Chapter 6, I will focus on the political actors: how the importance of a particular political actor depends on the political organization of education. The political structure can be organized to favor the influence of one group over another, enhance equality of educational opportunity, and possibly raise student scores on standardized achievement tests.

NOTES

1. John E. Chubb and Terry Moe, *Politics, Markets & America's Schools* (Washington, D.C.: Brookings Institution, 1990); Kenneth J. Meier, Joseph Stewart, Jr., and Robert E. England, *Race, Class, and Education: The Politics of Second-Generation Discrimination* (Madison: University of Wisconsin Press, 1989); Kenneth Meier and Joseph Stewart, Jr., *The Politics of Hispanic Education* (Albany: State University of New York Press, 1991).
2. For a discussion of these political changes, see Joseph Cronin, *The Control of Urban Schools* (New York: Free Press, 1973), pp. 39-123; Joel Spring, *Education and the Rise of the Corporate State* (Boston: Beacon Press, 1972), pp. 85-135; David Tyack, *The One Best System* (Cambridge, Mass.: Harvard University Press, 1974), pp. 126-167.
3. Ibid.
4. Chubb and Moe, *Politics, Markets*, p. 4.
5. Meier and Stewart, *Politics of Hispanic Education*, p. 8.
6. Chubb and Moe, *Politics, Markets*.

7. Meier, Stewart, and England, *Race, Class, and Education*.

8. Meier and Stewart, *Politics of Hispanic Education*.

9. Lawrence Cremin, ed., *The Republic and the School: Horace Mann on the Education of Free Men* (New York: Teachers College Press, 1957), pp. 94-97.

10. William Gellerman, *The American Legion as Educator* (New York: Teachers College, Columbia University, 1938), pp. 20-39.

11. Quoted in ibid., p. 68.

12. Quoted in ibid, pp. 90-91.

13. Quoted in ibid, pp. 225-227.

14. Gellerman, *American Legion*, p. 122; Harold Hyman, *To Try Men's Souls: Loyalty Tests in American History* (Berkeley: University of California Press, 1959), pp. 323-326.

15. David Hulburd, *This Happened in Pasadena* (New York: Macmillan, 1951); James Boyle, "Pasadena, Calif.," *Saturday Review of Literature* (8 September 1951), pp. 7-8.

16. For a general description of this anticommunist crusade against public schools, see Joel Spring, *The Sorting Machine Revisited* (White Plains, N.Y.: Longman, 1989), pp. 1-35.

17. See Molefi Kete Asante, *Afrocentricity* (Trenton, N.J.: Africa World Press, 1989).

18. Mark Walsh, "Black Private Academies Are Held Up as Filling Void," *Education Week*, (13 March 1991), pp. 1, 28.

19. M. A. Farber, "'Africa Centered' School Plan Is Rooted in 60's Struggles," *New York Times* (5 February 1991), pp. B1, B2.

20. Ibid.

CHAPTER 6

Reinvention of the School, Systemic Reform, and Federal Policies

"We will abolish the Department of Education, end federal meddling in our schools, and promote family choice at all levels of learning," proclaimed the 1996 Republican National Platform.[1] In contrast to the Republican platform, the Democrats offered federal programs "to make sure America has the best public schools on earth."[2]

Behind these opposing promises are political efforts to reinvent the school and cause systemic reform in the educational system. There are four major political and economic forces pressuring the school system to change.

1. The revolt of Christian Fundamentalists
2. Conservative and business proponents of the free market ideas of Austrian economics
3. The web of conservative foundations including the Heritage Foundation, the Hudson Institute, and Olin Foundation
4. Corporate demand that schools educate workers for the new global economy

The Christian Coalition was responsible for the anti-federal government and pro-school choice sections of the 1996 Republican platform. In fact, the revolt of Christian Fundamentalists against the supposed secular humanism in public schools is the major political force behind the whole concept of reinventing the school. Central to this reinvention are provisions for school choice and charter schools. In the 1970s and 1980s, Christian fundamentalists received public support and financial support from Austrian economists and conservative foundations. Austrian economists support the notion of Christian fundamentalists being given a choice of public schools. For Austrian economists, school choice for Christian fundamentalists is an important step in turning public schools over to the forces of the free market.[3]

Corporate leaders, conservative foundations, governors, and New Democrats advocated systemic reform of the educational system through the creation of national academic standards. They believe that national standards will force changes on the entire educational system. By creating national standards, state governments, it is hoped, will enforce tight academic standards and ensure compliance through statewide examinations. Faced with state standards and examination requirements for students, teachers and school administrators would be forced to change their practices. In this manner, federal and state standards are to cause systemic reform by forcing change throughout the school system.[4]

REINVENTING THE SCHOOL

David Osborne and Ted Gabler's *Reinventing Government: How the Entrepreneurial Spirit is Transforming the Public Sector* heralded the concept of the reinvention of schools. The book serves as a guide for President Clinton and the New Democrats. Osborne and Gabler argue, "The kind of government that developed during the industrial era, with their sluggish, centralized bureaucracies, their preoccupations with rules and regulations, and their hierarchical chains of command, no longer work very well."[5] It was during this industrial period the public school system was shaped. Consequently, the authors argue that the school system also needs to be reshaped. Based on this thesis, Osborne and Gabler offer suggestions for reinventing government and public schools.

There are seven basic principles to their reinvention idea.

1. Create competition between government agencies and private organizations. For education, this means applying Austrian economics to create competition between public schools through a *choice plan*.
2. Moving control from the government bureaucracies to the community. For schools, this means *site-based management* teams or local governance boards consisting of parents, teachers, community members, and school administrators.
3. Accomplishments should measure government performance. For education, this means determine performance from student-grades achievements.
4. Goals should guide government agencies and not rules and regulations. For education, this means national and state academic standards.
5. Government agencies should consider citizens as customers. For schools, this means *choice*.
6. A government that prepares for future problems. Osborne and Gabler do not discuss education in this context.
7. Replace hierarchical control with teamwork. For school systems, this means trimming back the bureaucracy and delegating decision-making power to a *site-based management team* at the school level.

In their final chapter, Osborne and Gabler stress school choice, decentralizing authority, and creating "a system of accountability that focuses on results, rather than compliance on rules and regulations."[6] In this context, state governments and local school boards would set minimum educational standards, enforce social equity, and arrange financing of schools. Osborne and Gabler proposed that, "school districts would not *operate* public schools. Public schools would be run—on something like a contract or voucher basis—by many different organizations: teachers, colleges, even community organizations."[7] In addition, public schools would earn extra tax money by attracting more students in a competitive market created by school choice.

Reflecting the influence of Osborne and Gabler on the Democratic Party, the *1996 Democratic National Platform* calls for an expansion of public school choice and the promotion of public charter schools.[8] In addition, the *Platform* promises to reduce federal regulations and to "give local schools, teachers, and principals the flexibility they need to meet those [Goals 2000] standards."[9]

Of course, the Republican Party is also a strong advocate of school choice. The difference between the two political parties is over how much choice. Republicans favor choice between public and private schools, while the Democrats, because of the important influence of the two teachers' unions, would limit choice to public schools.

ANALYZING NATIONAL EDUCATION POLICY

For "the first time in the nation's history a statutory framework defining an appropriate role for the federal government in education has been enacted," Secretary of Education Richard Riley proclaimed in 1995 with the passage of President Clinton's Goals 2000: Educate America Act.[10] As I discussed in Chapter 1, Goals 2000 is the heart of the New Democratic approach to school reform and national education policy. It is debatable whether it defines an "appropriate role for the federal government." Ironically, recent Republican demands for a limited role of the federal government in education are at odds with the historical record. Extensive federal involvement in education occurred during the Republican administration of President Dwight Eisenhower in the 1950s. During the 1950s, Eisenhower's administration linked public schools to national defense policies. During the 1950s the military and industrial establishment influenced the federal government to adopt policies designed to change public school curricula so that they would educate more engineers and scientists to meet the needs of military competition with the Soviet Union. However, the current objection to federal education policies stems from gaining federal support in the 1960s of educational programs designed to reduce poverty and aid dominated groups. Also, federal involvement in education expanded in the 1970s when the business community gained federal support for establishment of career education programs and expansion of vocational education.

For national-level analysis, I am making a distinction between the politics of policy and the politics of implementation. Politics of policy refers to the struggles between interest groups and politicians that result in the formulation of national educational policy. On the other hand, politics of implementation involves the struggles among politicians, interest groups, and bureaucrats over the implementation of policy.[11] These two analytical categories, as indicated in

TABLE 6-1. Politics of Policy and Implementation

Origins of Federal Educational Policy
    Grass-roots movements
    Political strategy
    National policy concerns
Causes of Struggles over Implementation
    Bureaucratic conflict
    Political strategy and interest groups

Table 6-1, can be divided according to the origins of political action. For instance, federal policy can originate from grass-roots movements that pressure politicians to enact legislation. The civil rights movement is a good example of a grass-roots movement that produced federal educational legislation. For this book, I am defining a grass-roots movement as a group of citizens who are outside government and the educational establishment and who organize to cause educational change.

In some situations, politicians advocate educational policies to win votes and build a constituency. In 1980, the Republican Party organized a constituency of private-school supporters and religious reformers around educational policies that included tuition tax credits, school prayer, and abolishing the Department of Education. Educational policy also originates in debates about other national problems. Historically, concern with national defense and the economy resulted in a variety of federal education legislation.

The responses of politicians to voters are part of the politics of implementation. In the 1980s, Republicans promised voters less federal regulation and intrusion into state and local governments. They actualized these campaign promises in deregulation, and by the shifting of partial control over federal programs to state and local school authorities. President George Bush's administration continued this policy into the 1990s. In addition, struggles occur among bureaucrats at different levels over the control of federal programs. For instance, local school authorities often object to the authority of state educational agencies.

Like many categories used in this analysis, those in Table 6-1 are interconnected and overlapping. Grass-roots movements catch the eye of politicians, who see another source of votes. Politicians quickly translate concerns with unemployment or defense into proposals for more and better education. Local school authorities pressure their political representatives to free them from federal paperwork and red tape.

GRASS-ROOTS MOVEMENTS

The revolt of Christian Fundamentalists and the political influence of the Moral Majority and the Christian Coalition are prime examples of the ability of a grass-roots movement to influence national education policies. Historically, the civil rights movement is another good example. The lack of response from state and local governments forced the civil rights movement to turn to the courts and the federal government. The civil rights movement dates back to the nineteenth century, when southern states passed laws requiring segregation in education, public accommodations, transportation, and other public facilities. The black community, disenfranchised by southern voting laws, was unable to exert political power at the local level to end school segregation. Consequently, black organizations, led by the National Association for the Advancement of Colored People (NAACP), carried their battle into the courts and successfully achieved school desegregation with the 1954 U.S. Supreme Court decision *Brown* v. *Board of Education.*

The *Brown* decision, along with its implementation decision in 1955, could not, however, force southern school systems into desegregating. The civil rights movement had to pressure the federal government. In addition, it had to resort to nonviolent sit-downs and demonstrations to force the desegregation of public facilities and transportation. They formed a variety of civil rights organizations, including the Congress on Racial Equality and the Student Nonviolent Coordinating Committee. The most important of these organizations was the Southern Christian Leadership Conference under the direction of Martin Luther King, Jr.

The activities of these civil rights organizations are examples of how failure to change government policies at local and state levels results in groups seeking federal intervention. Dominated by whites, many southern municipal and state governments defied the law of the land. Unable to get southern communities to comply with Supreme Court rulings, civil rights activists took to the streets.

In the 1950s and early 1960s, desegregation struggles persuaded liberal political leaders in the Democratic Party that federal action was necessary. They proposed a series of civil rights bills, the most important of which they passed in 1964. The 1964 Civil Rights Act gave teeth to federal desegregation efforts by decreeing that federal monies would be withheld from institutions that discriminated according to race, religion, or ethnic origin. This legislation established the precedent of policing civil rights violations (including, eventually, discrimination based on gender and disabilities) in institutions that received federal monies.[12]

To be an effective weapon against school segregation, the 1964 Civil Rights Act required major federal funding of education. This funding came in 1965 with passage of the Elementary and Secondary Education Act (ESEA), which contained Title I (now called Chapter 1) supporting compensatory education. ESEA was part of the War on Poverty conducted by the federal government in the 1960s.

ESEA was one response to the civil rights movement and a growing national concern with poverty during the administrations of presidents John F. Kennedy and Lyndon B. Johnson. In the early 1960s, King shifted the emphasis of the civil rights movement to a poor people's campaign to eradicate poverty in the United States. The Democratic Party—which during the New Deal years of the Great Depression had structured its voter support around the poor, organized labor, urban blue-collar workers, Catholics, and minority groups—responded to the rising tide of protest from minority groups and the poor.

Illustrating the tension that pressures from different groups can cause, President Kennedy faced the problem of drafting educational legislation that would please civil rights groups and Catholic school leaders who wanted to receive some benefit from any federal education legislation.[13] In addition, education lobbyists feuded over whether to emphasize funding of elementary and secondary education or higher education. President Kennedy's commissioner of education, Francis Keppel, recalled the antagonism that existed in 1962 between the education lobbyists. "It was obvious that the best hope that one could have would be to keep a program before the Congress . . . and try to keep the lobbyists from killing each other, oh, because the higher education fellows were so mad at the NEA fellows they wouldn't speak to them."[14]

While education lobbyists bickered with one another over the emphasis in federal legislation, they were united opposing aid to religious schools. For instance, Edgar Fuller, executive secretary of the Council of Chief State School Officers, testified before Congress in 1962 for the American Association of School Administrators, the American Vocational Association, the National Congress of Parents and Teachers, the National School Boards Association, and his own organization against aid to sectarian schools. He argued that it was unwise public policy and would result in educational legislation being declared unconstitutional.[15]

Exemplifying how political strategy determines educational policy, the resolution of the differing demands from civil rights organizations, Catholic groups, and educational organizations shaped federal legislation. After President Kennedy's assassination, President Johnson decided to overcome religious conflicts and squabbles among education lobbyists by linking educational legislation to his War on Poverty. In addition, Johnson developed a strategy for overcoming fears about federal control of education. In his study of education legislation during the Kennedy and Johnson years, Hugh Graham describes the problem for the Johnson administration: "the best way to avoid the charge of federal control was to provide general aid to the states as what the Bureau of the Budget abhorred as the leave-it-on-the-stump-and-run variety." But, according to Graham, "if this aid was to be for public schools only, so as to keep church and state separate, it of course aroused the intense opposition of the Roman Catholic lobby and thereby split the Democratic constituency."[16]

They resolved the problem in a brilliant stroke of political strategy contained in a 1964 memo written by Commissioner of Education Francis Keppel. Keppel outlined three legislative options, the first of which was to provide general aid to public schools. This, he argued, would cause a negative reaction from Catholic groups and spark a battle between Catholics on one side, and the National Education Association (NEA) and the Council of Chief State School Officers on the other. The second option was to provide general aid to both public and private schools. This, he predicted, would cause a strong reaction from the NEA and would split the Democratic Party, since southern Democrats objected to any aid to Catholic schools. In addition, there was the issue of the constitutionality of federal aid to religious schools.

The third option, and the one that eventually became the Elementary and Secondary Education Act of 1965, was to drop the idea of general aid and focus on educational aid to the children of the poor. Keppel believed that most education lobbyists would support the proposal, as would the many southern Democrats who represented depressed rural areas. They could include Catholic schools because the money would go to benefit poor children, not religious institutions. In addition, in response to charges of federal control, the legislation would provide money to strengthen and expand state departments of education so that they could administer the legislation.[17]

This political strategy produced one of the most important pieces of federal education legislation in modern times and had major consequences for future federal legislative action. First, it signaled the abandonment of general federal aid to education in favor of categorical aid. One consequence was to tie federal aid to other national policy concerns, such as poverty, defense, and economic growth. Second, it solved the religious issue by linking federal aid to educational programs that could be used in parochial schools to benefit children, not religion. However, this would remain a constitutional issue as the courts continually refined the extent of federal involvement in religious schools. And last, to avoid charges of federal control, the reliance on state departments of education to administer federal funds resulted in an expansion of those bureaucracies and a much larger role for state government in a local education. This trend accelerated in the 1980s, when, in an attempt to reduce federal control, Ronald Reagan's administration consolidated educational legislation into block grants to be planned and administered at state and local levels.

POLITICAL STRATEGY

There is a thin line between federal education policies caused by pressure from grass-roots movements and policies initiated by politicians to win votes. Although it is often hard to determine original causes and effects, it is possible to point to some specific situations in which politicians have acted consciously to organize and please an educational constituency. In these situations, federal policy has been linked directly to political strategy.

For instance, consider the political strategy in President Reagan's appointment of educational politician William Bennett as secretary of education in 1985. During the 1980 presidential campaign, the Republican Party formed its educational constituency around interest groups concerned with private schooling, school prayer, and moral values in the curriculum. On the other side of the fence, organized educational interests supported Democrats, including the NEA and the American Federation of Teachers (AFT).

The most prominent religious and conservative groups forming the educational constituency of the Republican Party were the Moral Majority, the

Heritage Foundation, and Phyllis Schlafly's Eagle Forum, which, with other organizations, formed a coalition under the umbrella organization Committee for the Survival of a Free Congress. These conservative organizations, and other conservative appointees to the Department of Education, complained that Terrel Bell, President Reagan's first secretary of education, was being un-duly influenced by the education community.

For instance, during the early years of the Reagan administration, conser-vatives within the Department of Education drafted regulations to provide stiffer enforcement of the Hatch amendment. The Hatch amendment was passed in 1978 but remained unenforced until the Reagan administration. It re-quired parental approval before any child in a public school could be given psy-chiatric, psychological, or behavioral testing or questioning. Conservatives be-lieved that the amendment provided protection against public school meddling in student values. Based on the Hatch amendment, Schlafly's Eagle Forum issued a form letter to parents that they could use to advise their local school districts that they did not want their children to be involved in any psychiatric, psychological, or behavioral questioning or testing. The form letter objected to school activities such as values clarification, death education, discussion and testing of interpersonal relations, sex education, drug and alcohol education, and "anti-nationalistic, one-world government, or globalism curricula."[18]

Conservative appointees within the Department of Education complained when Secretary Bell dragged his feet in enforcing the provisions of the Hatch amendment. Charlotte Iserbyt, an employee of the Department of Education, wrote in a memorandum to other conservatives, "Bell doesn't like them [the Hatch amendment regulations], and he does not want to offend his education-alist friends by signing off on regulations that will disturb their modus operandi." Iserbyt believed that educators were trying to change "the values, attitudes, and beliefs of students to conform with those necessary to bring about a socialist/humanist one-world government."[19]

Conservatives were therefore pleased when Bell resigned in 1985 and Reagan appointed William Bennett. Reagan failed to accomplish his campaign promises to abolish the Department of Education and gain passage of a school prayer amendment and tuition tax credit legislation. Bennett's appointment was an attempt to hold the Republican educational constituency together and silence conservative critics.

With the appointment of Bennett, the Moral Majority report of 1985 proudly announced in headlines, "Finally a Friend in Education."[20] The Moral Majority has steadily gained strength within the Department of Education. For instance, in 1985, Thomas Tancredo, the Department of Education's Region VIII representative in Denver, distributed at government expense a speech written five years previously by the executive director of the Moral Majority at the time, Robert Billings. The speech declared, "Godlessness has taken over America." President Reagan appointed Billings to direct the Department of Education's ten regional offices.[21]

During confirmation hearings before the Senate Committee on Labor and Human Resources, Bennett, under oath, admitted that twelve conservative organizations meeting under the umbrella of the Committee for the Survival of a Free Congress had screened him for the position of secretary of education. He claimed that he was forced to attend that meeting under pressure from the White House. Bennett told the Senate committee that he received a call from Lynn Ross Wood of the Office of Presidential Personnel. "The advice to me," Bennett said, "was to attend the meeting, that they requested that I should attend this meeting."[22]

To please his educational constituency, Reagan transformed the philosophy and style of the Department of Education. Bennett announced that he was going to use the office as a "bully pulpit" to influence educational policy through rhetoric and pronouncements. In addition, Bennett championed a core curriculum emphasizing the humanities in the context of Western civilization—a curriculum that ignored the culture of many ethnic groups supporting the Democratic Party. This political bias was evident in a statement to the Senate confirmation hearings by Arnoldo S. Torres, national executive director of the League of United Latin American Citizens (LULAC). About Bennett's emphasis on Western civilization in the core curriculum, Torres stated: "Yet Western Europe is merely one continent on the globe; the melting pot of North America also has its roots in the cultures of the East, of Africa, of the Pacific, and finally of the rest of the Western Hemisphere—Central and Latin America."[23]

Concerns about pleasing a particular educational constituency extended into the Bush administration. Like Reagan, Bush did not receive the support of the two teachers' unions. A story illustrates the gulf between the two teachers' unions and the Republican Party told to Maurice Berube by the Washington lobbyist for the NEA. At the time, Berube was doing research for his book *Teacher Politics: The Influence of Unions*. The NEA played a major role in Democratic President Jimmy Carter's election campaign. During the years that Carter occupied the White House, Dale Lestine, manager of NEA lobbying, would walk the six blocks from the NEA headquarters to the White House for early morning breakfasts with representatives of the administration. In contrast, during the Republican Reagan and Bush administrations, telephone calls to the White House had gone unanswered, and lobbyists from the NEA had not been invited to frequent early morning breakfasts.[24]

Directing his energies at the same educational constituency that had backed Reagan, Bush, during the 1988 election campaign, announced that he would be the "education president." And, like Reagan, Bush called for choice in education, a school prayer amendment, and excellence in education. Shunning the two teachers' unions and the educational establishment, Bush decided to develop his educational plan in cooperation with the National Governors Association.

For building a strong political image regarding education, the Bush administration turned the development of educational goals for the year 2000 into a media event. Meeting at the University of Virginia in 1990, the president and the National Governors Association issued a joint statement outlining six national goals for education to be achieved by the year 2000. But, as Democratic Governor of New York Mario Cuomo pointed out, the national goals were issued with a great fanfare but with no promise of federal financial aid.[25]

As part of his strategy to use education to build a political image, Bush appointed a new secretary of education, Lauro Cavazos, who played a different role than his predecessor, Bennett. Unlike Bennett's outspoken manners that often caught the attention of the media, Cavazos's quiet deportment kept him out of the media spotlight. This meant that Bush did not have to share media exposure regarding educational issues with his secretary of education.

Bush's strategy of building a strong image in educational issues by keeping the media spotlight focused on him eventually backfired. Ironically, the Bush administration was criticized for appointing a weak and indecisive secretary of education. In addition, Bush's educational proposals went down to defeat in Congress. Typical of the criticism was a statement by A. Graham Down, president of the Council for Basic Education: "I would give him [Bush] a C-minus, maybe a D-plus. I mean, he hasn't really done much except talk, and talk is cheap."[26]

Trying to recoup his political losses, Bush in 1991 replaced Cavazos with Republican stalwart Lamar Alexander. Given the nature of the criticism of the Bush administration, Alexander appeared as an ideal appointment. While governor of Tennessee, Alexander made education a central focus of his administration. He gained national prominence for instituting a state program of career ladders for teachers. Familiar with political maneuvering, Alexander could be a stronger political manager than Cavazos. And unlike Bennett, Alexander did not threaten to steal the media spotlight from Bush.

Alexander won immediate support from Bush's educational constituency. The Heritage Foundation, which played a major role in shaping the educational constituency of the Republican Party, reacted positively to the appointment. Jeanne Allen, education analyst for the Heritage Foundation, stated that Alexander "has an enormous head start. . . . He is a former governor at a time when governors are playing a crucial role in education reform." Denis Doyle, a conservative educational thinker and favorite of the Republican administration during the 1980s, called Alexander the first real secretary of education because he is "a mainstream person with superb education credentials, a genuine education agenda, and no personal ax to grind."[27]

To hold onto support from the religious right and private school constituency, Bush announced that his fiscal 1992 budget would include money to reward school districts that developed plans allowing parents to choose between public and private schools. Unlike previous Republican attempts to gain choice for parents between public and private schools through tuition tax credits (Republican administrations in the 1980s found it impossible to get tuition tax credit legislation through Congress), the Bush strategy was to persuade local school districts to develop choice plans.[28]

There are many other examples of educational policies being shaped by politicians consciously trying to gain votes. One of the more interesting is the issue of bilingual education. In the previously cited study of federal education policy in the Kennedy and Johnson years, Hugh Graham provides the example of liberal Democratic Senator Ralph Yarborough of Texas, who, believing that he would lose the 1970 election to a wealthy and conservative Democrat, decided that Hispanic support was crucial for his coalition of blacks, Mexican-Americans, and poor whites.[29]

To win Hispanic support, Yarborough, after being appointed to a special subcommittee on bilingual education of the Senate Committee on Labor and Public Welfare, launched a series of hearings in major Hispanic communities. Ethnic political lobbyists—not educational experts or linguistic theorists—gave most of the testimony. The hearings concluded in East Harlem, with Massachusetts Senator Edward Kennedy and the Bronx Borough President Herman Badillo decrying the fact that there were no Puerto Rican principals and only a few Puerto Rican teachers in the New York City school system.[30]

Yarborough supported bilingual legislation that focused on students whose "mother tongue is Spanish." The legislation included programs to impart knowledge and pride about Hispanic culture and language and to bring descendants of Mexicans and Puerto Ricans into the teaching profession. The legislation was clearly designed to win political support from the Hispanic community.

The opportunistic nature of Yarborough's legislation was highlighted in Congressional hearings when Commissioner of Education Harold Howe pointed out that bilingual education programs were already being funded to the level of $13 million under Title I of the 1965 ESEA and that Yarborough's bill provided only $10 million. Furthermore, the needs of other children such as those of Korean or Chinese descent were ignored in the legislation. In Graham's words, "Senator Yarborough was not primarily interested in the bloc vote of Korean Texans."[31]

The Johnson administration opposed a separate bilingual education bill because of the programs developed under the ESEA and the explicit Hispanic bias of the proposed legislation. But in the end, according Graham, the political arguments won out. The administration compromised by supporting the legislation, and Congress compromised by removing the Hispanic bias. The result was separate legislation for bilingual education. As an ironic comment on the political value of educational issues, Yarborough lost the 1970 Democratic Senate primary to Houston millionaire Lloyd Bentsen.

The above examples illustrate how politicians and educational politicians use educational issues to win votes. Of course, there is a direct relationship between this process and the effect of grass-roots movements. In the cases of both choice and bilingual education, politicians are trying to win support from well-defined grass-roots movements. As discussed earlier in Chapter 2, the religious right and Catholic organizations have pressured for some form of a choice plan that would include both private and public schools. Hispanic organizations have struggled for bilingual education. In both situations, politicians shaped their educational policies to win support from these movements.

NATIONAL POLICY CONCERNS

National political, social, and economic issues are a major source of change in federal education policy. In response to national issues, the schools often become both scapegoats and citadels of hope. For instance, in the Cold War years of the 1950s, the schools were criticized for being the weakest link in national defense. One aspect of the arms race was the competition between U.S. and Soviet schools to educate the best scientists, mathematicians, and engineers. One result of the Cold War was the 1958 National Defense Education Act, which supported math, science, and foreign language programs in the public schools. In the 1960s, national concerns focused on the issue of poverty, and the schools were blamed for being racist institutions and perpetuating poverty. Within this climate, the ESEA was passed in 1965. In the 1980s the schools were blamed for not preparing students to help the United States compete in international markets against the Japanese and West Germans.

Educational interest groups tend to jump on the bandwagon with each new shift in national policy concerns. For example, the "Sony war" of the 1980s turned federal education policy around and caused a struggle among educational interest groups for a share of the federal budget pie. The battle cry of the Sony war in education was given in 1983 by the National Commission on Excellence in Education when it declared in its report *A Nation at Risk*, "Our nation is at risk. Our once-unchallenged preeminence in commerce, industry, science, and technological innovation is being overtaken by competitors throughout the world." The report placed the blame on the schools with the warning, "The educational foundations of our society are presently being eroded by a rising tide of mediocrity that threatens our very future as a nation and a people." The report specifically warns of Japan's efficient automobile manufacturing, South Korea's steel production, and West German products.[32]

A Nation at Risk was issued after a period in the 1970s and early 1980s of relatively high unemployment (particularly among youth), declining productivity, and dwindling capital investment by U.S. industry. In part, the high unemployment was caused by the large number of youth from the baby-boom generation entering the labor market combined with a slow increase in the number of jobs. The result was a decline in wages, particularly for entry-level occupations, and a tendency by American business to limit capital investment and rely on inexpensive labor. The resulting decrease in capital investment caused a slow growth in productivity in U.S. industry. Between 1960 and 1978, the average annual rate of increases in labor productivity in the United States was 1.7 percent; in Japan, by contrast, it was 7.5 percent.[33]

Therefore, the claim by *A Nation at Risk* and by other educational reports in the early 1980s, that the poor academic quality of schools was responsible for the slow growth in the nations' productivity was inaccurate. The cause was to be found in decisions made by business management. In fact, it takes twenty years for a high school graduate to affect the economy. A poorly educated high school graduate does not walk out of school and immediately bring down the economy. If one is going to blame the schools for the economic problems of the 1980s, then one has to blame the schools of the 1950s and early 1960s, not the schools of the 1970s.[34]

Clearly, most education reports in the early 1980s were using the public schools as a scapegoat for economic problems caused by factors outside the realm of education. But, against the background of these general economic concerns, there emerged a school reform movement that emphasized teaching traditional academic subjects, increasing the quality and number of science and mathematics courses, and changing the career structure of teachers.

THE POLITICS OF IMPLEMENTATION

The implementation of federal legislation often causes political struggles among various levels of the educational bureaucracy. State education agencies and local school districts have always complained about federal red tape and regulations. In addition, local school districts have complained about the heavy hand of state government. For their part, federal and state administrators have claimed that, without their respective guidance, the goals of federal legislation would not be achieved.

Paul Peterson and Barry Rabe outlined the relationships that develop between the different levels of government with the implementation of federal legislation.[35] Eventually, they conclude, the struggle over the implementation of federal legislation is resolved with a cooperative relationship between new bureaucratic structures and professionals. But before this occurs, there are several stages of development.

In stage one, according to Peterson and Rabe, Congress passes legislation with imprecise guidance on its implementation. This was the situation with the compensatory education programs of the 1965 ESEA. The legislation contained only a vague framework for creating compensatory education programs, and professionals at the local school district level were unprepared to deal with the new federal programs.

Federal regulations during the early years of the ESEA were minimal and sometimes nonexistent. Consequently, local school districts organized their own programs without much intrusion from state and federal officials. In fact, state and federal governments lacked the staff to supervise the spending of federal money. For instance, in 1976, 14,000 school districts spent $120 million for compensatory education. Also, there were only 100 Office of Education staff members to supervise compensatory education programs. As a result, complaints were made that local school districts were improperly using federal money designated for compensatory education programs.[36]

In response to these complaints, federal control moved into what Peterson and Rabe designate as stage two. During this stage, the federal government attempts to control the actions of local school districts by drafting more specific guidelines and regulations. Interest groups also begin to exert influence over any amendments to the original law and over the regulations. In compensatory education, these interest groups included the National Advisory Council for the Education of Disadvantaged Children, the Lawyers' Committee for Civil Rights under Law, the Legal Standards and Education Project of the NAACP, and the National Welfare Rights Organization. These groups demanded more specificity in federal regulations to correct what they believed to be the failure of local school systems to implement compensatory education programs properly.

Stage three results, according to Peterson and Rabe, from complaints about federal red tape and control and repeated conflicts between federal bureaucrats and local leaders over guidelines and expectations. Federal control begins to loosen, but it does not return to the conditions that existed under stage one. Instead, the administration of federal programs at state and local levels is now in the hands of experienced professionals who understand and conform to the objectives of federal legislation. For instance, regarding compensatory education programs, Peterson and Rabe write: "State-based professionals became increasingly aware of what was and was not expected by the federal government, and what was and was not feasible locally."[37] These state-based professionals, they argue, take pride in enforcing federal requirements. Therefore, according to Peterson and Rabe, cooperation develops between local, state, and federal administrative structures. This cooperation is established between a new set of bureaucrats at each government level whose primary purpose is to deal with particular federal programs. It is not necessary, Peterson and Rabe argue, for every federal program to go through each evolutionary stage. For instance, federal programs for the disabled were launched under the stringent controls of stage two. But eventually there developed a new cadre of professionals at the state and local levels, and disabled programs moved to stage three.

Although Peterson and Rabe provide evidence of administrative cooperation in the implementation of federal programs, there is also evidence of continuing conflict between local and state bureaucrats. During the Congressional hearings on the Elementary and Secondary Education Consolidation Act of 1981, local school administrators voiced their fear of greater state control of local schools. Ironically, this legislation was designed to provide greater discretionary power to local and state governments in the management of federal programs.

For instance, one new professional whom Peterson and Rabe consider to be part of the cooperative administrative structure, Dan Foster (administrative director, Projects, Compliance, and Research, Hayward Unified School District in California), told the House subcommittee holding hearings on the 1981 legislation, "The LEA's [local education agency's] problem is not with federal interference in education, but rather with the state legislatures, state boards of education, and state departments of education."[38]

At oversight hearings later in the year, Tom Rosica, executive director of the Office of Federal Programs in the Philadelphia school district, stated, "As I speak to my counterparts around the country, I think one of the concerns expressed is that we not replace federal bureaucracy with a state bureaucracy and federal regulations with state regulations."[39] At the same oversight hearings, Foster again appeared, but this time as president of the Western Association of Administrators of State and Federal Programs, to express the fear by local administrators of more control by state government.[40]

In summary, Peterson and Rabe might be correct about the development of cooperative relations among the new professionals responsible for federal programs at the state and local levels. But it should also be recognized that these new professionals struggle with one another for control over the implementation of federal legislation. This results in political tension between the new professionals responsible for federal programs in local school districts and similar professionals in state education agencies. Therefore, the general evolution of the politics of implementation tends to be the following:

1. Federal legislation is implemented with minimal controls.
2. Interest groups and federal officials complain that state and local education agencies are not fulfilling the intent of federal legislation.
3. Federal regulations are tightened and made more specific.
4. New professionals appear in local and state education agencies to handle federal programs.
5. Complaints are voiced about federal red tape and regulation.
6. Federal controls are eased, and cooperation develops among the new professionals in charge of federal programs.
7. Conflict continues between the new professionals at the state and local levels.

POLITICIANS AND INTEREST GROUPS

In recent years, politicians have made the issue of federal red tape and control a major campaign issue. As part of its strategy to please conservative groups that were critical of federal involvement in education, the Republican Party in the 1980s and 1990s advocated limiting federal regulations over educational programs and increasing local and state control. Such a policy entailed a major change in the way federal education laws are enforced. Of course, any change in the administration of federal programs brings an immediate response from interest groups. The methods of implementation of federal programs are a product of actions by politicians, pressures from interest groups, and, as discussed in the last section, conflict between bureaucrats.

In the 1980s, the Republican administration's plan for reducing federal regulations over educational programs and increasing local and state control was embodied in the Elementary and Secondary Education Consolidation Act of 1981. The general plan of the law was (a) to lump large groups of categorical programs into block grants and (b) to have local and state educational agencies plan and administer the use of the money allowed for each grant.

The most controversial of the original proposals, which did not appear in the final legislation, was to combine money for the disadvantaged and the disabled in the same block grant. Objections to this proposal were immediately raised by Representative Carl Perkins of Kentucky when introducing Secretary of Education Terrel Bell during the House hearings on the legislation. Perkins warned of potential conflict between interest groups representing the disadvantaged and groups representing the disabled: "I am concerned about your bill because it could pit the disadvantaged and the handicapped against one another at the local level. It could also allow the use of these funds for local tax relief."[41]

Secretary Bell's response to Representative Perkins and other critics of the proposal contained an interesting analysis of the political power of interest groups. Bell argued that the pressure of interest groups at the state level would ensure the proper allocation of federal funds. Bell told the committee, "The parents and those others who express themselves in lobbies when the legislature is in session, those forces would be at work, those handicapped children's advocates, the education associations and that big school lobby that is around every state house would be there."[42]

Referring to his own experience in state politics, Bell assured the committee that interest groups would determine the use of federal money. "I have lived in that arena," he claimed in reference to state politics. "We would presume that those forces would be protecting these interests. That state education lobby is a big one and it is powerful and the interest groups inside of education are getting more and more capable and powerful. We have the state school boards' association and the state teachers' associations. You know the scene. It is all that."[43]

From Bell's perspective, therefore, less federal regulation of educational programs would create more conflict among interest groups at the state level. On the other hand, interest groups objected to the withdrawal of federal control because they believed that their interests would not be protected. M. Hayes Mizell, chair of the National Advisory Council for the Education of Disadvantaged Children—an organization claiming to represent 6 million children who depend on Title I funds—complained to the House oversight committee, "The effect of the secretary's position is to create even more passive compliance with federal education law. . . . The federal bureaucracy has abandoned its responsibilities."[44]

Also objecting to the freedom provided under block grants were the new professionals described by Peterson and Rabe. Like some interest groups, the new professionals were protected by stringent federal controls, and they objected to deregulation. They feared the potential battle with interest groups and legal problems. Members of the Florida, Georgia, North Carolina, Alabama, and California departments of education appeared before the House oversight committee and expressed fear about the lack of federal guidelines. Speaking for the state administrators, Steve Sauls of Florida stated, "Normally, we would be among the last to be complaining about the prospect of too little regulation. But we are concerned that too little regulation by the U.S. Department of Education will leave too many unanswered questions, with the result being that the courts will be asked to play a greater role in education policy making."[45]

State politicians are also worried that less federal regulation means less federal money. In 1991, some governors accused President Bush of wanting to turn control of federal programs over to states as a cover for reducing federal aid. Bush proposed turning control of more than $15 billion worth of federal programs to state governments. While governors hailed this transfer of power, they worried that they would be accompanied by a 25-percent to 30-percent reduction in funding. Republican Governor Richard Snelling of Vermont argued that Bush should be encouraged in providing block grants but warned, "We've been there before. . . . If we get block grants with a third or a quarter reduction in the funding, we can't do it."[46]

In summary, the implementation of federal legislation is part of the political battle between interest groups and bureaucrats. Conservative interest groups such as the Christian Coalition and the Eagle Forum advocate a reduction in federal regulation and control. On the other hand, some interest groups such as those representing the disadvantaged and the disabled feel protected by strong federal control. The new professionals at the state and local levels are concerned with any changes in regulations that threaten their interests. In addition, these new professionals compete for power over federal programs. Although state politicians welcome control over federal programs, they worry about reduced federal spending. It is within this complex arena of political struggles that federal regulations are developed and federal programs are administered.

CONCLUSION

Between the 1950s and the 1990s, federal involvement in education increased as (a) grass-roots movements sought federal aid to overcome injustices in educational opportunities; (b) politicians, after blaming the schools, called for educational reform to improve the economy and national defense; and (c) politicians discovered that organized groups interested in education could be a source of aid in campaigns and of votes.

Ironically, the debate between Republicans and New Democrats in the 1990s symbolized the importance of education in national politics. In 1980, the Republican Party made educational issues an important part of its presidential campaign. In 1997, the Democratic administration advocated greater involvement by promising to make universal the first two years of college through a system of scholarships and tax deductions.

As national education policy continues to change, the following guidelines can be used to analyze federal educational politics:

I. Federal Legislation
  A. Determine the causes of the federal legislation:
    1. Is the legislation a result of the failure of local and state educational authorities to respond to a grass-roots movement?
    2. Is it the result of a politician or politicians seeking to form or please a particular educational constituency?

      3. Is it the result of politicians using education as a scapegoat for other national problems?

      4. Is it intended as an easy cure for a complex national problem?

   B. Determine the reasons for the content of the federal legislation:

      1. What interest groups and politicians supported or opposed the legislation?

      2. What political strategy was used to balance the desires of politicians and interest groups?

      3. How was the above political strategy reflected in the content of the legislation?

      4. Did an iron triangle develop between interest groups, federal administrators, and particular politicians?

II. Appointment of Federal Educational Politicians

   A. Determine the reasons for the appointment:

      1. Was there pressure from a particular interest group?

      2. Did the administration want to form a particular educational constituency?

      3. Was the administration paying off a political debt?

   B. Determine the consequences of the appointment:

      1. What educational policies does the educational politician support?

      2. How does the educational politician balance her or his educational interests with pressures from interest groups, bureaucrats, and politicians?

      3. What effect does the educational politician have on the implementation of legislation?

III. Implementation of Federal Legislation

   A. Determine the reasons for the implementation methods:

      1. Did the political party in power promise a particular method of implementation (e.g., deregulation and block grants under Republicans)?

      2. What was the role of interest groups in developing the methods of implementation?

      3. What role did local and state educational agencies play in developing the implementation methods?

   B. Determine the consequences of the implementation methods:

      1. What government agency or agencies controls the federal program?

      2. What interest group benefits?

NOTES

1. *The 1996 Republican Platform*, p. 21.

2. *The 1996 Democratic National Platform*, p. 6.

3. For a more detailed discussion see Joel Spring, *Political Agendas for Education: From the Christian Coalition to the Greens Party* (Mahwah, N.J.: Lawrence Erlbaum Associates, Inc., 1997), chapters 1-3.

4. Ibid., chapters 2-5.
5. David Osborne and Ted Gabler, *Reinventing Government: How the Entrepreneurial Spirit Is Transforming the Public Sector* (New York: Penguin Books, 1993), pp. 11-12.
6. Ibid., p. 315.
7. Ibid., p. 316.
8. Ibid., p. 7.
9. *The 1996 Democratic National Platform,* p. 6.
10. Quoted by Hanne Mawhinney, "The New Focus on Institutions and the Reinvention of Schooling," in *The Politics of Education and the New Institutionalism: Reinventing the American School* (Washington, D.C.: The Falmer Press, 1996) edited by Robert L. Crowson, William Boyd, and Hanne Mawhinney, p. 23.
11. Richard K. Jung's review of research on the politics of education at the federal level, "The Federal Role in Elementary/Secondary Education: Mapping a Shifting Terrain," in Norman Boyan, ed., *Handbook of Research on Educational Administration* (White Plains, N.Y.: Longman, 1988) references only studies dealing with the implementation of policy.
12. Hugh Davis Graham, *The Uncertain Triumph: Federal Education Policy in the Kennedy and Johnson Years* (Chapel Hill: University of North Carolina Press, 1984), pp. 26-52.
13. Ibid.
14. Quoted in ibid., pp. 43-44.
15. Ibid., p. 48.
16. Ibid., pp. 71-72.
17. Ibid., pp. 73-75.
18. Phyllis Schlafly's letter was reprinted as "Please Excuse My Child from . . ." in *School and Community,* vol. 72, no. 1 (Fall 1985), p. 8.
19. Quoted in Bert Greene and Marvin Pasch, "Observing the Birth of the Hatch Amendment Regulations: Lessons for the Education Profession" *Educational Leadership* (December 1985/January 1986), p. 44.
20. Quoted by Senator Lowell Weicker in U.S. Senate, Committee on Labor and Human Resources, Hearing on William J. Bennett, of North Carolina, to Be Secretary of the Department of Education, 97th Cong., 1st sess. (28 January 1985), p. 61.
21. Ibid., pp. 173-174.
22. Quoted in ibid., pp. 60-61.
23. Quoted in ibid., p. 188.
24. Maurice Berube, *Teacher Politics: The Influence of Unions* (Westport, Conn.: Greenwood, 1988).
25. Reagan Walker, "Accord on Goals Hard to Attain, Executives Find," *Education Week* (31 January 1990), pp. 1, 13; William Welch, "Governors," *Compuserve Executive News Service, Associated Press* (27 February 1990).
26. Quoted in Lynn Olson and Julie Miller, "The 'Education President' at Midterm: Mismatch between Rhetoric, Results," *Education Week* (9 January 1991), pp. 1, 30.
27. Quoted in Julie Miller, "Educators Hail Nomination of Alexander as Secretary," *Education Week* (9 January 1991), p. 1.
28. Mark Ptisch, "Bush Seeks to Reward District Plans that Include Private-School Choice," *Education Week* (13 February 1991), pp. 1, 29.
29. Graham, *Uncertain Triumph,* p. 155.
30. Ibid., p. 156.
31. Quoted in ibid., p. 157.
32. National Commission on Excellence in Education, *A Nation at Risk: The Imperative for Educational Reform* (Washington, D.C.: U.S. Department of Education, 1983), pp. 5-7.

33. See Daniel Quinn Mills, "Decisions About Employment in the 1980s: Overview and Underpinning"; and Michael Wachter, "Economic Challenges Posed by Demographic Changes," in Eli Ginzburg et al., eds., *Work Decisions in the 1980s* (Boston: Auburn House, 1982).

34. Pamela Walters and Richard Robinson, "Educational Expansion and Economic Output in the United States, 1890-1969," *American Sociological Review*, vol. 48 (August 1983), pp. 480, 493.

35. Paul Peterson and Barry Rabe, "The Evolution of a New Cooperative Federalism," in Norman Boyan, ed., *Handbook of Research on Educational Administration* (White Plains, N.Y.: Longman, 1988).

36. Ibid.

37. Ibid., p. 28.

38. Quoted in U.S. House of Representatives, Subcommittee on Elementary, Secondary, and Vocational Education and Subcommittee on Select Education and Labor, Joint Hearing on the Elementary and Secondary Education Consolidation Act of 1981, 97th Cong., 1st sess. (28 May 1981), pp. 113-114.

39. Quoted in U.S. House of Representatives, Subcommittee on Elementary, Secondary, and Vocational Education, Oversight Hearings on Title I, ESEA, and the Chapter 2 Education Block Grant, 97th Cong., 1st sess. (6 October 1981), pp. 21-22.

40. Ibid., pp. 23-27.

41. Quoted in U.S. House of Representatives, Joint Hearing on ESEA, p. 44.

42. Quoted in ibid., p. 95.

43. Ibid.

44. Quoted in U.S. House of Representatives, Oversight Hearings, pp. 30-31.

45. Quoted in ibid., pp. 44-45.

46. Quoted in Lynn Olson, "Governors Greet Bush Plan to Turn Programs Over to the States with Cautious Enthusiasm," *Education Week* (13 February 1991), pp. 1, 30.

CHAPTER 7

State Politics of Education

State involvement in local school districts expanded with systemic reform and efforts to equalize financing between school districts. Even classroom teachers feel the greater presence of the state government as academic standards and statewide examinations are enforced. School administrators worry about how their schools will do on state tests. Both teachers and administrators fear that test scores will damage their careers. "Teach to the test" is now an important factor in many school districts. Systemic reform's promise of affecting all parts of the school system may be fulfilled. Consequently, state governments exert greater control over the knowledge distributed in local schools.

Also, other factors have contributed to the expansion of educational activity by state governments. State politicians are increasingly involved in educational issues, and some members of state legislatures have become expert in educational policies. Also, the new federalism has given state governments more control over federal education programs. Also, the National Governors Association continues to play a role in carrying out academic standards. Fourth, during the Reagan and Bush administrations the National Governors Association cooperated in the development of reform policies for the public schools. Last, throughout the 1980s and early 1990s, the business community complained that higher academic standards and better teachers were required for the United States to maintain leadership in world markets. Of course, other factors also are leading to increased centralization.

On the surface, the trend toward centralization at the state level appears to contradict efforts to increase school autonomy through site-based management and encourage greater teacher and parental involvement in local school decisions. Making a distinction resolves this contradiction between controlling the knowledge distributed by schools and getting schools to dispense that knowledge efficiently. Centralization of power at the state level is designed to control the type of knowledge distributed by schools; thus, state standards define the parameters in which local groups can work. On the other hand, it can be argued, plans for differing forms of site-based management are designed to

111

make schools more effective in dispensing the knowledge required by the state. Of course, conflict can result between local control and state control when local managers decide to reject state requirements.

Centralization varies from state to state, depending on differences in political climate and government organization. Although the U.S. Constitution gives the power to control education not to the federal government but to state governments, state involvement in local schools has evolved slowly since the nineteenth century. In the nineteenth century, state governments were primarily concerned with laws creating school districts, general academic requirements, and compulsory education. In the early twentieth century, most states began to license teachers and establish teacher certification standards. During these early years, state education agencies remained relatively small.

In the 1960s, state control over local schools increased with the administration of federal programs and the enforcement of civil rights policies. It was estimated that by 1983, federal funds supported 50 percent of the staff in state education agencies. Also, court decisions in the 1970s requiring equitable financing of schools forced state governments to become more involved in local school finance and caused some state legislators to become experts in educational policy.[1]

In addition, governors and state legislators aided the trend toward centralization when, for a variety of political reasons, they declared that improved schools would cure the states' economic problems. The resulting school improvement campaign increased state control over teacher certification and school curricula. Some states established statewide competency testing of teachers and students. In other states, legislatures restructured the teaching profession by establishing career ladders and master teacher plans. States such as California, which have the power to influence textbook adoption in local school systems, pressured publishers to change the content of textbooks.

In summary, the historical trend is increased centralization of control by state governments over educational policies. The continuation of this trend will depend on the shifting nature of educational politics at the national level and on how much resistance from local school systems. Of course, with greater centralization of power comes greater uniformity. Statewide testing and detailed curriculum requirements result in uniformity of content and curriculum in public schools and teacher training institutions. In addition, greater involvement in educational finance strengthens state control over local schools.

My discussion of state educational politics will begin with descriptions of the similarities and differences among states and of the major political actors. I will then discuss the causes for political action at the state level and present a method analyzing state educational politics.

PATTERNS OF STATE EDUCATIONAL POLITICS

The increasing centralization of control over state educational policies can be understood by analyzing differing patterns of state educational politics. Joseph McGivney provides the best synthesis of categories of state educational politics.[2] His theoretical framework assumes that as social organizations de-velop, they become more centralized and bureaucratized.

McGivney's categories are based on Lawrence Iannaccone's pioneering work, *Politics in Education*.[3] Iannaccone used four categories to describe state educational politics. In the first category, *type I (local-disparate)*, political deci-sions are primarily the result of linkages between state politicians and local school board members and superintendents. In other words, power is found at the local level. In the second category, *type II (monolithic)*, state educational pol-itics are dominated by a coalition of statewide educational interest groups, including teachers' associations and associations of school administrators. In this category a coalition of educational interest groups applies pressure to members of the state legislature. In the third category, *type III (fragmented)*, political decisions are a product of conflict between educational interest groups and between educational interest groups and state agencies. The cooperation of type II politics is replaced with competition. Iannaccone modeled the last cate-gory, *type IV (syndical)*, on the Illinois School Problems Commission, which tried to establish a cooperative effort among government officials, education groups, and private citizens for the development of state educational policy.

Iannaccone assumes that state educational systems evolve from the local-based character of type I to the statewide syndical model of type IV. In this evo-lutionary process, different states are at different levels of development. McGivney accepts the idea of stages of development but recasts Iannaccone's categories, using new research on state politics.

In McGivney's categories, state educational politics evolve to a centralized, bureaucratic form. McGivney's stage I is similar to Iannaccone's type I, in which educators represent primarily a local constituency, and state educational agencies and legislatures work to maintain local control. Like Iannaccone, McGivney labels stage II "monolithic" and describes a statewide coalition of educational interest groups working with key members of the legislature. For development, the concerns of stage II are broader than the local concerns of stage I. In stage III, the monolithic structure is replaced with competition among educational interest groups, and new interest groups such as parochial schools become active.

For McGivney, stage III is an important step in centralization because indi-vidual interest groups direct their attention to specific state agencies. In the lobbyists monolithic stage II, interest groups primarily interact with one another and, as a group, with members of the state legislature. In stage III, interaction among interest groups decreases as individual interest groups interact with specific state agencies. McGivney argues that stage III is a product of increasing bureau-cracy and centralization. At this stage, competition among interest groups results from a desire to protect their respective share of advantages won from government. In other words, as the role of state government in education increases, each educational interest group becomes dependent on a continua-tion of a particular state program or funds. In stage III, interest groups begin to compete for more state support of their particular programs. This competition causes the coalition of stage II to disintegrate.

McGivney replaces Iannaccone's type IV or stage IV with a model of statewide bureaucracy in which iron triangles form among members of education lobbies, members of the state legislature, and representatives of the chief executive. In McGivney's words, "Over time . . . increasing influence is gained by or is delegated to the bureaucracy as the former lobby becomes more the bureaucracy. . . . Conflict is adapted to through an impersonal, rational, and legalistic process that becomes dominated by the bureaucracy."[4]

McGivney matches his stages of development with Frederick Wirt's national study of state centralization. After closely examining the laws, constitutions, and court decisions in each of the fifty states, Wirt constructed a *school centralization scale* to rate the degree of centralized state control as opposed to local control. Although Wirt found varying degrees of centralization among states, the major gatekeeping functions of teacher certification, accreditation, and attendance were under rigid control even in the most decentralized state.

Overall, Wirt concluded, state politics controls local school policies. Any reform movement that attempts change at the local level will have only a marginal impact. "If the locus of reform is the district or school site," says Wirt, "efforts at reform, even if successful, win only a skirmish; the massive structure beyond it remains unengaged or unaffected." Therefore, Wirt argues, state politics of education is the key to understanding the organization and operation of local schools. "Too often, then," Wirt writes, "local politics is a marginal politics, a struggle over things at the fringe, with the major decisions about how children will be taught having already been made elsewhere and therefore almost untouchable locally."[5]

Accepting Wirt's argument about the power of state educational politics over local schools, McGivney matches Wirt's scale to his political stages. States that rate low on the school centralization scale are in stage I of state educational politics, and states that rate high on Wirt's scale are in stages II and III. Only one state, Hawaii, with complete state control over schools, ranks at the top of Wirt's scale and is placed in McGivney's stage IV. Examples of states in stage I that rank low on the centralization scale are Connecticut, Massachusetts, Maine, and New Hampshire. Missouri, Texas, Rhode Island, Georgia, Illinois, and Tennessee are in stage II; Wisconsin, New York, California, Colorado, New Mexico, Nebraska, Michigan, New Jersey, Minnesota, and Florida are in stage III.[6]

The general patterns in state educational politics found by Iannaccone, Wirt, and McGivney create a picture of increasing centralization and control by state governments over local education. During the 1990s, this pattern of centralization is occurring at the same time that there are calls for site-based management in local schools and parental choice of schools. As discussed in Chapter 6, this apparent contradiction between increased state control and increased local choice and management can be understood as a difference between controlling the objectives of a school system and organizing for efficient management. Plans for choice and site-based management are based on the premise that they will increase the efficiency of local schools in achieving the academic goals established by the state.

PATTERNS OF STATE CONTROL

By the 1990s, state governments developed differing methods for controlling local school systems. The differences among states ranged from states helping local school systems develop goals to threats of a takeover of failing local school systems. One common feature of many of these state systems is a reliance on testing. In 1991, forty states mandated some form of student testing, and forty-five states required some form of teacher testing. Testing is an important tool of control because it defines a particular content that must be learned to pass the test.[7] Anecdotal reports suggest that school administrators and teachers frequently teach according to test requirements. In addition, during the 1980s many states tightened control of academic requirements for schools.

One way of comparing state systems is by examining the mechanisms used to influence local schools. James Cibulka identifies three types of state educational policy systems: *lightly coupled, assessment driven; tightly coupled, instructionally guided;* and *loosely coupled, instructionally guided.*[8] As the name suggests, a *tightly coupled assessment-driven* system uses the results of statewide tests of student achievement to determine actions toward local school systems. Cibulka places South Carolina and Illinois in this category. South Carolina's 1985 Basic Skills Assessment Act requires statewide testing in reading and math. The assessment program is coupled with a combination of rewards and punishments. The state might declare low-performing schools "educationally impaired," or it might give merit rewards to high-performing schools. As Cibulka indicates, the key to the South Carolina system is performance on the statewide tests. State action is taken based on these test results. Legislation mandates the establishment of school improvement councils, which must plan according to the results of the testing system.

A 1991 plan for Illinois is another example of a tightly coupled, assessment-driven state system. A report issued by State Superintendent Robert Leininger, "Linking Accountability to Student Performance and School Improvement," calls for linking school accreditation with results from the state's testing program. Test results for individual schools, not school systems, would be compared with past results and state standards. The state would have the power to intervene in low-performing schools and reward high-performing schools.

California is Cibulka's example of a *tightly coupled, instructionally guided* educational system. Local school systems in California are guided by curriculum frameworks adopted at the state level. In addition, local schools must adopt textbooks from an approved state list. According to Cibulka, many of these textbooks were written in response to the state's curriculum frameworks. Local school systems retain the right to decide how they will organize and teach the curriculum material.

California is a good example of the combination of centralized control to achieve particular educational objectives and local management to attempt to assure efficient achievement of those objectives. Overseeing textbook selection and adopting curriculum frameworks is more controlling than administering statewide tests. Statewide tests open the door to teachers teaching for the tests. On the other hand, controlling textbooks and the curriculum provides direct state control over the content of knowledge distributed to students.

Cibulka uses Minnesota as an example of a *loosely coupled, instructionally guided* system. Minnesota requires local school systems to develop individual learning programs for each student. State assistance is provided to help local school systems develop the goals and methods to assess these individual programs. There is no statewide system of testing, but the state does make recommendations for methods of assessment. Unlike many other states, Minnesota attempts to avoid specifying what will be taught. The major requirement, rather, is that local districts plan an outcome-based system.

Of course, the realities of conditions often frustrate attempts at greater state control in local school systems. This is particularly true of urban school districts that face problems of many at-risk youth, rapid turnover in chief executives, and continuing issues of desegregation. In addition, strong teachers' unions can frustrate state plans. Consequently, one result of state-testing plans for urban school districts are to push students out of the system. The affluent school districts have been most active in responding to new state requirements.[9]

POLITICAL INFLUENCE

With centralization, the control of state educational policy is primarily a product of interaction between leading politicians and educational politicians, and between educational associations and business groups. In stage I of state politics, local school people and communities exert a major influence over state policies. By stages III and IV, teachers' associations—usually the strongest of the educational interest groups—and the business community compete for influence over politicians and educational politicians.

During the 1980s and 1990s with the growing concentration of educational policy making at the state level, state governors made education a central focus of their political campaigns. As politicians, governors tried to please teachers' organizations and the business community. To the business community, governors promised an improved economic system through better schooling. To teachers, they promised improved salaries and a restructured profession. Sometimes governors were forced to choose one group over another; most often, the choice was the business community.

Although there is a trend toward centralization and increased influence of statewide teachers' organizations and business groups, differences remain in patterns of influence in different states. Catherine Marshall, Douglas Mitchell, and Frederick Wirt conducted an important study of influence in state education politics. They synthesized previous studies of influence in state politics and identified by order of influence the major political actors in Arizona, West Virginia, California, Wisconsin, Pennsylvania, and Illinois. Their study is useful for discussing general patterns of influence in state politics.[10]

One problem with the study is that it blurs distinctions between the influence of elected politicians and educational politicians, and that of groups acting outside the official sphere of government. Of course, this distinction is important at all levels of government. Obviously, elected politicians and educational politicians responsible for state educational policy will exert a great deal of influence. The issue is, Which government actor has the most influence over education? Is the major influence in the government exerted by the governor, members of the state legislature, the state legislature as a whole, the chief state school officer, or the state education agency?

The next problem is identifying the group outside government that exerts the most influence over politicians and educational politicians. If the governor is influential in educational policy making, then identifying the group outside government that influences the governor is important. Is the governor influenced by the business community, teachers' associations, or other interest groups? The same question can be asked about members of the state legislature and state educational agencies.

Unfortunately, Marshall, Mitchell, and Wirt do not distinguish between influences on government and influences on members of government from groups outside government. Nevertheless, even with this limitation, generalizations about influences on state educational policies can be made from their study. For the six states in their study, Marshall, Mitchell, and Wirt established the following list, in descending order of influence, of policy actors at the state level:

1. members of the state legislature specializing in educational issues;
2. legislature as a whole;
3. chief state school officer and senior state officials in state departments of education;
4. coalitions of educational interest groups (teachers, administrators, school boards, and other educational groups);
5. teachers' associations;
6. governor and executive staff;
7. legislative staff;
8. state board of education;
9. school board associations;
10. associations of school administrators;
11. courts;
12. federal policy mandates;
13. noneducation interest groups (business leaders, taxpayers' groups);
14. lay groups (PTAs, school advisory groups);
15. educational research organizations;

16. referenda; and
17. producers of educational materials.

This list can be divided into those inside and those outside government. For instance, the following is a list, in descending order of influence, of those within government:

1. state legislature;
2. chief state school officer and senior members of the state department of education;
3. governor and executive staff;
4. legislative staff; and
5. state board of education.

Focusing on influences within state governments, Marshall, Mitchell, and Wirt found that certain legislators specialized in educational issues and guided the votes of others, while most legislators gave educational issues only occasional attention. Obviously, the lawmaking power of a legislature would give it the greatest control over educational policy.

Next in order of influence, the power of chief state school officers varied significantly within the six states. Overall, they functioned as long-term bureaucrats who worked patiently to establish educational policies. An earlier study of chief state school officers found them to be primarily white males in their middle 50s with rural backgrounds. Most chief state school officers come from the ranks of public school administrators and teachers. They exert their greatest influence within state departments of education and in their leadership of state boards of education. Elected chief state school officers, as opposed to appointed, tend to exert more influence among legislators.[11]

As Marshall, Mitchell, and Wirt note, governors increased their involvement in educational policy in the early 1980s. Before that time, governors were concerned mainly with school finance issues. A major study done in the 1970s concluded, "State tax burden, educational effort, and educational expenditures were associated most strongly with gubernatorial involvement in educational policy making."[12]

Members of legislative staffs gain their influence by acting as links between interest groups and members of the state legislature. Both legislators and interest groups depend on staff expertise. The most influential staff members work for legislators who specialize in educational legislation.

At the bottom of the scale in influence are the state boards of education. Usually, state boards of education are strongly influenced by the chief state school officer, who often sets the agenda for their meetings. State legislators and educational interest groups consider state boards of education as having only a minor role in policy making. In fact, very few board members believe they have any meaningful influence on legislative actions.[13]

The important issue is which groups outside government have the greatest influence over policy makers in government. In the six states, the following groups influence government officials in descending order of importance:

1. educational associations;
2. noneducational groups (business leaders, taxpayers' groups);
3. lay groups (PTAs, school advisory groups);
4. educational research organizations; and
5. producers of educational materials.

In the six states, educational associations have the greatest influence on government officials. Teachers' associations are the most influential, with a coalition of other educational associations running a close second. School board associations are more influential than organizations representing school administrators. The combined figures for all six states give education groups more influence than noneducation groups—except in Arizona, where the Phoenix 40, a group of prestigious businesspeople that meets informally once a month, exercises strong influence over state educational policy.

In addition, the courts and federal policy mandates influence state educational policy. Court decisions forced states to act in areas such as school finance, segregation, and education for the mentally retarded and disabled. As discussed in Chapter 6, federal policy mandates created a new group of professionals at the state level and established new educational programs. The courts and the federal government can, in some situations, exert more influence than any state government officials.

Important differences in influence exist within the six states. In West Virginia, the courts became active in 1979, when a ruling in *Pauley* v. *Kelley* mandated a very detailed reform of the state school system that included defining minimum standards and changing the system of educational funding. In Illinois, the chief state school officer and the state department of education have little influence, while teachers' associations are ranked very high.[14]

Different patterns of influence in each state cause variations in educational policies. In West Virginia, under the influence of the courts, equalizing access to education is a major concern. In Illinois, because of the strong influence of teachers' associations, collective bargaining is a major concern. In Wisconsin and Illinois, which have strong teachers' and local school board associations, there is a high level of interest in mandating local development of student tests. On the other hand, in West Virginia, California, and Pennsylvania, the influence of local school board associations is low and is related to a high interest in statewide student testing.

These variations highlight the ultimate impact of centralization. With centralization there are fewer groups and individuals influencing educational politics. Only the most powerful have meaningful influence—the most powerful being the teachers' associations and the business community.

In highly centralized states, the educational associations protect their interests and support educational changes that will enhance their power and position. On the other hand, the business community supports educational policies that serve their economic interests, which usually means ensuring that the schools prepare students to meet their labor needs and taxes on corporations are kept at low levels.

CENTRALIZATION AND TEACHERS' UNIONS

The increasing centralization of control over educational policy and the financing of schools at the state level has made it necessary for teachers' unions to focus more attention on state politics. Of particular concern is the importance of the state in financing local school systems. In many states, teachers can no longer be content with bargaining and taking strike actions in local school districts. In many situations, higher salaries depend on actions by state legislatures. Consequently, teacher strikes are, in some places, occurring statewide.

For instance, in 1990, statewide strikes occurred in Washington, Utah, and West Virginia. In early February 1990, 13,000 teachers in 35 of Washington's 296 school districts announced they were planning a walkout for higher salaries. Eight thousand other teachers pledged to attend after-hour rallies and marches. The state affiliate planned the protest of the National Education Association (NEA), the Washington Education Association, to demand that the state surplus of funds be used to increase teacher salaries by another 10 percent. In 1989, the state legislature approved a 10-percent increase but the teachers' union demanded an additional 10 percent. In Washington in 1990, the average starting pay was $18,000 and the average pay for all teachers was $33,100.[15]

Focusing on the relationship between the economic competitiveness of Washington state and the quality of teachers, Teresa Moore, spokesperson for the 49,000-member union, stated that low salaries have an "impact on national competitiveness, the ability to keep good teachers, and . . . on how we can attract new people into the profession." Ignoring union demands for higher salaries, Governor Booth Gardner, who called himself the "education governor," told a rally of school board members and administrators that, while he is committed to creating a world-class education system, there could be no salary increases because the state's $611-million budget surplus was a one-time phenomenon.[16]

In Utah, the issue was the passage in the state legislature of a $38-million reduction in state taxes. Like Washington, Utah's state government was hardly in bad financial straits since it could afford a large tax reduction. On the other hand, the average teacher's salary in Utah in 1990 was $22,621, and the state's teacher-student ratio of 25.4/1 was the highest in the nation. On February 16, 1990, most of the 16,000 members of the state affiliate of the NEA, Utah Education Association, authorized their union board to call a strike. On February 19, teachers rallied in front of the state legislature demanding more spending for education. Because of union activity, the state legislature granted a $1,000 salary increase for all teachers and a 4-percent increase in state money to local school districts.[17]

Union actions in Washington and Utah set the stage for one of the largest and longest state teachers' strikes in history. The only previous strike of this nature was a 3-week strike by Florida teachers in 1968. On March 7, 1990, two-thirds of West Virginia's 22,000 teachers walked off the job for what would be an 11-day strike. The strike idled half the 328,000 students in West Virginia schools.

Led by the 3,000-member West Virginia Federation of Teachers (of the American Federation of Teachers [AFT]) and the 16,000-member West Virginia Education Association (of the NEA), teachers began their protests for higher salaries with a rally on February 15, 1990, which ended when state troopers were called in to restrain teachers as they pounded on the doors of the state legislature demanding higher pay. The average salary for West Virginia teachers was $21,904, ranking from 49th among other states. On March 2, teachers skipped school chanting, "Pay raise or strike." Twenty-one counties canceled classes, and pickets in one county turned away buses at three schools. A group of 5,000 teachers met at the state legislature, where members of the United Mine Workers and other unions joined them. A group of 100 teachers surrounded Education and Arts Secretary Steve Haid, screaming questions and complaints. At the rally, the president of the West Virginia Education Association, Kayetta Meadows, complained that while the state was not able to raise teachers' salaries, they could give raises of 5 percent to 25 percent to the division of highways engineers and were considering raising state troopers' salaries by $7,000 per year. In response to the governor's claim that there was no money for increasing teachers' salaries, she retorted, "Do they think we're so dumb that we can't read the paper, that we can't tell what's going on?"[18]

As the strike continued into a second week, the state education superintendent closed all schools for a cooling-off period. Governor Gaston Caperton urged county superintendents to fire all teachers who did not go back to work after the cooling-off period. As the tension built, the state attorney general's office issued a statement that the teachers were striking illegally and could be suspended or fired, and charged with a misdemeanor. Pressured by threats of being fired or refusing to back union demands, some teachers crossed picket lines. In one county, it was estimated that 30 percent of the teachers crossed picket lines.

Lasting antagonisms developed between striking teachers and those who crossed picket lines. Strikers greeted teachers crossing picket lines with handouts and with demands that they honor the line. Jeanne Taylor, a home economics teacher who crossed a picket line, reported, "We drove slowly, we rolled down our window, we stopped and we listened to what the pickets had to say. We respect their view. It would be nice if they respected ours." After entering the school building, she said, "I cried . . . the emotions are like a roller coaster. You're up and down. You're taking Maalox and Rolaids." Lois Swineford, a math teacher who crossed a picket line, complained, "I haven't slept, I've had nightmares over this. It's hard to know what's right any more."[19]

On March 17, the two unions urged teachers to return to work after leaders of the state legislature agreed to call a special session to develop a long-range plan for the educational system and raise teachers' salaries. In addition, the unions were feeling pressured by a series of court decisions regarding back-to-work orders. After agreeing with legislative leaders, Kayetta Meadows, president of the West Virginia Education Association, told a news conference, "We've moved education to the forefront, so it just isn't something that you pay lip service to during elections."[20]

These three teacher strikes highlight a major source of tension in state educational politics. Demands by teachers that state legislatures increase funding puts politicians in a difficult position. Politicians fear that tax increases will cost them support from voters. In this regard, governors are most vulnerable because voters often do not know the names of their state representatives but do know who is governor. Consequently, voters most often direct their anger at the governor. In addition, since the business community resists increases in corporate taxes, there will probably be increased tension between the business community and teachers' unions as school funding becomes increasingly centralized at the state level.

SOURCES OF POLITICAL CHANGE

As in federal politics, there are three major, often overlapping sources of political change at the state level. For analysis, one source of political change can be identified as *grass-roots movements*. An example of grass-roots movement is the successful campaign in Minnesota for tuition tax credits. Another source would be the *political strategies* of elected politicians and educational politicians. As an example, I will discuss the activities of a master political strategist, Bill Honig, the superintendent of California schools. Third, the actions of Governor James B. Hunt of North Carolina demonstrate how changes in educational issues are linked to *general policy concerns*.

GRASS-ROOTS MOVEMENT

Tim Mazzoni and Betty Malen provide an excellent example of a grass-root movement in their research on tuition tax credit legislation in Minnesota between 1971 and 1981. They analyzed the lobbying techniques of the Minnesota Catholic Conference (MCC), representing six Catholic dioceses, and the Citizens for Educational Freedom (CEF), an organization composed of private school supporters.[21]

These two organizations formed an alliance in the late 1960s to campaign for state transportation aid for private schools. Following this campaign, the MCC-CEF alliance sought state tax concessions for non-public school pupils. As a single-issue lobbying group, the alliance constantly hounded state legislators about financial aid to private schools. Their persistent efforts forced many legislators to bow to the pressure to avoid harassment or being labeled as opponents. According to Mazzoni and Malen, legislators placed the issue in the same category as gun control or abortion, where nonsupport of that single issue, no matter what other issues a politician stood for, would be considered sufficient reason for voters not to support him or her.

In other words, a single-issue interest group will force a politician to support its position by making all other issues secondary. One unidentified member of the Minnesota legislature stated, "Their people [the MCC-\CEF alliance] spoke out: 'We'll beat you if you vote against our bill.' And it didn't matter if you had done 5,000 things right . . . . That gave me and a lot of other people real concern . . . and it was, I think, a statewide effort."[22]

The alliance campaigned with phone calls, orchestrated mailings, and persistent contact with state legislators. During the 1971 legislative debate on tuition tax credits, the alliance sent busloads of supporters to the state capitol to make direct contact with their representatives. Legislators reported that constituents would look them in the eye and say, "You aren't going to let us down now, are you?"[23] Mazzoni and Malen quote legislators who pleaded for passage of the bill just to get alliance supporters off their backs. In addition, the alliance brought private school supporters to legislative hearings to remind lawmakers of their promises. There were complaints that during the hearings on non-public school aid, parents and kids flooded the hallways and legislative chambers.

The unanimous opinion of Minnesota legislators is that the successful passage of tax concessions for private schools in 1971, 1978, and 1981 resulted primarily from the power of the MCC-CEF alliance. The key tactics of the alliance were identified as: "(a) keep the issue continuously on the legislative agenda; (b) energize sympathetic lawmakers to carry its bills, attract supporters to these bills, and maneuver them through the legislative process; and, most important, (c) mobilize grass-roots constituency pressure to sway votes in the Legislature." And, from the standpoint of Mazzoni and Malen, the constant face-to-face contacts between lobbyists and lawmakers were the most effective lobbying technique.[24]

Another factor to the success of the MCC-CEF alliance was the lack of a well-organized opposition. Traditionally, the two teachers' unions have led strong national opposition to any form of tax concession to private schools. Nevertheless, according to Mazzoni and Malen, the Minnesota Education Association and the Minnesota Federation of Teachers did not concentrate any effort on the issue raised by the MCC-CEF alliance. Unlike the alliance, the two unions did not try to impose a political price on legislators who supported tax concession legislation. With no strong opposition from such a major influence in state educational politics, the alliance could achieve an easy victory.

POLITICAL STRATEGIES

Bill Honig, California state superintendent of schools, is a master of political strategy. He set out, after being elected in 1982, to build a state coalition that would support his proposed educational reforms. Honig decided that he needed the support of the education community. California teachers' unions and school administrators had given a great deal of time and money to the campaign of Honig's opponent. In fact, after the 1982 election, teachers wore black armbands to school. Honig decided to combine proposals for increased academic requirements, more homework, and the firing of incompetent teachers with support for a $950-million increase in state educational funding. This, he stated, was his carrot to the educational community.

First, Honig made the proposal for increased funding to the national State School Boards Association and leading school administrators. Then he turned his attention to the local school superintendents, who were complaining that their communities did not support increased academic requirements for math, science, and English. To these local educational politicians, he held out the promise of more state money for their support of his reforms.

Money was also Honig's method for wooing the teachers' unions. He recognized that their support was crucial for any reform movement: "Education reform without their [the teachers'] support would be like Normandy Beach without the landing craft—a nonevent. It is they who command the classroom."[25] To outstanding California teachers he promised an extra $4,000 per year. In addition, he established regular meetings with leaders of the California Teachers Association and the California Federation of Teachers to discuss the future training of teachers and to prevent misunderstandings regarding his reform program. Nevertheless, even with these efforts, Honig admitted, teachers were reluctant to give full support to his reform package.[26]

Honig recognized that the two most influential groups in state educational politics were the teachers' associations and the business community. To win support of the business community, he spoke at local meetings of the Kiwanis Club, Rotary Club, and chambers of commerce. On encountering a clipping in *The Los Angeles Times* listing the heads of California's top 100 corporations, Honig phoned each corporate head and requested that they write a letter to the governor supporting additional state funding for the public schools.[27]

His appearances before local business clubs were supplemented with community rallies organized by a nonprofit organization called the Quality Education Project (QEP). This organization's manual gives procedures for organizing local education rallies designed to attract 1,000 to 10,000 people. The QEP provides videotapes to local groups on how to use the school auditorium or stadium and how to function as rally leaders. Certainly a very innovative method of gaining political support, the rallies are held with balloons and flags, emotional speeches and songs; and against this background, parents are asked to sign pledges to support the schools. The emotional quality of these rallies was captured by comments made by a World War II veteran in San Luis Obispo, California, to a newspaper reporter: "I haven't had feelings like this since I was in uniform. I realized something for the first time tonight. It's just not American to be against the public schools."[28]

Building support from minority groups was another important part of Honig's strategy. He went directly to the black and Hispanic communities in California with speeches promising quality education. "The response," Honig writes, "was enthusiastic; the audiences themselves suggested that the main victims in the decline of the public-school standards had been their children."[29]

Careful organization of business leadership, minority leadership, community rallies, and school leadership (without the support of the teachers' associations) was the key to Honig's eventual victory. Yet Honig admits, not all of it was sheer political brilliance on his part. For instance, when he was fighting the governor to gain the carrot of his plan, increased state funding, luck became a major factor. According to Honig, in the middle of the debate on the state budget, President Reagan visited a predominantly Hispanic high school in Los Angeles that was noted for its academic success. Surrounded by reporters, President Reagan stopped to chat with a student who complained that possible cutbacks in state funds would reduce the school's programs. After a resulting article was published in *The Los Angeles Times*, Honig said he received a call from the governor's office with a promise to increase the state school budget.[30]

Honig's methods embody all of the important elements in state educational politics. Linkages were established with important power groups, including business and school leaders. Honig admits that his major failure was not winning the support of the teachers' associations, but the support he did receive from the minority community is an important element in states with large minority populations. In addition, Honig made direct linkages to local communities through his public school rallies.

GENERAL POLICY CONCERNS

In the early 1980s, many governors tried to capitalize on apparent public dissatisfaction with the public school system. Most often, they would link claims of school failure with economic problems. This action paralleled the political use of education by national leaders. First, governors would use schools as scapegoats for general problems facing their states. During the early 1980s, this meant blaming the schools for problems in their states' economies. Second, they claimed that school reform would solve their states' problems.

Governor James B. Hunt of North Carolina typified this pattern, claiming, "Our economic future is in danger because our students, unlike those in other leading industrial nations, are not learning the fundamental skills they need in a modern economy."[31] Blaming the public schools for the United States' low rate of increase in productivity compared with those of Japan and what was West Germany, Hunt argued that one cause lay in the differences in academic requirements and the quality of teachers.

Reflecting his participation on the Task Force on Education for Economic Growth of the Education Commission of the States, Hunt advocated the establishment of state task forces that would include leaders of business, education, and labor. Each task force, he argued, should develop a plan that matches educational objectives with economic objectives. In addition, each plan should include a timetable and a method for evaluating results. Alongside the work of the state task forces would be partnerships between education, business, and government. Hunt was clear in his determination to have business play the dominant role in these partnerships: "A central element of our plan is the involvement of business as a genuine partner with the schools, to help determine what is taught, to assist in marshaling the resources needed to provide top-quality education, and to convey to educators the skills that are needed in the workplace."[32]

When Hunt created the North Carolina Commission on Education for Economic Growth, he included no representatives of organized labor; yet in his role on the Task Force on Education for Economic Growth, he had called for labor's involvement. The fifty-member group consisted of legislators, top business and corporate leaders, educators, school board members, and students. In other words, the planning of education for economic growth involved an alliance of government, business, and education.

Besides the Commission on Education for Economic Growth, Hunt created the North Carolina Business Committee on Math/Science, with the specific goal of expanding local business involvement in public school math and science programs. He proudly boasted, "We have involved North Carolina businesses and industries in the schools to an unprecedented degree."[33]

Against this background of linking educational policies to economic problems, North Carolina instituted a variety of reforms in the early 1980s. Minimum competency tests in reading, writing, and mathematics were required of public school students. A tuition-free residential high school for mathematics and science was established. Students were honored through the North Carolina Scholars Program. Money was provided for additional summer training of high school math and science teachers, and the Quality Assurance Program was begun to monitor teacher-education programs.

In summary, state politicians, in a manner similar to national politicians, link schools to general policy issues. First they blame the schools, and then they declare that they are the cure. With the growing centralization of state control and the decreasing number of influential groups outside government, the business community has begun to wield a major influence over state educational policies. Of course, this pattern can be modified through the pressure of organized interest groups such as the MCC-CEF alliance in Minnesota.

THE NATIONALIZATION OF STATE POLICIES

In recent years, several nongovernmental organizations have contributed to the nationalization of state educational policies. In this context, *nationalization means creating uniformity in policies among states*. Three of these organizations, the National Governors Association, the Council of Chief State School Officers, and the Education Commission of the States, serve as forums for the discussion of educational policies and for the coordination of state educational efforts. The third type of nationalizing organization, private foundations, attempts to advance programs for educational change by influencing politicians at the state level.

In a larger sense, these organizations represent centralization of educational policy beyond the state level because they tend to coordinate their efforts. In the 1980s and early 1990s such coordination was directly related to the increased involvement of governors in educational issues and, as a result, the strengthening of ties among governors through the Education Commission of the States. Educationally active governors have also been recruited by educational foundations to serve on task forces.

A good example of how these activities interrelate is the report of the Task Force on Education for Economic Growth of the Education Commission of the States. The Education Commission of the States was founded in 1966 as a nonprofit, nationwide, interstate compact to help state governments develop educational policies. The organization strongly depends on outside funding from foundations and private corporations to support its coordinating activities. For instance, the Task Force on Education for Economic Growth received support from fifteen leading corporations and foundations, including the Aetna Life & Casualty Insurance Foundation, AT&T, Control Data, Dow Chemical, Xerox, Time Inc., Texas Instruments, RCA, Ford Motor Company Fund, and IBM. The task force membership, which was almost evenly divided between state politicians and business leaders, exemplifies state politicians and the business community coming together in the formulation of educational policy. The chairperson of the task force was Governor James Hunt of North Carolina, and co-chairs were Frank Cary, chairman of IBM's executive committee, and Governor Pierre S. DuPont of Delaware. In addition, there were eleven other governors and three members of state legislatures.

A comparison of task force financial supporters with its members reveal that the corporations represented on the task force were also its major financial supporters. This created the interesting situation of corporations funding a task force that brought together state leaders and the business community for formulating state educational policy.

This combination of forces produced a report, *Action for Excellence,* that supported increased business influence over educational policy. The report's introduction declares, "We believe especially that businesses, in their role as employers, should be much more involved while setting goals for education in America." Linking education to economic concerns, the report states, "If the business community gets more involved in both the design and the delivery of education, we are going to become more competitive as an economy." The report used the schools as a scapegoat for economic problems and singled out the reform of the teaching profession as the key to school and economic improvement.[34]

The National Governors Association has also tried to coordinate educational policies among the states. Until the 1980s, the organization paid little attention to broad educational issues, but in 1985 it established seven task forces to plan state educational improvement to the year 1991. Task force topics included teaching, leadership and management, parent involvement and choice, school readiness, technology, facilities, and college quality.[35]

A logical interest of governors is to enhance their prestige and power by concentrating control of education at the state level. This interest was reflected in a controversial proposal to allow states to declare school districts academically bankrupt. Taken as a last resort, the declaration would allow states to oust local officials and assume state control of a local school district. The major supporter of the idea, Governor Thomas Kean of New Jersey, stated, "As Governor of New Jersey, I couldn't sleep at night if I thought our schools were continuing to turn out unqualified graduates year after year after year, and I wasn't doing anything about it."[36]

The National Governors Association played a leading role in developing educational goals for the Bush administration. Bush's reliance on the National Governors Association meant that the nationalization of state policies would be linked to federal goals. In 1989, the Bush administration and the National Governors Association worked together to formulate a set of national educational goals for the year 2000. These goals were proclaimed in Bush's "1990 State of the Union" message.[37]

In the 1980s, the Council of Chief State School Officers shared the same economic concerns as the governors. Many members of the organization—leading state educational politicians—were influenced by the same pressure groups as governors were. For instance, in 1985 the organization studied the relationship between education and economic development. It decided to focus on the decreasing supply of high school graduates available for entry-level employment, the employment needs of small business, the impact of technology, and how education officials could attract new industry to their states.[38]

Of course, this agenda was dear to the hearts of the business community within each state. Of particular concern were at-risk youth. In the 1980s, the decreasing supply of high school graduates forced employers to dig deeper into the labor pool of poor and minority youth. After a decade of neglect, improving the education of the urban poor returned to the top of the policy agenda. In September 1986, David W. Hornbeck, president-elect of the Chief State School Officers and Maryland superintendent of schools, told the council's study group that aiding at-risk youth was closely linked to state economic growth. He stressed that the way in which schools dealt with this problem would affect the rate of economic growth within communities.[39]

Therefore, national organizations representing leading state politicians and educational politicians in the 1980s and 1990s are primarily concerned with how a state's educational system can help solve its economic problems. Although not conclusive evidence, this suggests that the present business community is exerting the greatest influence on these nationalizing organizations. Interestingly, one focus of the effort to improve the economy by changing educational policy is on changing the teaching profession through career ladders, master teacher programs, and certification requirements. If teachers' associations are rivals with the business community for influence in state politics, then one must question the motives of those attempting to change the profession. The basic political question that should be asked is whether the changes will increase or decrease the political influence of teachers. One might assume that the business community would want to decrease teacher power.

In fact, concern with reforming the teaching profession in the 1980s and 1990s linked the National Governors Association and another nationalizing influence, private foundations. The association recommended the establishment of a national board of teacher standards, an idea championed by the Carnegie Corporation of New York. In fact, the Carnegie Corporation's campaign for a national certification board and school reform provides a good example of how foundations can influence state policies. In its national campaign, the Carnegie Corporation tried to persuade states to change their teacher training and certification laws to conform to the recommendations of their Task Force on Teaching as a Profession report, *A Nation Prepared: Teachers for the 21st Century.* As part of this effort, the Carnegie Corporation granted $890,000 to the National Governors Association for the purpose, in the words of Marc Tucker, executive director of the Carnegie Forum on Education and the Economy, of "helping states that want to empower teachers to do so." With this money, the National Governors Association planned to aid states and local communities in carrying out the foundation report.[40]

In addition, members of the Carnegie task force traveled to twenty-nine states between June and September 1986 in an attempt to sell the ideas in the report. They sold 35,000 copies of the report and provided information and assistance to state legislative and gubernatorial aides. Tucker defended the methods as not just an advertising campaign: "We have not been marketing this report in the sense in which most people would use that term, developing advertising campaigns, trying to change people's opinions in an aggressive way. I don't think it's appropriate for us to do that." While denying being aggressive in the campaign, Tucker told an audience in Massachusetts, which included Governor Michael Dukakis, "The bottom line as I see it is that Carnegie has really fashioned a house of the future of teaching in the twenty-first century. They believe, and we believe, that Massachusetts is in a good position to take those proposals and run with them."[41]

If the Carnegie Corporation report were put into practice, then changes in state educational policy would include recognition of a national certification board, changes in state teacher-education requirements, and development of performance goals for schools. In fact, within three months of issuing the report, Carnegie Corporation staff members were claiming that they had directly influenced some state legislation. For instance, Carnegie Corporation staff members held small, informal meetings with the governor of Washington, Booth Gardner, who then went on to propose legislation based on the Carnegie Corporation report for graduate-level teacher-education degrees and for giving more power to teachers at the school site. In Oregon, an education commission was organized with the aid of Vera Katz, a member of the Carnegie Corporation task force and speaker of the house in Oregon. A commission member claimed that its recommendations would "parallel what was in the Carnegie report." When a two-and-a-half-day conference was organized in North Carolina by former Governor James Hunt, it was announced that an attempt would be made to see the state "put together a comprehensive package of ideas that would move some Carnegie proposals to reality." Similar claims of state activity occurred in Minnesota, California, and New Jersey.[42]

The combination of activities by various foundations, the National Governors Association, the Council of Chief State School Officers, and the Education Commission of the States increases the centralization rate of state educational policies. This nationalization of state educational policies move the pattern of state politics beyond McGivney's stages III and IV. Consequently, it reduces the number of groups outside government that influence educational policy, while increasing the importance of the governor.

The nationalizing trends in state educational politics adds a new stage to McGivney's patterns of state politics. McGivney stops at stage IV—centralization—which, as discussed above, does not explain the full range of political patterns. A stage V called *nationalization* should be added to complete the description of patterns of state educational politics.

CONCLUSION

For the future, the pattern may be toward steady centralization of control of educational policy in state government. This centralization of control includes teacher certification, teacher education, school curriculum, graduation requirements, and school financing. Obviously, increased control by state government means less control by local school districts and by the federal government. Block grants from the federal government and the reform movement of the 1980s and 1990s has sped up this process of centralization.

A major consequence of centralization of control at the state level is a decrease in the power of the individual citizen acting alone to influence educational policy. To influence state educational policy, the individual citizen must work through her or his state legislator, the state educational bureaucracy, or a well-organized interest group. Currently, the best organized of these groups are those representing the business community and the teachers' unions.

The centralization of control in state government creates an interesting paradox. As school reformers call for more citizens and teacher control of local schools through site-based management, choice, and other local governance plans, the number of policies that can be controlled at the local level steadily declines. From this standpoint, increased local control might just be a method for more efficiently achieving the goals established by state and federal governments.

I. Method of Analysis of State Educational Politics
   A. Political Style
      1. Are the most important political contacts in educational policy-making between government officials and local school authorities?
      2. Do the major state educational groups work together to influence policy-making in state government?
      3. Are iron triangles established between particular educational interest groups and state agencies?
      4. Do educational interest groups compete with one another for influence over state educational policies?
      5. Is there centralized control of state educational policy-making?
   B. Educational Policy-Making in Government
      1. Whom are the key legislators interested in educational issues?
      2. Has the governor made educational issues a primary focus of his or her campaign?

3. Does the chief state school officer have a strong influence in the state legislature?
4. Does the chief state school officer have a major influence on public opinion regarding educational policies?
5. Is the state board of education highly visible to the public and influential in the state legislature?

C. Interest Groups

1. Which educational interest group has the most influence in state government?
2. What organizations represent business interests at the state level?
3. In the consideration of educational issues, does the governor or do other major state government leaders favor one interest group over another?
4. Is there a single-issue interest group operating in the state? Does the interest group exact a political cost for nonsupport of its issue?

NOTES

1. Lynn Olson, "Governors Greet Bush Plan to Turn Programs Over to the States with Cautious Enthusiasm," *Education Week* (13 February 1991), pp. 1, 30.
2. Joseph H. McGivney, "State Educational Governance Patterns," *Educational Administration Quarterly*, vol. 20, no. 2 (Spring 1984), pp. 43-63.
3. Lawrence Iannaccone, *Politics in Education* (West Nyack, NY: Center for Applied Research in Education, 1967).
4. McGivney, "State Educational Governance," p. 54.
5. Frederick Wirt, "School Policy Culture and State Decentralization," in Jay D. Scribner, ed., *The Politics of Education* (Chicago: University of Chicago Press, 1977), pp. 186-187.
6. McGivney, "State Educational Governance," pp. 56-57.
7. As reported at the session entitled, "A Decade of Reform: District Responses to State Policies and Other Factors," at the annual meeting of the American Educational Research Association, San Francisco (6 April 1991).
8. James Cibulka, "State Education Agencies and State-Local Relations: The Weak Links in Education Reform," paper presented at the annual meeting of the American Educational Research Association, San Francisco (3 April 1991).
9. *"A Decade of Reform."*
10. Catherine Marshall, Douglas Mitchell, and Frederick Wirt, "The Context of State Level Policy Formation," paper presented at the annual meeting of the American Educational Research Association, San Francisco (16-20 April 1986).
11. R. Campbell and T. Mazzoni, *State Policy Making for the Public Schools* (San Francisco: McCutchan, 1976), pp. 81-134.
12. Ibid., p. 172.
13. Ibid., pp. 46-47.
14. Marshall, Mitchell, and Wirt, "State Level Policy Formation," pp. 13, 29.
15. David Ammons, "Teacher Walkouts," *Compuserve Executive News Service, Associated Press* (13 February 1990).
16. Ibid.

17. Hilary Groutage, "Utah Teachers," *Compuserve Executive News Service, Associated Press* (27 February 1990).

18. Kelly Kissel, "Teacher Strike," *Compuserve Executive News Service, Associated Press* (17 March 1990); Jill Wilson, "Teacher Strike," *Compuserve Executive News Service, Associated Press* (20 March 1990).

19. Quoted in Wilson, "Teacher Strike."

20. Ibid.

21. Tim Mazzoni and Betty Malen, "Mobilizing Constituency Pressure to Influence State Education Policy Making," *Educational Administration Quarterly,* vol. 21, no. 2 (Spring 1985), pp. 91-116.

22. Quoted in ibid., p. 102.

23. Quoted in ibid., p. 103.

24. Quoted in ibid., p. 104.

25. Bill Honig, *Last Chance for Our Children* (Reading, Mass.: Addison-Wesley, 1985), p. 147.

26. Ibid., pp. 149-163.

27. Ibid., pp. 118-119.

28. Quoted in ibid., p. 198.

29. Ibid., pp. 113-114.

30. Ibid., p. 119.

31. James B. Hunt, "Education for Economic Growth: A Critical Investment," *Phi Delta Kappan,* vol. 65, no. 8 (April 1984), p. 538.

32. Ibid., p. 539.

33. Ibid., p. 541.

34. Carnegie Foundation Task Force on Education for Economic Growth, *Action for Excellence* (Denver: Education Commission of the States, 1983), p. 18.

35. Chris Pipho, "Governors Push Better Schools Coalition," *Phi Delta Kappan,* vol. 68, no. 2 (October 1986), pp. 101-102.

36. Quoted in Bill Montague, "State Takeovers Debated as School-Reform Tactic," *Education Week* (24 September 1986), pp. 1, 17, 18.

37. "Text of Statement of Education Goals Adopted by Governors," *Education Week* (7 March 1990), p. 16.

38. Bill Montague, "Citing Link to Economy, School Chiefs Plan Study of 'At Risk Students' Needs,' " *Education Week* (1 October 1986), pp. 1, 13.

39. Ibid., p. 13.

40. Lynn Olsen, "Carnegie Backs Reform Agenda with Money, Effort," *Education Week* (15 October 1986), pp. 1, 16.

41. Quoted in ibid., p. 16.

42. Ibid., p. 16.

CHAPTER 8

Local Politics of Education

"As school boards have become battle grounds for many special interests," writes James Cibulka, "it is less credible for them to argue that they speak for the community as a whole."[1] These special-interest groups, according to Cibulka, include "teachers' unions, administrators, other employee groups, and contending external constituencies such as business, African-Americans, Mexican-Americans, and many others."[2]

Cibulka's claim differs strikingly from conservatives claiming domination by educational administrators. In 1996, I received a phone call from an English supervisor in a small town in Ohio. In the 1980s, the supervisor had taken my Politics of Education course as part of her program in Educational Administration. "I used to believe you," she complained, "about bureaucracy and administrators. I know they can be bad. But they don't control things. My problem is the Christian Fundamentalists on the school board. They want to throw out books for all sorts of reasons—Satanism, secular humanism, vegetarianism, one worldism. Administrators are more progressive than board members."

I explained that in the 1970s and 1980s bureaucracy and school administrators dominated discussions of problems in local school districts. Nevertheless, by the 1990s, local school districts were immersed in conflict because of the Christian Coalition and under-represented minority groups. As I explain in Chapter 1, school board meetings are filled with debates over religion, multiculturalism, and racism. In the language of this chapter, school boards and local politics of education are being swept up in factional politics.

While surrounded by factionalism, the majority of school board members are conservative. According to a 1997 report of the National School Boards Association, most of the 95,000 school board members in 14,700 school districts do not support proposals for broad changes in education. The author of the report, Professor Joan Curcio of Virginia Polytechnic Institute, says, "The tradition from which school board members come and their positions with public schools suggest keeping things as they are, and not trying things that are new or not proven."[3]

The report gave the following characteristics for school board members.

- Sixty percent were men
- Ninety-five percent were white
- Forty percent were between 41 and 50 years old
- Fifty-four percent described themselves as religious conservatives
- Sixty-five percent described themselves as political conservatives
- More than forty percent reported family incomes of $40,000 to $80,000 a year[4]

Despite being religious and political conservatives, most school board members opposed vouchers and tuition tax credits for private and religious schools. Most school board members retained a faith in the importance of public schooling. One respondent to the survey stated, "The voucher system seems unfair, discriminatory and elitist, as does school choice. Public school is for all Americans to learn how to live together and be tolerant."[5]

The reported 95 percent white membership on boards of education is a major concern for many cultural and racial minorities. The support of public schooling for building tolerance is at odds to the pressures from Christian Fundamentalists. What the findings of this report suggests is that political turmoil and factionalism will continue in the local politics of education.

LOCAL SCHOOLS AND STATE CENTRALIZATION

Accompanying the factionalism of local politics is the increasing tension between local and state control of schools. This tension highlights the trend to state centralization and site-based management. The power of site-based management is limited by academic requirements established by state governments and monitoring by statewide testing programs. In addition, federal influence over the content of instruction might increase as national tests are developed. Within the context of state control and federal influence, site-based management becomes a method for accomplishing state and federal objectives without the exercise of meaningful power.

The same could be said about the power of local school boards. Increasing demands from above can reduce the range of decisions made by local school boards. Certainly, the centralization of power in state governments has reduced the ability of local school boards to decide the curriculum. On the other hand, school boards do retain important prerogatives concerning (a) the hiring of teachers and administrators and (b) the organization of schools in the district. As discussed in Chapter 2, representation of African-Americans and Hispanics on school boards affects the degree of second-generation segregation. The importance of this representation is directly linked to the hiring of African-American and Hispanic administrators and teachers. In addition, school boards play an important role in organizing school districts and distributing money.

For instance, each school district adapts educational policies to the characteristics of its population. Upper-middle-class suburbs emphasize the education of students for jobs requiring a college education. In contrast, graduates of poor school districts enter jobs that require little formal education. In these communities, the emphasis is on a solid general or vocational education with college preparatory courses being offered to a select few. Urban schools must educate for a diversified labor market and deal with many poor and minority students. Consequently, urban schools offer a variety of educational programs ranging from advanced academic programs to highly specialized vocational training.

Of course, every local school district must deal with problems peculiar to its setting and population. The most divisive issues center on religious values and censorship. In some school districts, Protestants and Catholics war over support of public schools and the moral content of instruction. In these communities, health and sex education and increases in school taxes can be major areas of dispute. Reflecting attitudes in the national Republican Party, Protestant fundamentalists in some school districts have battled against secular humanism and demanded censorship of school texts.

Value conflicts pose a major problem for public schools in a democratic and highly diverse society. No matter what values are reflected in the curriculum, they are bound to offend some group. And when schools try to avoid any teaching of particular religious values, then, as with Protestant fundamentalists, they are charged with being "godless."

Therefore, local educational politics will vary according to the needs of the local economy and the existence of factional disputes. Let us consider four models for analyzing local educational politics. These four models include most aspects of local school politics; they do not, however, consider the issues of site-based management, the power of local teachers' unions, and the role of local school bureaucracies. These aspects of local power will be discussed later in the chapter. Also, like most analytical models, they leave a great deal of room for variation; for instance, some communities might show the characteristics of several different models.

PATTERNS IN LOCAL POLITICS OF EDUCATION

For this discussion, I am assuming a relationship between a community's labor needs and the community power structure that controls the schools. In some situations, labor market needs are secondary to strong factional disputes. I am also assuming that the nature of the power structure determines the type of school board and superintendent, although, as will be discussed in a later section, this may not be the case with local educational bureaucracies and teachers' unions.

The analytical models developed in this section are based on the work of Donald McCarty and Charles Ramsey.[6] They provide classifications of community power structures, school boards, and administrative styles. These classifications assume that the community power structure determines the nature of the school board and the superintendent's administrative style. The types of community power structures are as follows:

1. dominated,
2. factional,
3. pluralistic, and
4. inert.

In a dominated community, a few persons or a single person exercise majority power. Usually, these people are part of the community's economic elite, though sometimes they are leaders of ethnic, religious, or political groups. Dominated power structures exist primarily in small towns and urban areas in which the school system serves the needs of a labor market that is either diversified or dominated by a single industry. A major characteristic of a dominated power structure is the lack of a strong opposition.

Factional communities, as described by McCarty and Ramsey, usually have two factions that compete for influence. Very often these factions hold different values, particularly religious values, and each faction often shares equal power over school affairs. In these communities, concerns with the needs of the labor market are often secondary to religious issues.

In pluralistic power structures, there is competition among several community interest groups, with no single group dominating school policies. Often, a pluralistic power structure shows a high degree of community interest in the schools, with many groups active in school affairs. McCarty and Ramsey found pluralistic power structures to be characteristic of suburban school systems in which there is a high interest in students entering occupations that require a college education.

Inert communities are without any visible power structure. McCarty and Ramsey claim that this situation most often occurs in rural communities in which the power is latent in the status quo of the community. In inert communities, there is little competition for positions on the school board. Membership usually goes to anyone who is willing to take on the job, and there is little public interest, as compared with other communities, in the schools. In these communities, most students do not intend to enter occupations for which education is a major factor. The primary concern is with a solid general or vocational education for most students and a college preparatory curriculum for a select few.

Table 8-1 lists McCarty and Ramsey's types of community power structures as related to types of school boards.

A dominated school board shares the beliefs and values of the community elite. Often, economic control is a factor in an elite's influence on board members. There is usually no organized opposition for positions on the school board, and the community elite can be represented by a majority or by several powerful individuals.

In factional communities, elections to the school board are often disputed, with board members representing the beliefs and values of particular factions. Power between factions can shift with the election of new members. Members

TABLE 8-1. Community Power Structures and School Boards

Community Power Structures	Types of School Boards
Dominated	Dominated
Factional	Factional
Pluralistic	Status congruent
Inert	Sanctioning

of a status-congruent school board are not bound to a particular ideological position.

In a pluralistic power structure, board members represent many community groups. Board meetings emphasize discussion and consensus, with little influence from any particular community group.

Sanctioning school boards exist in communities with inert power structures. This type of board is relatively inactive, and its members do not represent factions within the community. The term "sanctioning" refers to the tendency of this type of board to follow its leadership and approve the recommendations of the school administrative staff.

McCarty and Ramsey argue that school boards hire compatible superintendents. In other words, there are direct relationships among the community power structure, the nature of the school board, and the style of the superintendent. And, as we will see, these relationships are all connected to the occupational aspirations of the local community.

Let us now consider the interrelationships in dominated, factional, pluralistic, and inert communities. Again, the reader is cautioned that the models developed in each section are for analysis and that some communities might exhibit traits of several models.

DOMINATED COMMUNITIES

In a community where an elite power structure dominates the school board, the superintendent will reflect the values of the power structure and act in its interests. Usually, this type of superintendent carries out board policies but does not initiate new policies.

For example, in a dominated community studied by McCarty and Ramsey, the elite power structure acted in private, and direct control of the school system was exercised by a superintendent who reflected its values.[7] In this town of 35,000, the school board was composed of seven members who were not high in the power structures and who were not troublemakers. The superintendent gave the appearance of being a strong decision maker with a firm hold on his job.

The event that began the community's elite power structure was the decision by four members to fire the superintendent because they felt he was overly involved in educational research and publication and was neglecting the school system. The superintendent was incredulous when first informed of the decision and did little to find other employment or prepare to leave the position. At a later board meeting, members asked if he had sought other employment, and when informed that he hadn't, they voted four to three to fire him. Immediately, the superintendent called the vice president of one of the two largest banks and the general manager of the largest company in the community. The firing surprised both, and the company manager got in contact with the presidents of two other banks, the local newspaper editor, and a lawyer from a highly prestigious family in town.

First, this group of community leaders met in the office of the bank vice president and decided to meet as a group with the superintendent before making a decision. At the next meeting, also held at the bank, the superintendent demanded a new contract and an increase in salary. After lengthy discussion, the town leaders decided to avoid community conflict and let the superintendent be fired.

The power of this elite group was evidenced in the plans that followed their decision. First, the group felt that the school board had gotten out of control. The most respected member of the elite group was made chairperson of the school board's nomination committee, and its members were selected to ensure elite control. This committee recommended candidates for the school board who were either members of the power structure or loyal followers. Traditionally, those recommended by the nomination committee had been elected without opposition to the school board. And finally, the leading members of the community kept a close watch on the nominating committee for several years to ensure the selection of the right candidates. In addition, a new superintendent was selected whom, it was believed, would act in the interests of the town leaders.

McCarty and Ramsey argue that in this situation the superintendent made several mistakes. His major error was not recognizing that he was a servant of the power structure. He should have immediately gone to the elite group about the possible firing. Instead, the superintendent tried to play a political strategist by bringing the elite group together and demanding a new contract and increased pay. These demands alienated the elite and created the possibility of open conflict.

From McCarty and Ramsey's analysis of dominated communities, there emerges a pattern of educational policies resulting from elite control. First, elite leaders, particularly business leaders, want low taxes. Second, the leaders want the school to provide a curriculum that meets their needs. In most situations, this means a college preparatory curriculum for their children and a curriculum to prepare future employees. Finally, elite leaders want to reduce community conflict. This was precisely how the new superintendent acted in the dominated community studied by the two researchers.

In their book *Political Strategies in Northern School Desegregation*, David Kirby, T. Robert Harris, and Robert Crain highlight the important role of elite groups in urban school politics. They studied ninety-one cities ranging in size from 50,000 to more than 250,000. Their major conclusion is that urban elites are the most important political actors in determining school desegregation plans. In their words, "School desegregation is a political decision made by the elites rather than the masses."[8]

Kirby, Harris, and Crain identified urban elite decision makers as drawn primarily from the business community. In their study, more than 50 percent of the elite was bankers, industrialists, and heads of local businesses. Only 5 percent of this decision-making group was composed of liberals who represented labor and civil rights organizations. The remainder of the elite decision makers were heads of local utilities, newspaper people, members of civic associations, executives, clergy, university administrators, and professionals.

Elite domination does not result in a uniform political style in all urban areas. Kirby, Harris, and Crain found that large, slow-growing cities with identifiable ethnic populations have liberal elites. (They defined a liberal as someone who is willing to change the social structure to solve social and economic problems, and a conservative as someone who wants to maintain existing social arrangements and expects individuals to adapt to those arrangements.) They found conservative elites in smaller, faster-growing cities with relatively small ethnic populations.

School board elections that are nonpartisan aid elite domination in urban areas and at large. Of course, in cities such as Chicago, the mayor appoints the board of education. In these situations, the political obligations of the mayor determine board appointments. Very often these political obligations are linked to the power of local elites. For instance, in Chicago in the early 1980s, the mayor appointed the entire slate recommended by the local business group Chicago United.[9]

Ending the power of political parties made nonpartisan and at-large elections in the early twentieth century to clean up corrupt, big-city school systems. In effect, these changes ensured the domination of school board elections by business groups. An at-large election, as opposed to an election from a small district in a city, requires that a candidate campaign throughout the urban area. Campaigning within a small district in an urban area requires only small expense and organization. In many situations, the candidate can campaign simply by going door-to-door. Therefore, at-large elections require more money and organization. Since nonpartisan elections remove the influence of political parties, the candidate must turn to other sources of financial and organizational support. Usually, these other sources are community business groups.[10]

Studies of nonpartisan urban elections have revealed a bias in favor of business and conservative groups. In his book *Nonpartisan Elections and the Case for Party Politics,* Willis Hawley argues that nonpartisan elections create a partisan bias in favor of Republicans.[11] These Republican politicians receive most of their support from the business community. Hawley studied nonpartisan elections in eighty-eight cities and concluded that they definitely favored the Republican business community. This was particularly true in cities with populations more than 50,000 that had many unemployed persons with low incomes and levels of education.

Hawley believes that the relationships established through informal business ties and civic organizations cause the Republican bias in nonpartisan elections. Without the active involvement of political parties, these informal networks assume a dominant role. Hawley emphasizes that there is a positive association between high socioeconomic class and participation in community organizations. It is almost impossible for a poor person to become part of an informal business network or join the local chamber of commerce.

It is these informal business networks, as McCarty and Ramsey also found, that control nominations to the school board in dominated communities. Sometimes community leaders will create an actual nominating committee. In dominated communities this nominating committee often controls school board elections. In other situations, actual business organizations will recommend candidates.

In the 1980s and 1990s, the linkages between business groups and urban school systems were formalized by attempts to make education serve the needs of local labor markets. One pioneer agreement was the Boston Compact, which was signed among the Boston public school system, the Tri-Lateral Council, and the Private Industry Council in Boston. The Tri-Lateral Council originated in 1974 and grew out of elite concerns with the desegregation of Boston schools. It is composed of representatives from the Greater Boston Chamber of Commerce, the National Alliance of Businessmen, and the Boston School Department.

The Boston Compact specifically links the goals of Boston schools to the needs of the local labor market. The compact states, "As the largest school system in Massachusetts, the Boston public schools must improve to sustain economic growth in the city." The school system agrees to improve the employability of its graduates, and the business community agrees to give hiring priority to job applicants residing in Boston.[12]

In Atlanta a similar arrangement exists between the schools and the business community. The state of Georgia chartered the Atlanta Partnership of Business and Education in order "to enhance the economic development potential of Atlanta and to improve the standard of living of its people by raising the educational achievement of its citizenry." To meet this goal, magnet schools in Atlanta are organized so that each program is answerable to business needs. Each magnet school has an advisory committee formed from the membership of the Atlanta Partnership. This committee, according to the report of the Atlanta Partnership, "provides continual counsel so that the curriculum and its delivery stay attuned to the developments within the industry."[13]

In other parts of the nation, formal ties between business and the schools were increased through adopt-a-school programs, with local businesses and industries adopting individual schools. Governors across the nation backed this national movement, designed to increase the influence of business interests over public school curricula.

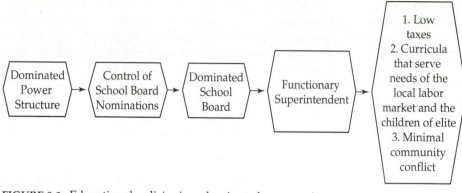

FIGURE 8-1. Educational policies in a dominated community

Compacts between schools and businesses, partnerships, and adopt-a-school programs are visible signs of the informal control traditionally exerted by local business groups. In dominated communities, business groups maintain their influence through their informal control of school boards. The primary goal, of course, is to ensure that the schools serve the needs of the local labor market.

Based on McCarty and Ramsey's study, Figure 8-1 describes the development of educational policies in dominated communities. A local elite group indirectly controls the school board by controlling the nomination of its members. In turn, this dominated board selects a functionary superintendent who supports policies favored by the elite. These policies involve low taxes, a curriculum that meets the needs of the local labor market, a curriculum for the children of the elite, and a school system that operates with minimum conflict.

FACTIONAL COMMUNITIES

In contrast to the calm appearance shown by dominated school boards, factional boards display a great deal of conflict. Unlike the functional superintendent, the superintendent in the factional community must be a political strategist who can balance competing groups.

In a factional community studied by McCarty and Ramsey, the major competition occurred between a permissive Jewish group and a conservative Catholic group.[14] With almost equal populations in the school district, the control of the school board shifted between groups in each highly contested election. The campaigns were very emotional, with each group accusing the other of undermining the quality of education.

When McCarty and Ramsey arrived in the community, the liberals on the school board had lost their majority to conservatives, who immediately fired the superintendent. The fired superintendent, according to McCarty and

Ramsey, failed as a political strategist because he appeared to favor the previous liberal majority. Interviews with community members revealed that they clearly recognized the existence of the two factions; each side admitted to holding secret meetings to plan strategy against its opponent. The researchers found, however, that factionalism in this community did not always mean a split vote. Many educational issues do not relate to factional divisions, and sometimes there is an attempt to avoid factional voting.

An example of a situation that did result in factional votes in this community is when elementary school report cards became a heated issue. Liberals favored a card that simply reported "satisfactory," "unsatisfactory," or "excellent," according to a child's potential learning rate. Conservatives wanted a card that gave grades of A through F, based on percentage test scores. The conservative majority rewrote the report card in one-and-a-half hours, with four conservative board members voting for the new card and three liberals voting against it.

In other communities, the most frequent types of factions are:

1. religious groups,
2. racial groups,
3. ethnic groups,
4. taxpayers' groups, and
5. town people versus gown people (college communities).

Religious divisions make up one of the most frequent causes of community factionalism. Usually, this involves Catholics struggling against Protestants or Jews. Since most Catholics send their children to parochial schools, they are primarily interested in keeping down the costs of local public schools and ensuring that the teachings of the public schools are not in conflict with Catholic doctrines. For instance, a major debate in communities with large Catholic populations usually takes place over teachings about birth control and abortion in sex-education courses.

Racial factions often develop over concerns with minority students gaining equal access to the labor market. Since the civil rights struggles of the 1950s, dominated groups have campaigned to place their representatives on boards of education. Once on the board, representatives of dominated groups back decisions directly related to the interests of their constituencies. In recent years, this has meant support for quality integrated education and additional programs for the disadvantaged. A major goal is to provide equal educational opportunities to ensure that minority students gain equality of opportunity in the labor market. In certain areas, ethnicity is an important factor. A Jewish, Italian, Irish, or Scandinavian name on the ballot might be attractive to ethnic-oriented voters.[15]

Sometimes communities will divide over school taxes. Many taxpayers' associations oppose increased spending by any part of the local government. McCarty and Ramsey assert that the true leadership of taxpayers' associations is often unknown; such groups count on the support of the "silent majority" in a community to defeat attempts to increase school taxes and expenses.[16]

Town-and-gown conflicts often plague college towns, with faculty members wanting a more liberal and academic schooling than town people do. Town people usually disdain the ivory tower demeanor of professors, and professors often regard town people as culturally backward. This division can result in factional conflict over the curriculum, school activities, and grading policies.

The issue of secular humanism has divided many communities. A classic dispute occurred in 1974 over textbook adoptions in Kanawha County, West Virginia. In varying degrees, the extreme emotional outbursts in this situation were later repeated in other communities. Ann Page and Donald Clelland provide an insightful analysis of the Kanawha County controversy. They identify the source of the controversy as the attempt to protect a fundamentalist lifestyle against the pressures of modernity. In contrast to school battles that center on economic issues, lifestyle politics involves conflicts over beliefs and ways of living. In the words of Page and Clelland, "Lifestyle concern is most evident when fading majorities come to recognize the eclipse of their way of life through loss of such control" over socialization in the schools.[17]

In Kanawha County, the lifestyle issue erupted in June 1974, when a school board member demanded greater board control of textbook selection and, after speaking at a local Baptist church, organized a demonstration by 1,000 anti-textbook protesters at a school board meeting. By September, protesting parents picketed local businesses and mines in the county and withheld approximately 10,000 children from the school system.

Violence quickly escalated with the firebombing of two schools, the shooting of a picketing protester, the destruction of school property, and the dynamiting of the county education building. In the midst of this violence, a citizens' review board split into two factions, with the anti-textbook group in the minority. The majority faction recommended that all but 35 of the 325 books under protest be returned to the classroom, and the minority faction recommended that 180 books be permanently banned. Of course, the majority faction had its way, and most of the books were returned to the classroom, with 35 of the most controversial books being placed in the school library. The protesters reacted to this decision by having four board members and the superintendent arrested for contributing to the delinquency of minors.

Page and Clelland found that the most significant difference between the two factions was level of education. About occupational and economic indicators, both groups were similar. The differences in educational level reflected the differences in lifestyle. Page and Clelland feel that the protesters were trying to protect a lifestyle—which they call cultural fundamentalism—that has been under attack throughout the twentieth century.

This cultural fundamentalism is reflected in concerns with the content of modern textbooks. Cultural fundamentalists object to textbooks that appear to show disrespect for God and the Bible, use vulgar language, support secular humanism, and, most important, show disrespect for authority. In Kanawha County, the cultural fundamentalists were most concerned with the writings of Mark Twain, George Bernard Shaw, and Norman Mailer because these authors were considered disrespectful of authority and institutionalized practices. In the words of Page and Clelland, "Cultural fundamentalism was once the dominant lifestyle in the United States. Its strength has been eroded by such master trends as urban heterogeneity, consumer-oriented affluence, and the pervasive drive of rationalization in all spheres of life."[18]

School administrations in factional communities must learn to walk a political tightrope. At any moment, the community might be plunged into highly emotional conflict that would require the superintendent to attempt to reconcile both sides. In addition, because control of the school board might change, the superintendent cannot afford to take sides. For the school administrator, a factional community is one of the worst places to work. McCarty and Ramsey describe the superintendent in the factional community they studied as so affected by the pressures of the job that he could barely light his cigarette at board meetings and was rapidly developing ulcers.

The most effective technique for a school administrator in a factional community is to avoid taking sides and remain as silent as possible on most issues. For instance, a superintendent should give the appearance of working hard for both factions. Each faction should think that he or she is on its side. Silence is the best rule for an administrator in major factional disputes; this avoids any appearance of taking sides. In addition, if the majority on a factional school board decides, then the superintendent should avoid giving wholehearted support in case there is a shift in power. Another recommendation is the creation of large committees composed of community members to study any potentially explosive educational issue. This allows negative feelings by board members to be directed at the committee, not the school administrators. Also, the large number of reports from these committees can diffuse the strong emotions surrounding the issue under consideration.

Figure 8-2 provides a summary of education decision making in a factional community. Factional power structures result in factional boards of education, which require superintendents who act as political strategists. The best political strategies include remaining neutral toward both factions, maintaining silence,

FIGURE 8-2. Educational policies in a factional community

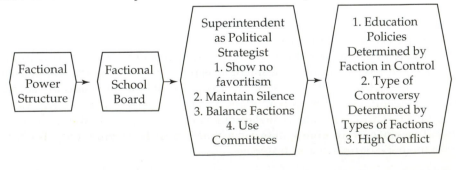

balancing factions, and using committees extensively. School board debates depend on the nature of the factions and the faction in control of the board. Factional communities are noted for their high degree of conflict.

PLURALISTIC COMMUNITIES

McCarty and Ramsey are full of praise for what they consider to be the ideal community power structure: pluralistic. In these communities they found model school boards and superintendents. The problem with their praise, as William Boyd discusses in an insightful review of their study, is that these model boards and superintendents seem to exist only in stable, and often upper-middle-class, suburbs.[19] In our model, these communities are concerned about training their children to enter occupations that require a high level of schooling. Consequently, they focus on a college preparatory curriculum.

In McCarty and Ramsey's pluralistic community, the power structure had passed through a phase of domination by a single industry to a period of competition among groups. Unlike a factional community, no group had ever gained a majority on the board of education. In this community, power was diffused through competition among an organized group of Catholics, two Protestant churches, the chamber of commerce, a labor union, and the parent teacher association (PTA).[20]

These groups did not tend to form lasting coalitions. At the time the researchers entered the community, a bond issue was being opposed by Catholics, the chamber of commerce, and the labor union, and was supported by the Protestant churches and the PTA. Regarding the elementary school report card, the PTA, the Catholic organization, and the two Protestant churches worked together to develop a progressive report card on which progress was measured against the potential learning of the student, as opposed to mastery of subject matter. Members of the chamber of commerce opposed the progressive report card because they believed employers needed an accurate record of a future employee's achievements.

The superintendent in this community played the role of a professional advisor. He supported the bond issue in professional statements about the need for additional classrooms and teachers. On the report card issue, he helped to organize the committee and quoted research information on the effects of various report cards on student learning. In most situations, he acted as an expert who gave the board information to aid in their decision making and then faithfully administered their decisions.

McCarty and Ramsey argue that pluralistic communities are typically open minded and rely on facts. On most major issues, community-wide investigative committees are established to report to the board of education and the administration. Boards of education in these communities, which they call "status congruent," do not meddle in the administration of the schools, but are active in the formulation of policy. Status-congruent boards encourage open debate with the hope of reaching a consensus.

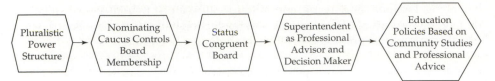

FIGURE 8-3. Educational policies in a pluralistic community

Interestingly, status-congruent boards are selected in a relatively closed system. McCarty and Ramsey claim that if selection to the board depends on the vote of the mass public, then candidates will be elected because they are identifiable representatives of special-interest groups. With status-congruent boards, members are selected in a caucus system and the actual voting is pro forma. The caucus system, they argue, limits the number of members who serve particular special interests and, consequently, reduces the possibility for developing factions on the board. Therefore, status-congruent boards tend to be self-perpetuating, with members chosen by a nominating caucus and elections rubber-stamping the caucus.

In acting the role of a professional advisor to a status-congruent board, the superintendent moves cautiously to avoid adverse community reaction to proposals for change. She or he should not surprise the board or the community with any sudden new proposals. In addition, the superintendent should study each board member carefully to avoid any explosive situations. A superintendent in a status-congruent community will sometimes function as a decision maker. In these situations, the superintendent will surround him- or herself with expert administrative advisors. The role of superintendent may fluctuate from a professional advisor to a decision maker, depending on the mood of the board of education.

Figure 8-3 summarizes educational policy development in a pluralistic community. A nominating caucus controls the membership of the school board, with the superintendent functioning as a political advisor. Educational policies are the result of broad community investigations and professional advice.

INERT COMMUNITIES

Finally, inert communities give the superintendent most of the power over school issues. In our model, the labor market in inert communities is not dependent on a high level of education. Most jobs in these communities are in agriculture and small factories. As McCarty and Ramsey describe them, inert communities are ideologically homogeneous, have no sense of purpose, and confine their energy to one community activity, such as trying to attract new industries. An inert community has no clear group structure, and most community members follow an individualistic philosophy.

Within this community framework, it is difficult to get people to run for the school board. In most situations, the superintendent indirectly controls the composition of the board. Board members turn to the superintendent for leadership and decision making. Sometimes, McCarty and Ramsey report, superintendents claimed that board members accepted 99 percent of their proposals. Very seldom in inert communities does the board turn to leaders outside the school system for advice on educational matters. McCarty and Ramsey therefore call the board sanctioning because it primarily accepts the recommendations of the superintendent. In this situation, the decision-making superintendent assumes that the board will accept any reasonable recommendations and therefore does not consult outside community leaders.

In an inert community studied by McCarty and Ramsey, the superintendent held his position for 29 years and maintained firm control over the selection process for board elections. School board members reported that the superintendent always recommended names of candidates to them. In turn, board members would urge those whom the superintendent had selected to run for office. These candidates usually ran without any opposition. When nomination committees were used, the superintendent would recommend the names for membership.

To maintain his relationship with the board, the superintendent avoided any issue that might upset its members. Most of his activities were conducted in private by contacting board members about issues to be discussed before future meetings. Therefore, the superintendent knew how each member was planning to vote on a particular issue and could avoid confrontations. McCarty and Ramsey found the actions of this superintendent to be typical of other inert communities. They conclude that the decision-making superintendent tries to avoid any controversy with the board, and between the board and the community. The superintendent is aided by his influence over the selection of board candidates. An important method of control for this type of superintendent is the giving, withholding, and slanting of information about the school system to the board. In addition, the decision-making superintendent is the source of new ideas for change and refinement of educational policies. While working in private, the superintendent tries to ensure open discussions at board meetings to give the members a sense of freedom.

In his book *Growing Up American,* Alan Peshkin describes a rural Illinois community in which the primary educational concern is with the weekend football or basketball game.[21] Advanced educational training is unimportant to the needs of the local labor market. Of the approximately 360 full-time working people in the community, 240 work in factories, 90 in agriculture, and 33 in business. Women in the community are employed in equal proportions as clerks, factory workers, and secretaries. Within this economic context, Peshkin found the goal of the schools to be providing a good basic education.

Traditionally, the school board in this community was composed of farmers and, with one exception, men. As in other communities of this type, the major responsibility for running the school system is given to the superintendent. During Peshkin's study of the community, the superintendent of 17 years died

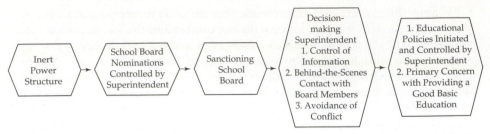

FIGURE 8-4. Educational policies in an inert community

and was replaced by a similar type of leader. Both superintendents acted as strong decision makers.

In Peshkin's words, the "school board prefers a strong superintendent who can run their schools, but this preference rests on a critical condition—that the superintendent act in a way that fits [the community]."[22] In other words, the superintendent is the decision maker if she or he remains in tune with the community's values.

Peshkin sat in on the board's discussions of candidates for the superintendent's position. According to Peshkin, board members rejected candidates for having "big-city ideas," being "too intelligent for the community," having "too many ideas," and being "a little slow on discipline problems." They selected a superintendent who shared their values and background. They felt comfortable giving the decision-making power to this type of person.[23]

The role of the decision-making superintendent in a community with an inert power structure is summarized in Figure 8-4. The superintendent controls by influencing school board nominations, monitoring the flow of information about the school system to the board, avoiding controversy, and working in private with each board member. And finally, the superintendent initiates and controls most education policies.

It is important to remember that the application of any one of the four models depends on the type of power structure in the local community. Also, it is assumed that the nature of the community power structure determines the political style of the board of education and the school superintendent, and that these are all related to the community's occupational needs. A problem with these models is that they neglect the political power of educational bureaucracies and teachers' unions. The next two sections will integrate these political forces into the patterns of local governance.

EDUCATIONAL BUREAUCRACIES

Most studies of local school politics stress the domination of educational policy making by the superintendent and local educational bureaucracy. In fact, Boyd criticizes the study by McCarty and Ramsey because it emphasizes the importance of community power structures. In his review of the literature, Boyd writes: "Most research shows that instead of being dominated by a powerful elite or being influenced by coalitions that shift with the issue . . . local educational policy making is generally dominated by the influence of the top school administrators." Boyd argues that it is often difficult to discern where the power of the community ends and the power of school administrators begins. In many situations, Boyd argues, administrators act according to what they perceive to be the wishes of the community.

Administrators are free to exert control over educational policies if they operate within the values and desires of the community. Boyd calls this the "zone of tolerance." In Boyd's words, "Since for pragmatic political reasons . . . schoolmen usually seek to avoid conflict, it is unlikely that they will very often attempt to give the community other than what the community wants." In another study, L. Harmon Zeigler and M. Kent Jennings found that the policy-making process of local school boards is controlled by superintendents.[25]

Obviously, the degree of administrative control is dependent on the nature of local school politics. Of the four models discussed in the previous section, the superintendent assumes significant political power in pluralistic and inert communities. In dominated and factional communities, the superintendent is either the pawn of the power structure or an astute political strategist. For instance, school administrators were not in control of the political events in the previously discussed textbook controversy in Kanawha County, West Virginia.

Studies of communities controlled by educational administrators provide an analysis of the techniques and methods of administrative domination. In addition, many of these studies are critical of administrative control and blame many educational problems on the existence of rigid bureaucracies.

Certainly, the most widely recognized method of administrative control is the ability of superintendents to act as gatekeepers of information. Through this method, a superintendent can ensure that school board members receive only information that is favorable to her or his policies. In the words of Zeigler and Jennings, "A superintendent who occupies a gatekeeping position with respect to the flow of information to the board is ideally situated to select only what he wants the board to hear." According to their study, "Most observers acknowledge that many, if not all, superintendents occupy a strategic gatekeeping position, particularly where technical information is concerned."[26]

Through the gatekeeping of information, according to Zeigler and Jennings, superintendents can control the types of issues considered by school boards. In addition, superintendents can define alternative methods of action, which gives them control of the major part of the policy-making arena. Superintendents determine for the board what is to be considered and how it is to be considered. Quoting one political scientist, Zeigler and Jennings write, "Consequently, the superintendent who controls issue definition indirectly controls the type of educational-political market within which policies are decided. As Schattsschneider once observed, 'The definition of the alternatives is the supreme instrument of power.'"[27]

Another method used by school administrators is to convince boards of education that only administrators have technical expertise in most areas of educational policy. In the twentieth century, this became a classic technique used by administrators to justify control of the policy-making process. The claim is made that educational decisions require expert opinion and that professional educators, and not elected board members, are the only people qualified to decide. If elected school board members accept this argument, then they often defer to the expert opinion of the superintendent.

As part of the method of gatekeeping, superintendents often exercise control over the agenda for school board meetings. This ensures that only the issues the superintendent wants to be discussed will be discussed. In 70 percent of the school districts studied by Zeigler and Jennings, superintendents had primary control of the agenda, and in almost as many districts the superintendent had sole responsibility. Also, to build political support, superintendents rely on informal contacts with individual board members and spend time socializing new board members to district policies. Occasionally, superintendents try to build their own political coalitions among community members.[28]

Although superintendents might control policy through gatekeeping, informal contacts, and community coalitions, the central office staffs of local school systems also exercise a degree of control. These middle managers (associate and assistant superintendents, supervisors, and heads of special projects) generally resist any public input into the school system and try to maintain control over all educational policies in their local school systems.

McGivney and Haught argue that the most important need of the central office staff is to perceive itself as in control of a situation. The desire to control a situation, they argue, has the greatest explanatory and predictive power about the actions of the central office staff.[29] Also discussed in Chapter 1 is the tendency for educational bureaucracies to pursue policies that increase their salaries and job opportunities. As it is for the superintendent, the gatekeeping of information is an important method of control for the central office staff. For instance, McGivney and Haught cite examples of central office efforts "to establish and maintain central control over communications to such agencies as city hall, the state education department, principals, and teachers, and other extra-school-system groups."[30]

Concerning control of the policy-making process, McGivney and Haught argue that informal networks within the central office bureaucracy play a major role. In their study, they found that the central office was divided into two major subgroups, and each subgroup comprised minor subgroups. Each subgroup met informally every day; one subgroup was oriented toward the board of education and the other toward building principals and teachers. The location of offices played an important role in determining the membership of each subgroup. The actions of each of these subgroups were essential parts of the informal power structure. The general pattern of decision making, according to McGivney and Haught, was for each subgroup to try to reach a consensus over an issue. A proposal accepted by a minor subgroup would then be considered for acceptance by the major subgroups. McGivney and Haught found that proposals considered by the major subgroup without first receiving acceptance by a minor subgroup were delayed until they received that acceptance; furthermore, "Proposals submitted in major subgroups by isolates [were] either rejected or delayed."[31]

After going through this informal network of subgroups, the whole central office submits a proposal to an administrative council for agreement. A proposal introduced into an administrative council without major subgroup approval is delayed until that action occurs. If a consensus by the central office staff is reached in favor of a proposal, then the proposal is sent to a school board study meeting for consideration. The central office staff "utilizes the board's study session to produce a predictable vote for or against a proposal at the official board meeting."[32]

Over the years there has been a great deal of criticism of the power and control of educational bureaucracies. They have been accused of being insulated from community influences and of focusing most of their attention on internal struggles for power. Often, it is argued, members of an educational bureaucracy are more concerned with extrinsic rewards than with service to a client. Principals and teachers in the system are often faced with many contradictory statements coming from different parts of the bureaucracy, and the bureaucratic units are more concerned with their own prestige and advancement than with helping the schools. In his study of the New York City school bureaucracy, David Rogers writes,

> These loyalties, cliques, and internal power struggles were an essential element in headquarters politics. . . . Predictably the divisions [within the school administration] competed in trying to secure larger shares of the scarce resources of the system. "What will this do to our unit?" was the usual question when reforms were discussed.[33]

Educational bureaucracies tend to have the greatest power in urban school districts and in large consolidated school districts. "As the size of the school system increases," Boyd states, "the visibility of lay opposition groups tends to decrease, and school system bureaucracy, the social distance to school authorities, and the ability of the system to maintain 'business as usual' in the face of lay opposition tends to increase."[34]

Therefore, in dominated and factional communities, educational bureaucracies have more power when the school district is large. For instance, a faction boycotting a school in an urban area will not have so much of an effect as a factional boycott in a small school district. In addition, ruling elites in urban areas might complain about their inability to change the local schools because of an entrenched bureaucracy.

Criticisms of educational bureaucracies reveal another aspect of the issue of control in local school districts. The issue is not the desire by bureaucracies to control, but the inability of bureaucracies to change in response to outside demands. This issue cuts across every type of community power structure. In other words, a distinction should be made between educational bureaucracies that are in control and educational bureaucracies that are out of control.

Remember, educational bureaucracies are most likely to be out of control in large, as opposed to small, school districts. And even if the superintendent and the central office give the appearance of exerting major control over local educational policies, there is still the possibility that they are acting within the range of community expectations, or what Boyd calls the zone of tolerance.

TEACHERS' UNIONS

Teachers' union contracts affect policies in local school districts. Union contracts are often negotiated outside the range of direct public control; therefore, teachers' unions can affect school politics that is independent of the local community power structure. This condition is reflected in the wide variation of union practices that seem to operate independently of any particular type of community environment or power structure. In fact, it is difficult to generalize about the effect of teachers' unions on local school politics because of the wide variations in labor relationships. In her book *Teachers' Unions in the Schools*, Susan Moore Johnson writes about her study of local teachers' unions: "It would have been nice to have derived a simple, neatly predictive model to explain the great diversity in educational labor practices, but none was to be found."[35]

Johnson's study was limited to six communities, of which three were urban, one was suburban, one was a suburban consolidated district, and one was rural. Based on this limited sample, Johnson made the common-sense conclusions that (a) there is more trust and cooperation between unions and local school officials in smaller school districts; (b) communities with a strong local labor tradition are more supportive of teachers' unions; and (c) union negotiations are more difficult when there is a shortage of funds for local schools. Nonetheless, she was unable to provide a model that could be used to predict labor relations in a particular type of community.

Any discussion of the effect of local teachers' unions on school politics must therefore recognize wide variations in practice. These variations occur even when negotiated contracts contain similar language. According to Johnson, much of the variation is a result of individual personalities, personal relationships between school administrators and teachers, and teachers' attitudes toward their school and school system. She writes,

> The experiences of these districts suggest that teachers and principals remake even this locally derived policy [union contract] until it is their own—until it is consistent with past practices and current preferences. Contract implementation, like program implementation, demands ongoing mutual adaptation between the rules and local school practices.[36]

Even with variations between school districts, there is an increasing trend for local teachers' union contracts to include policy matters along with wage settlements. The negotiation of noneconomic items has removed many policy discussions from the traditional arena of school politics. In fact, one important consequence of the expansion of noneconomic items in teachers' union contracts is the possible loss of public control. It can be argued that during negotiations, a board of education represents the public. The assumption is that the board functions as elected representatives of the public in bargaining with teachers' unions. A major problem with the argument is that boards of education tend not to play an active role in negotiations and give most of the responsibility to either professional negotiators or members of the administrative staff.

In their study of trends in teachers' union contracts, Lorraine McDonnell and Anthony Pascal suggest that it is naive of the public to assume that a board of education plays a major role in union negotiations: "Citizens may assume that their elected representatives on the school board take an active part in negotiations, but we have seen that this rarely happens."[37] McDonnell and Pascal found a lack of community participation in most contract negotiations and discovered that school boards were often divorced from negotiations except approval of the final contract. In many districts, it was found, collective bargaining was being handled by a director of personnel and/or an employee in public relations. Consequently, one effect of labor negotiations is to strengthen control by school administrators and teachers over school district policies concerning school boards and the public.

McDonnell and Pascal found that since the early 1970s, items in teachers' union contracts have steadily expanded to include areas traditionally controlled by school administrators. For instance, items in some contracts now include (a) teacher participation in the evaluation of other teachers, (b) teacher supervision of other teachers, and (c) the establishment of school building committees and grievance procedures. The latter two items have helped teachers counter the power of school administrators. Additional general policy issues in some teachers' contracts include class size, working hours, number of faculty meetings, policy review committees, and textbook committees.[38]

Johnson found the same range of contract provisions. In the six school districts in her study, contract items dealt with the following: grievance procedures, union privileges in schools, building committees, evaluations and ratings, personnel files, personal leave, lunch duty, meetings, extracurricular assignments, teacher assignments, length of work day, evening meetings, preparation periods, extra duties, teaching load, and class size.[39]

McDonnell and Pascal found that the noneconomic provisions in contracts had their greatest effect at the school building level: "The noneconomic effects of collective bargaining are more perceptible at the school than the district level. Because of contractual provisions . . . principals have less latitude than before in managing their own buildings."[40]

Union contracts have formalized and made complex the internal governance of school systems. Charles Kerchner uses the term *multilateral* to describe the style of governance resulting from collective bargaining. He argues that the traditional hierarchical structure of schooling with a unitary command structure has broken down and has been replaced with one that involves continuous negotiations between a variety of actors in a school system.[41]

Kerchner uses one incident in a California elementary school to depict both the changes in the command structure in education and the role of teacher-building committees. In this school a group of vandals entered over a weekend, destroying equipment and stealing the master key for all of the classrooms. The teachers became concerned that the thieves could enter their classrooms and steal personal property. The principal called the central office to have the locks changed and received a firm refusal because of the expense. As Kerchner points out, before there was a union, that would have been the end of the issue. But here, the building representative for the California Teachers Association got on the phone and told the central office that if they didn't change the locks there would be a major grievance. The locks were changed in a few days.[42]

Any general analysis of the effect of teachers' unions must consider the pursuit of the collective interests of teachers in relationship to other interests within a school district. For instance, demands for higher wages affect how much money can be spent on other things. In addition, the pursuit of greater power for teachers conflicts with the interests of administrators in protecting their power.

Randall Eberts and Lawrence Pierce examined the effect of collective bargaining on the battle over resources in 1,336 school districts in Michigan and New York.[43] They argue that during periods of declining enrollments and budgets, school administrators have many options:

1. Leave vacant teaching positions unfilled.
2. Defer any salary increase for teachers.
3. Cut nonprofessional staff.
4. Reduce expenses by (a) requiring teachers to teach more and larger classes, (b) reducing or eliminating teacher preparation periods, and (c) eliminating in-service training.
5. Cut teaching supplies.
6. Replace older, more experienced teachers with younger, cheaper teachers.

If one considers these options in light of union concerns, it is easy to see the possible effects of union demands on resource allocations and educational policy. For instance, unions would certainly fight against replacing an older staff with a younger staff. In fact, most union contracts contain language protecting the seniority rights of teachers. Unions would also fight any attempt to defer salary increases for teachers. Protection of seniority rights and salaries are the most important priorities of most unions and have been major issues in most strikes, forcing authorities to select other means for reducing the budget.

Most teachers' unions would also fight against larger class sizes and the elimination of teacher preparation periods, but these issues would not have so high a priority as salaries and job protection; no teachers' union has conducted a strike solely over class size and preparation periods. Indeed, it is hard to imagine a teachers' union striking because of a freeze in hiring, the cutting of nonprofessional staff, or a reduction in supplies.[44]

In other words, as Eberts and Pierce found in their study, the existence of a strong union has a major impact on decisions about the allocation of resources. Given the goals and structure of teachers' unions, their primary concern is to protect jobs and seniority rights and to increase wages. Unions will tend to resist any educational policies that threaten those primary concerns.

Collective interests of strong teachers' unions not only affect resource allocations and educational policies, but they also threaten the interests of school administrators. As teachers' unions gain more power, they reduce the power of other school administrators. In fact, school principals complain that their interests are often not represented during collective bargaining sessions. Johnson recorded complaints by principals about the impact of contract provisions on local schools. In one community, she reported, "there were principals who objected that teachers had been granted a duty-free lunch without the provision of cafeteria aides to supervise students." In another community, principals complained of the vagueness of contract language regarding supervision of preparation periods.[45]

The most dramatic example of the struggle for power between administrators and teachers' unions occurred in 1987 in Rochester, New York, when the local administrators' union sued the local teachers' union over its mentor teacher program. The suit contained objections similar to those raised the previous year by administrators in New York City against a master teacher program. The argument in both situations was that the programs gave teachers duties and power that were normally part of the job of principals and assistant principals.

In Rochester, the mentor teacher program was agreed on in collective bargaining sessions between the Rochester Teachers Association and the school district. The program relieves some teachers of teaching duties so that they can help improve the skills of first-year teachers and tenured teachers who are having difficulties.

The suit filed by the Association of Supervisors and Administrators of Rochester claimed that the mentor teachers were doing administrative and supervisory tasks without proper state credentials. The head of the administrators' association, Patricia Carnahan, stated, "As far as I am concerned, this program encroaches on the jobs of those currently involved in the evaluation process. . . . The district and teachers' union are saying that evaluations of new teachers done by administrators are to be shared with the panel [includes mentor teachers], and we are saying 'no.' "

Similar objections were raised by Ted Elsberg, president of the Council of Supervision and Administration of the City of New York. He objected to the creation of the position of a master teacher, which would do functions similar to those of the mentor teachers in Rochester, because the role already existed in the schools as principals and assistant principals. What Elsberg wanted was for the city to hire 200 new assistant principals. Arthur Wise, director of the RAND Corporation's Center for the Study of the Teaching Profession, stated concerning the court action, "I think these are perhaps the first signs of administrative resistance to the emerging idea of teacher professionalism. . . . Unfortunately, we will probably be seeing more of this."[46]

Although it is difficult to generalize about the effect of teachers' unions on local school districts because of the wide variations in practice, where teachers' unions are strong they do affect local school district policies and resource allocations, and create power struggles with local administrators. Often, unions work outside the normal channels of community power. Like any union organization, teachers' unions are primarily concerned with the collective interests of their members—enhancing teacher power, increasing wages, and protecting jobs.

SITE-BASED MANAGEMENT

In this arena of school board politics, educational bureaucracies, and teachers unions, site-based management has been introduced as a reform strategy. Site-based management involves teachers, students, community members, and school administrators in shared decision-making about the management of individual schools. As suggested previously, however, site-based management does not involve the sharing of any meaningful power. It is primarily viewed as a method for carrying out educational policies more effectively. The movement for site-based management originated from research on effective schools, which concluded that cooperation and shared decision-making of school and community improves school climate, which in turn affects teacher performance and student achievement. Consequently, the major justification for site-based management is increasing student achievement.

For instance, the implementation of site-based management in the Chicago public schools is considered a means of improving school climate. During the 1988-1989 school year, site-based management was introduced in forty-two Chicago schools. In the Chicago plan, school climate includes the following factors:

1. staff morale,
2. job satisfaction,
3. professional development,
4. cooperative planning,
5. parent involvement,
6. student involvement,
7. student influence, and
8. self-concept/self-esteem.

It is also assumed that improvement in school climate will increase student achievement.[47]

To improve the effectiveness of site-based management, the Chicago public schools developed a school-based management training program that is part of a larger project to improve academic performance of underachieving students in racially segregated schools. This project created core planning teams (CPT) consisting of the school principal, teachers, students, parents, and community representatives. Evaluators for the Chicago public schools predicted, "The ability of the CPT to begin cooperative planning and management practices is expected to enhance school climate and to affect academic achievement."[48]

The evaluators studied ten of the forty-two Chicago public schools starting site-based management. They found that only two of these schools were effective in fully implementing site-based management methods. And, in these two schools, student academic achievement did increase: Retention rates and reading and math scores improved between the time that the project was started in 1988 and 1990.[49]

As discussed in Chapter 4, site-based management is a source of tension between administrators, who fear that their traditional power is being eroded by school-based councils, and teachers. The American Federation of School Administrators is opposed to many current attempts to carry out site-based management.

Clearly, site-based management is not intended to give meaningful power to teachers, students, and community members. Politically, it can threaten the power of school principals. It might improve student achievement, but it does not deal directly with the issue of what knowledge is of most worth for students. The political importance of site-based management would increase if individual schools were given the power to decide what students should learn and the content of achievement tests. Now, however, the power to decide is still in the hands of those determining academic requirements and the content of achievement tests.

CONCLUSION

Local educational politics varies according to the type of community power structure, the nature of the local labor market, the power of the local educational bureaucracy, and the militancy of the local teachers' union. Although these variations exist among school districts, a great deal of uniformity is imposed on local schools by state and federal educational policies. In fact, one can argue that local political battles are unimportant when compared with those that occur in state and federal politics.

An often-heard plea is to restore local control of the schools. It is not clear what this would accomplish. In the past, local control of schools often meant control by local power elites who discriminated against the poor and minority groups. It required political activity by civil rights groups to gain federal intervention to end discrimination by local school systems. Those who argue for local control might simply be advocating restoring power to these local elites.

On the other hand, local control of schools might free them from the constantly changing educational policies that result from state and federal politics. With greater local control, local school policies would not be linked to changes in national administrations or foreign policy. But, of course, greater local control might cause local educational policies that change to meet the needs of local business interests. In many ways, the choice is between the uncertainties and change of federal intervention, and the possibility of discrimination by local elites. As in any political issue, there is no easy solution.

The following list summarizes factors that must be considered in analyzing local educational politics. Each item in the list should be considered in the corresponding discussion in this chapter. Given the wide range of communities in the United States, there is no necessary relationship between these various factors. For instance, a community could have a dominated power structure that is constantly frustrated by the intransigence of the local school bureaucracy. On the other hand, the same type of power structure might operate in a community in which the bureaucracy is easily controlled.

Factors in Local Politics of Education
1. Nature of community power structure
   a. dominated
   b. factional
   c. pluralistic
   d. inert
2. Educational needs of the local labor market
   a. diversified
   b. single-industry
   c. suburban community (primary interest in preparation for college)
   d. rural, small town, or suburban (minimum educational concerns for future employment)
3. Governing style of school board
   a. dominated
   b. factional
   c. status-congruent
   d. sanctioning
4. Governing style of superintendent
   a. functionary
   b. political strategist
   c. professional advisor
   d. decision maker
5. Power of educational bureaucracy
   a. operating in zone of tolerance
   b. in control of policies
   c. out of control
6. Power of teachers' union
   a. range of noneconomic items in contract
   b. effect of contract on allocation of resources
   c. conflict with local administrators
   d. participation of union in politics of local school boards

Although communities in the United States vary widely, they share certain patterns. As argued in the first part of this chapter, the educational requirements of the local labor market often determine the type of power structure, which, in turn, determines the governing style of the superintendent. Dominated power structures tend to exist in communities with a single industry or a diversified labor market, and they tend to have dominated school boards and functionary superintendents. The educational needs of the labor market are of little concern in a factional community, which tends to have a factional school board and a superintendent who is a political strategist. Pluralistic communities are often oriented toward labor markets that require a college education, and they tend to have status-congruent school boards with superintendents who act like professional advisors. In inert communities, the local labor market usually requires a minimal level of education, and the school board tends to be sanctioning, with a decision-making superintendent. In addition, teachers' unions and school bureaucracies tend to have more power and influence in larger school districts.

NOTES

1. James Cibulka, "The Reform and survival of American public schools: an institutional perspective," in Robert L. Crowson, William Boyd, and Hanne B. Mawhinney, eds., *The Politics of Education and the New Institutionalism: Reinventing the American School* (Washington, D. C.: Falmer Press, 1996), p. 13.
2. Ibid.
3. Peter Applebome, "National Survey Finds School Board Members in Cautious Mood," *The New York Times* (12 January 1997), p. 11.
4. Ibid.
5. Ibid.
6. Donald McCarty and Charles Ramsey, *The School Managers: Power and Conflict in American Public Education* (Westport, Conn.: Greenwood, 1971).
7. Ibid., pp. 27-79.
8. David Kirby, T. Robert Harris, and Robert Crain, *Political Strategies in Northern School Desegregation* (Lexington, Mass.: Lexington Books, 1973), p. 84.
9. See Michael Timpane, *Corporations and Public Education,* a report distributed by Teachers College, Columbia University (May 1981), p. 34; and *Chicago United and the Chicago Board of Education,* a report distributed by Chicago United (March 1991). A general discussion of this relationship can be found in Kathy Borman and Joel Spring, *Schools in Central Cities* (White Plains, N.Y.: Longman, 1984), pp. 183-186.
10. For a discussion of these political changes, see Joseph Cronin, *The Control of Urban Schools* (New York: Free Press, 1973), pp. 39-123; Joel Spring, *Education and the Rise of the Corporate State* (Boston: Beacon Press, 1972), pp. 85-135; David Tyack, *The One Best System* (Cambridge, Mass.: Harvard University Press, 1974), pp. 126-167.
11. Willis D. Hawley, *Nonpartisan Elections and the Case for Party Politics* (New York: Wiley, 1973).
12. *The Boston Compact: An Operational Plan for Expanded Partnerships with the Boston Public Schools,* a booklet distributed by the Boston public school system (September 1982).
13. "A Community of Believers," in *The Atlanta Partnership of Business & Education, Inc.: Second Anniversary Report,* undated booklet distributed by the Atlanta Partnership of Business & Education.
14. McCarty and Ramsey, *School Managers,* pp. 79-127.
15. Ibid., pp. 87-97.
16. Ibid., p. 97.
17. Ann L. Page and Donald A. Clelland, "The Kanawha County Textbook Controversy: A Study of the Politics of Life-Style Concern," *Social Forces,* vol. 57, no. 1 (September 1978), pp. 265-268.
18. Ibid., p. 276.

19. William Boyd, "The Public, the Professionals, and Educational Policy Making: Who Governs?," *Teachers College Record*, vol. 77, no. 4 (May 1976), pp. 547-549.
20. McCarty and Ramsey, *School Managers*, pp. 127-143.
21. Alan Peshkin, *Growing Up American: Schooling and the Survival of Community* (Chicago: University of Chicago Press, 1978), p. 10.
22. Ibid., p. 58.
23. Ibid., pp. 74-82.
24. Boyd, "The Public, the Professionals," pp. 548, 551-552.
25. L. Harmon Zeigler and M. Kent Jennings, *Governing American Schools: Political Interaction in Local School Districts* (North Scituate, Mass.: Duxbury Press, 1974).
26. Ibid., p. 189.
27. Ibid., p. 189.
28. Ibid., pp. 190-194.
29. Joseph H. McGivney and James M. Haught, "The Politics of Education: A View from the Perspective of the Central Office Staff," *Educational Administration Quarterly*, vol. 8, no. 3 (August 1972), p. 35.
30. Ibid., p. 23.
31. Ibid., p. 30.
32. Ibid.
33. David Rogers, *110 Livingston Street: Politics and Bureaucracy in the New York City Schools* (New York: Random House, 1968), p. 301.
34. Boyd, "The Public, the Professionals," p. 560.
35. Susan Moore Johnson, *Teachers' Unions in the Schools* (Philadelphia: Temple University Press, 1984), p. 169.
36. Ibid., p. 172.
37. Lorraine McDonnell and Anthony Pascal, *Organized Teachers in American Schools* (Santa Monica, Calif.: Rand Corporation, 1979), p. 87.
38. Ibid., p. 190.
39. Johnson, *Teachers' Unions*, pp. 190-211.
40. McDonnell and Pascal, *Organized Teachers*, p. ix.
41. Charles T. Kerchner, "Unions and Their Impact on School Governance and Politics," in Anthony M. Cresswell and Michael Murphy, eds., *Teachers, Unions, and Collective Bargaining in Public Education* (Berkeley, Calif.: McCutchan, 1980), pp. 382-387.
42. Ibid., pp. 384-385.
43. Randall W. Eberts and Lawrence C. Pierce, *The Effects of Collective Bargaining in Public Schools* (Eugene, Ore.: Center for Educational Policy and Management, 1980).
44. Originally, I made this argument in Borman and Spring, *Schools in Central Cities*, pp. 134-159.
45. Johnson, *Teachers' Unions*, pp. 33-36.
46. Quoted in Blake Rodman, "New York Lawsuit Highlights Growing Tension between Principals, Teachers over Their Roles," *GEducation Week*, vol. 6, no. 16 (14 January 1987), pp. 1, 22.
47. William J. Evans and Carol Perry, "The Impact of School-Based Management on School Environment," paper presented at the Annual Meeting of the American Educational Research Association, Chicago, April 1991, p. 5.
48. William Kaufman, Kimberly Williams, Lisa Moultrie, Carla O'Connor, William Evans, and Geraldine Oberman, "School-Based Management: A Study of the Implementation Process," paper presented at the Annual Meeting of the American Educational Research Association, Chicago, April 1991, p. 1.
49. Evans and Perry, "Impact of School-Based Management," p. 11.

CHAPTER 9

The Knowledge Industry

There are three components to the politics of knowledge: first, there is the politics of the curriculum, which includes decisions about what subjects to teach in the public schools. Second, there is the politics of content, which deals with what is to be taught in each subject. Last, there is the politics of testing, which includes decisions about what students ought to have learned.

The preceding chapters focused on the politics of the curriculum, such as how national education policies have dictated the teaching of particular subjects. During the Cold War period of the 1950s, science, mathematics, and foreign languages were emphasized, and in the 1960s, priorities shifted to the needs of disadvantaged children. In the 1970s, emphasis was placed on career and vocational subjects to reduce unemployment. During the 1980s and early 1990s, concern with international trade prompted arguments for increased study of mathematics and science and more testing.

The politics of content primarily deals with the organization of the textbook industry, court decisions regarding textbooks, state laws, and the political and economic forces that affect publishing decisions. For most elementary and secondary students, a textbook is the major source of knowledge about a particular school subject. As we will see, decisions about the content of textbooks are made in a very heated and political environment.

Since the accountability movement of the 1970s, standardized test scores have been a major method by which schools tell the public what and how much students have learned. When test scores are high, newspaper headlines declare the triumph of local schools; when scores are low, they announce that the schools failed. When school systems use test scores to measure the effectiveness of teachers and principals, the result is the tyranny of testing. Any school system that reports test scores to the public, and any teacher or principal whose effectiveness is measured according to student scores, must, out of self-interest, "teach for the test." Thus the content of standardized tests has a direct impact on what is taught in the classroom.

Also, standardized tests and textbooks convey the idea that what is taught in schools is neutral and that all scholars agree about what kinds of knowledge are valuable. Of course, nothing could be further from the truth. In every field of study, scholars disagree about content, interpretation, and methodology. In addition, most subject matter areas contain values and assumptions that conflict with the values and beliefs of some public group. Knowledge is not neutral, and the knowledge taught in schools is the result of political and economic decisions.

With standardized tests, it is difficult to defend the idea of "standardized" knowledge in controversial areas of study such as history, economics, government, and other social sciences. In any society that claims to allow freedom of ideas, it is difficult to create standardized tests. For instance, what are the most important things to be learned in social studies and literature, and therefore measured on nationally standardized tests? Who would be presumptuous enough to decide? In the United States, testing companies presume to decide such things, and school systems agree to accept their decisions. Testing companies are motivated by profit, and government agencies are motivated by the desire for an instrument that can easily measure the supposed effectiveness of administrators and teachers.

In describing the politics of knowledge, I will discuss first the issue of the neutrality of knowledge, then the attitudes of the courts, and finally the politics of publishing and testing. The publishing and testing industries are money-making enterprises that operate in a politically controlled market. Consequently, both industries will be considered in their economic and political context.

THE MYTH OF NEUTRAL KNOWLEDGE

Professional educators, government officials, the publishing industry, and testing corporations help to perpetuate the myth of neutral knowledge. In this context, *neutral knowledge* refers to a universally agreed-upon standardized body of knowledge in a particular subject area. For instance, to avoid a loss of sales owing to controversies over content, publishers make their textbooks appear to present neutral knowledge. Being primarily interested in profits, the publishing industry tries to please all customers by avoiding any possible conflict over content. This avoidance of controversy often results in bland textbooks.

Professional educators and government officials also foster the idea of neutral knowledge when they report student learning in standardized test scores, as opposed to the content of what students have learned. Communities are told that their students scored above grade level on standardized tests in mathematics and reading, but they are never told what their students learned. Even standardized test scores lack substantive meaning for most people. What does it mean to read at grade level? Since a grade level is an artificial construct, the idea that all students should master a given body of knowledge by a particular grade level is also artificial. But in order for educators and officials to gain professional acceptance, and in order for the public to accept the use of standardized tests, everyone concerned must act as though there really was such a uniform body of knowledge.

The lack of uniform agreement about what knowledge should be taught is exemplified by the debate over standards for mathematics that occurred in 1991 after President George Bush outlined broad national standards for elementary and secondary students and called for tests to measure performance. It is often assumed that mathematics is the least controversial field of study. After making his pledge to establish national standards and tests, Bush told a meeting of the Mathematical Sciences Education Board, "Of the six national education goals, you're helping to realize one of the most important: that American students will rank first in the world in math."[1]

The members of the math board responded with skepticism that a math test could be produced because, according to *The New York Times,* "there is still much disagreement about what students should know, what they should be tested on, and even what kind of mathematics should be taught." For instance, the director of the National Center for Research in Mathematical Sciences, Thomas Romberg, criticized American teachers for teaching, "eight years of 15th century arithmetic, eight years of 17th century algebra and one year of third century B.C. geometry."[2] Of course, the development of a national test in mathematics will require the imposition of uniformity of the teaching of mathematics.

The size and bureaucratic organization of public schooling promote uniformity of content in classrooms. The use of only one textbook in a given classroom or grade creates the impression that there is a body of standardized knowledge. Most schools require the use of a particular text in a classroom; others require the use of the same textbook in *all classrooms* of a particular grade. Thus the public schools present a smaller variety of books and ideas than commercial bookstores do. It can be argued that the uniformity of subject matter in the public schools gives students the impression that an agreed-upon body of standard knowledge exists in every discipline. If this were true, then public schools would be educating people to accept the idea later in life that school knowledge is neutral.

Testimony given before the Texas commissioner of education and the Texas State Textbook Committee shows how value-laden school knowledge can be. For many years, the policy of statewide textbook adoption in Texas strongly influenced the publishing industry. Not wanting to lose big sales in Texas, publishers pay close attention to the testimony given before the Texas State Textbook Committee and to its decisions.

Testimony before the committee highlights some subtle but significant meanings that small changes in wording makes in textbooks. For instance, consider the 1986 testimony of a conservative textbook critic Mel Gabler regarding secondary-level texts on U.S. government. Having spent many years criticizing textbooks in all parts of the United States, Gabler and his wife are always vigilant for any sign of anti-Americanism, attacks on free-enterprise economics, and suggestions that federal controls might be needed to protect the environment.

Gabler complained to the committee about textbook treatment of the American Revolution. From his perspective, the American War for Independence was not a revolution but an instance of colonial obedience to British law. Gabler argued before the committee, "In other words, the colonists were obeying the laws. Actually, it was the parliament that was breaking the law. The parliament was passing laws contrary to the British rights, the British Constitution."[3]

The way in which U.S. history is interpreted in the public schools profoundly affects the way in which American students view their country. An interpretation that presents the colonial break with Britain as revolutionary creates the image of the United States as the first modern revolutionary power and as a leader of democratic revolutions in the rest of the world. Gabler's interpretation creates an image of a nation of law-abiding citizens whose primary concern is with the protection of rights under a system of laws. These two views of American history have striking implications for the conduct of foreign policy, the shaping of American attitudes toward other nations, and the development of political culture.

Directly related to the issue of neutral knowledge is the Texas law requiring text for grades 7 through 12 to advocate the free-enterprise system. In Gabler's language, the law requires books to be "unneutral." Concerning this law, Gabler complained of a text that "treats agricultural problems, on most pages, as something to be solved by government, rather than as problems that government helped to create by interfering with the free market."[4]

Obviously, students' ideas about economic and political problems can be shaped according to the way in which the sources of economic problems are identified and described. Certainly, the source of economic problems in agriculture is open to debate. It is also debatable whether or not America's prosperity is solely the result of free enterprise. Since the early days of the nineteenth century, the federal government was involved in financing roads, building railroads, managing the financial system, and helping business to accumulate capital. Whether or not government interference is a key element in economic development is therefore open to debate. But the Texas textbook law does not recognize this area of dispute. Essentially, Texas law defines what knowledge about economics should be standard.

Important issues also arise in subjects less controversial than history and government. Consider the testimony of Jane Boyd of the National Organization for Women on the content of basal readers: "My review of the basal readers for Grade 1 is primarily concerned with the equal representation of positive role models for both boys and girls." In her testimony she complained that "three of the four basal readers under review at this time practice a form of sexism that makes invisible the possible triumphs that girls and women can experience."[5] More specifically, she directed the attention of the committee members to a story about a toad and a frog, both male, who "experience winter and independence together." She recommended that one character be made female.[6] Changing the gender of the frog or toad would create a different image of appropriate sex-role behavior in the minds of students.

On a more humorous note, Suzanne Steinbach, a dietician, complained before the committee that an environmental studies text threatened the livestock industry by claiming, "Americans eat large quantities of beef. The conversion efficiency of plant material to beef is low. Is there any way to justify this kind of diet?"[7]

Such considerations make any subject taught in schools controversial. In addition, state textbook laws, like the one requiring advocacy of free enterprise, generate debate about whether or not the material is violating state law. State laws on the content of textbooks make it possible to object about many issues. Consider the Texas law stating, "Textbooks shall not contain certain material which serves to undermine authority." Based on this law, Lee Gaynier, a nurse, objected to a health book's definition of euthanasia because it made the act seem palatable. Gaynier reasoned, "Taking someone's life intentionally is murder. Murder is illegal. The book is teaching that murder is acceptable under certain circumstances, which is in violation of the General Content Requirement and Limitations [on undermining authority]."[8]

Although testimony before the Texas Textbook Committee points to the controversial nature of school knowledge, the greatest challenge to the neutrality of school knowledge has occurred in court cases brought by Protestant fundamentalists. Court decisions regarding the content of a public school instruction focus on the constitutional issues of interference with the free exercise of religion and the establishment of religion. Consequently, the only major court challenges to the neutrality of knowledge presented in public schools come from religious groups. In most situations, this means that a student or parent can object to ideas taught in the public schools on religious grounds only.

The courts' limited involvement in these matters creates the public impression that the only legitimate legal challenges involve religious issues. The issues that appear in the popular press deal primarily with creationism versus evolution and differences over moral instruction. In fact, court decisions dealing with the censorship of books by school officials assume that political neutrality can exist in the selection process. Seldom, if ever, are there court challenges over political and economic teachings outside the context of religion.

Some religious groups reject most public school textbooks (as in the West Virginia case in Chapter 8) because textbooks lack religious content and do not recognize the authority of God. For these groups, if a textbook does not tell a student to seek answers for personal problems from the Bible or from another religious source, then the textbook is antireligious. The same charge is made if the textbook teaches something contrary to a fundamentalist interpretation of the Bible such as the theory of evolution.

On the other hand, school authorities have resisted complaints from religious groups about textbooks with the argument that it is necessary to have a uniform system of instruction and textbooks. This was the defense used by school officials in *Mozert* v. *Hawkins Public Schools* (1986), when religious groups objected to the content of the 1983 edition of the Holt, Rinehart & Winston reading series, complaining that the content of the textbook series was inconsistent with their religious beliefs. According to the final decision rendered by Judge Thomas Hull, local public school officials argued that "to permit individual teachers, students, parents, or ministers to choose the textbook of their liking would inescapably result in widespread chaos not only within the Hawkins County School System but also within the State of Tennessee."[9]

The major limitation in this type of case is that the issues must be related to religion. The only part of the U.S. Constitution that concerns objections to the content of instruction is the Free-Exercise Clause of the First Amendment, which prohibits the government from interfering with the free exercise of religion. This means that public schools are prohibited from requiring students to do anything that will interfere with the practice of their religion.

Arguing in the context of the Free-Exercise Clause, the court required the Hawkins County schools to provide the plaintiff's children with alternative reading material. In the *Mozert* case, the court defined a two-step process for determining a free-exercise claim. The first step is to decide whether government action places a burden on the exercise of religion and whether a compelling government interest balances that burden. The second step is to determine "whether the beliefs are religious and whether they are sincerely held by the individual asserting them."[10] In the *Mozert* case, the court decided that the plaintiffs were arguing from a sincere religious position and that the government's interest in maintaining uniformity in textbooks was not a sufficient reason for interfering with the plaintiff's free exercise of religion.

Besides their concern with the free exercise of religion, the courts have used the Free-Speech Clause of the First Amendment to establish a standard for the selection of schoolbooks. This standard assumes that the free speech of students is violated only when clearly stated political opinions guide the selection process.

The standard for the politically neutral selection of texts was established in *Board of Island Union Free District* v. *Steven A. Pico* (1982), which involved the removal of books from the school library by the board of education because it believed that the contents of the books were unsuitable for high school students.[11] The case originated when several board of education members attended a conference of a politically conservative organization of parents concerned with educational legislation in New York State. While they were at the conference, the board members received a list of books considered morally and politically inappropriate for students. Upon returning from the conference, the board members investigated the contents of their high school library and ordered the removal of nine books that were on the list.

In rendering its decision, the U.S. Supreme Court recognized the power of school boards to select books and argued for the limitation of judicial interference in the operation of school systems. On the other hand, the Court recognized its obligation to guarantee that public institutions do not suppress ideas. Here, it argued that there was a clear intention to suppress ideas by removing books contained in a list from a political organization.

The Court balanced the right of school boards to select books against the protection of the free speech of students by arguing that the decisions about selection could not be based on partisan or political motives. In the words of the Court, "If a Democratic school board, motivated by party affiliation, ordered the removal of all books written by or in favor of Republicans, few would doubt that the order violated the constitutional rights of the students denied access to those books." In another illustration, the Court argued, "The same conclusion would surely apply if an all-white school board, motivated by racial animus, decided to remove all books written by blacks or advocating racial equality and integration."[12]

Although the Supreme Court decision was limited to the removal of books from the school library, it did establish a general standard for judging the actions of school officials regarding the content of books. The decision gave clear recognition to the power of school boards to select books. It also denied the right of school boards to select books according to a particular, and clearly recognized, political agenda. This standard does not preclude the possibility that the school board will select books that might be ideologically offensive to some members of the community, unless, of course, the books interfere with the free exercise of religion.

In summary, the examples from testimony before the Texas State Textbook Committee illustrate how unneutral the content of most school textbooks is. Knowledge in most areas of study is debatable by scholars and by those with differing ideological positions. The only protection for the free speech of students is against texts that interfere with the free exercise of religion or against texts that are selected according to a clear political agenda. Otherwise, school authorities, including school boards and state governments, have the right to select textbooks and require that they be read by students. In addition, states have the right to pass laws requiring that textbooks advocate the free-enterprise system or do not undermine authority. Clearly, these state laws advocate an ideological position, but one that has not been tested under the standard established in *Board of Island Union Free District* v. *Steven A. Pico*.

THE TEXTBOOK INDUSTRY

To understand how political forces determine the content of textbooks, one must examine the structure of the textbook industry. Most textbook publishers produce books that lack innovation and that reflect a politically conservative perspective. For instance, the very structure of the textbook industry works against innovation and creativity. Since its primary goal is to make a profit, the industry avoids risk by concentrating on mainstream textbooks. This reluctance to take risks is the result, in part, of the small number of companies in control of the textbook market.

When I wrote the first edition of this book in the mid-1980s, I stated that seven companies controlled 80 percent of the textbook market and that four of these companies operated independently. Two of those companies have since been bought by corporate conglomerates. Pearson plc, a global conglomerate that owns various types of companies, purchased Addison-Wesley, and Robert Maxwell purchased Macmillan. Of the top seven, the only remaining independent publishers are Houghton Mifflin and Harcourt Brace Jovanovich (which purchased Holt, Rinehart & Winston). Of the other textbook publishers, Scott, Foresman and Company was sold to HarperCollins, which is owned by Rupert Murdoch; Viacom owns Simon & Schuster and Prentice Hall; and Time owns Little, Brown.[13]

At the time of the consolidation, it was generally believed that these larger companies would force the remaining small companies out of the market. The larger companies were planning to offer textbooks in every area rather than specialize in particular subjects. According to an article in *Education Week*,

"Small houses will have their place in the new textbook market only if the large companies specialize in a particular curricular area, as they did in the 1960s."[14]

Most students of the textbook industry agree that consolidation results in less innovation and lower quality. In the most extensive sociological study of the publishing industry to date, Lewis Coser, Charles Kadushin, and Walter Powell argue that periods of high concentration in the publishing industry produce creative stagnation. One reason is that larger firms prefer "predictability, routine, and control, both for economic and for psychological reasons. Firms in concentrated industries, by virtue of their market power, feel no need to risk innovation though customers might be interested in new products."[15]

In a small firm an ambitious project requires a decision by only a small group of people; in a large firm the decision must go through an extensive chain of command, with each level of command acting cautiously. Coser, Kadushin, and Powell quote Townsend Hoopes, president of the Association of American Publishers: "The most fundamental measure of the health and vigor [of book publishing] is the number of active firms in the industry."[16]

Because publishing houses desire predictability and sure profits, their books are very similar in appearance and content. The reason is that publishers must rely on the success of previous publications to decide sales of new books. There is no method that accurately predicts the needs of the textbook market. Consequently, editors often examine the leading textbooks in the field to decide the type of book they want written. Very often, editors want a new textbook to resemble the leading seller in the field, but to contain some new features that make it slightly different. Consequently, particularly in a market dominated by only a few firms, all of the books in a given subject area look very much alike. Of course, this does not mean that a different type of text might not sell. What it means is that publishers are afraid to risk publishing a textbook outside the common mold. Thus the textbook market continually reproduces look-alike texts that might in fact sell, but only because of the lack of competition.[17]

One major role of acquisition editors is to help authors shape their prospective texts to fit the needs of the marketplace. What this means in practice is shaping the book to fit the content of the course as it is supposedly taught in most schools. Of course, this is difficult because no one knows exactly what is taught in courses across the nation, and the content of courses is often determined by textbooks. In the end, editors must rely on the content of existing textbooks to figure out course content. After fitting the book to meet course content, acquisition editors then compare the prospective text to existing texts.

In addition, publishers rely on an "invisible college" of reviewers in making publishing decisions. Before publication, a company sends copies of the manuscript to several reviewers, who are selected from the contacts that publishing houses make in the public schools and academic world. Most often, these reviewers are leading scholars in the field and are themselves authors of books.[18] By the time the process of comparison and review is completed, the acquisition editor has shaped a product that resembles other products in the field.

There is the possibility that this publishing process perpetuates the content and structure of certain courses. Consider the possibility that textbooks largely determine the content of classroom teaching. If this is true, then the inherently conservative process of textbook acquisition and marketing causes the same material to be used in classrooms year after year. Thus any hope that some have of changing public schools depends on changes in the organization of the text-book industry.

Fear of censorship and of attack by pressure groups also makes publishers less willing to take risks. Publishers live in dread that an organized group will object to the content of their textbooks. Any sign of opposition to a particular text can dissuade local school officials from adopting it.

The Harold Rugg story exemplifies the difficulties faced by a textbook pub-lisher when it publishes something that does not reflect a consensus viewpoint. The story also shows that even when textbooks are successful in the market-place and widely accepted in the public schools, attacks from special-interest groups can still destroy them.

It is estimated that during the 1930s nearly half the social studies students in the United States used Rugg's social-science textbook series.[19] Rugg's major goal in the series was to overcome what he called the "impasse in citizenship." "The impasse," he writes, "has been frequently revealed by indifference to matters of public concern and by lack of trained intelligence on the part of the rank and file of our people to deal with their collective affairs." Rugg believed that citizens act from impulse rather than from deliberative judgment and that the goal of orga-nized social studies programs should be to train future citizens to apply intelli-gent judgment to major political, economic, and social problems. In Rugg's words, "Knowledge about the issues of contemporary life and how they came to be what they are could be translated into tendencies to act intelligently upon them, provided the machinery of the social studies is properly organized."[20]

In the book *America Revised: History Schoolbooks in the Twentieth Century*, Frances Fitzgerald writes about Rugg's success: "Harold Rugg's social studies series for elementary–junior-high-school students . . . was in many ways the crowning achievement of the progressive-education movement in the field of textbooks; it was, in fact, a democratic history—a history of the common man."[21] Rugg's series of social studies texts were not radical in the sense of being Marx-ist, but it did portray many difficulties and failures in American society. During a period of racial intolerance, the books promoted racial understanding and so-cial justice. Rugg also advocated national economic planning and included problems related to unemployment, immigrants, and consumerism.

Protests against the Rugg series began in 1939. The Advertising Federation of America attacked the series for making negative statements about adver-tising. Cries of "socialist" and "communist" were heard from the National Association of Manufacturers, the American Legion, and newspapers. Local school boards banned the texts from the classroom because of attacks from many pressure groups. Rugg was forced to tour the country to defend his books against charges of communism and socialism. But there was little he could do about the attacks. School boards and public school teachers shied away from using the books because of the potential for being drawn into the controversy. Fitzgerald reports that in 1938, 289,000 copies of Rugg's books were sold, and that by 1944 the number had dropped to 21,000 copies.[22] The decline of the Rugg textbook series is a classic example of the powers that pressure groups have over the textbook industry.

Dean Jaros, author of the book *Socialization to Politics,* believes that because of community pressure on teachers and the blandness of textbooks, civics courses make almost no impression on students: "Probably in response to pressure—real or imagined—from influential groups in society, teachers may avoid discussion of all but the most consensual community and regime-level values." Because of these real or imagined pressures, Jaros continues, "most teachers, often abetted by the texts that they use, strike poses of explicit political neutrality." As a result, "teachers fail to communicate the fact that public policy involves social conflict and the resolution of different value positions."[23]

Political pressures can originate from a variety of sources. At the 1986 meeting of the Texas State Textbook Committee, there was testimony from groups ranging from the National Organization for Women to People for the American Way. People for the American Way represent an interesting type of pressure group because they specifically organized it to counter the actions of the religious right. Before the 1986 hearings of the textbook committee, Michael Hudson, director and general counsel of People for the American Way in Texas, stated that the purpose of the 250,000-member national organization was to ensure that content changes in textbooks are "based on sound academic educational criteria and are not based on sectarian or political bias, as we feel has been the case sometimes in past years." Hudson went on to attack complaints about terms used in textbooks, such as "values clarification" and "decision making." He told the committee, "Moreover, these are religious-right catchwords or code words that have been used for years across not only Texas but across the entire nation to object to content that is somehow inconsistent with a particular and narrow religious or political viewpoint."[24]

Besides their fear of pressure groups, state adoption policies influence textbook publishers. For instance, fifteen states adopt textbooks. The largest of these states, California, represents 11 percent of the textbook market. In the late 1970s, Bill Honig, then a member of the California State Board of Education and later state superintendent of instruction, was made aware of the state's power over the publishing industry. Honig recalls that at a textbook hearing in California in 1977, he made a casual comment about the television series "The Adams Chronicle." He suggested off the top of his head that students should know about Abigail Adams. "Sure enough," Honig later wrote, "in 1982, when the new batch of history books came up for adoption, almost every single major publisher had an insert on Abigail Adams."[25]

After learning that political power could be exerted over the textbook industry, Honig made it an important part of his political strategy for changing American education. Concerning influencing the publishing industry, Honig wrote, "It takes four or five years, from conception through writing, editing, field testing, and publishing, to prepare a new textbook for market [and] when textbook buyers talk, textbook publishers listen. It is up to the reform movement to make sure the message they hear is focused on excellence."[26]

Honig's particular concern was with the dumbing down of textbooks. The term *dumbing down* was used in 1984 in a speech by Terrel Bell, who was then secretary of education. The term was part of the conservative political attack on what was considered the poor quality of schools in the 1980s. By dumbing down of textbooks, Honig meant lowered reading levels and the lack of a point of view. He cited three causes for the dumbing down of texts. The first was the application of readability formulas to gauge the difficulty of texts. This, Honig believed, resulted in choppy and uninteresting sentences, limited vocabulary, and trivialized content. The second cause, which was a favorite complaint by conservatives, was the publishing world's overreaction to criticisms by women and minority groups of the existence of stereotypes in textbooks and the lack of relevant role models. Finally, Honig blamed the textbook market itself because easy textbooks full of visuals and graphics sell better than difficult textbooks.[27]

The actual process of textbook selection in California is described in a case study by a former member of the California State Board of Education, Michael Kirst, in his book *Who Controls Our Schools?* Kirst was on the state board with Honig and shares many of his views about the quality of textbooks. According to Kirst, the state board establishes a sixteen-member advisory commission to analyze the quality of textbooks. Of the sixteen-member commission, there are generally two subject matter specialists for each field of study. In Kirst's words, these specialists, "More often than not . . . decide what students should learn in the limited time available and determine the best techniques for conveying that body of knowledge." This gives these advisors a great deal of power in determining the method and content of instruction in California schools.[28]

As Kirst describes the situation during his tenure on the state board, board members did not know who the experts were in each subject matter field and had to rely on word-of-mouth recommendations. Once hired, subject matter specialists did not focus on the content of prospective textbooks, but on their appearance, methodology, and print size. In addition, the specialists were forced into tight schedules of review while they held other full-time jobs. This resulted in specialists doing what Kirst calls the "eight-second thumb test": They would just skim the books for appearance. Kirst reports similar situations in other states where textbook reviewers are forced to make quick decisions about many books. He writes that in 1984 a member of the North Carolina state board had only six weeks in which to review 700 books for one subject area.[29]

Kirst argues that dumbing down of textbooks was caused by the publishers' response to the political agenda of the 1970s: "The state board's agenda from 1974 to 1979 had been dominated by concerns about the bottom third of the achievement band—the disadvantaged, disabled, or limited-English-speaking pupils." As a result, he states, "publishers had responded to market demand; they were not the cause of the problems."[30]

After being elected to the post of state superintendent of public instruction in 1982, Honig changed the political agenda being used to select textbooks. The new agenda was for excellence, with an emphasis on improving the content and sharpening the point of view in textbooks. Because of this changed political agenda, California in 1985 rejected many seventh- and eighth-grade science textbooks because they lacked strong sections on evolution, human reproduc-tion, and other controversial topics. In 1986, California rejected K-8 mathe-matics books because they did not meet new curriculum guidelines.[31]

Arthur Woodward, former chairperson of the American Educational Research Association's special-interest group on textbooks, textbook pub-lishing, and schools, argues that California's rejection of textbooks resulted in only superficial changes by publishers: One or two paragraphs were added to books to comply with state demands. Woodward argues that the economic structure of the publishing industry determines textbook content, not the political actions of one state. He writes, "In any event, for all the influence of California and Texas, textbooks are basically consensus documents that will sell as well in Peoria as in San Diego."[32]

Political decisions by an individual state might not affect textbooks geared for a national market, but they do raise an important question about the legiti-macy of state power in determining the content of textbooks. Whether or not one agrees with Honig's criticisms, the fact remains that he attempted to apply direct political pressure to shape the content of public school textbooks. Cer-tainly, it is easy for many citizens to agree with Honig that school textbooks have been dumbed down and are boring reading. On the other hand, the appli-cation of direct political pressure to rectify the situation leaves the door open for the next political administration to shape textbooks in another direction. In other words, the attempted cure might just strengthen the political power that caused the problem in the first place.

Although profit and political pressures play a major role in shaping text-books, there is still an attempt by some editors to produce scholarly and imagina-tive textbooks. College textbook editor Naomi Silverman considers the content of textbooks to be a balance between the creative and scholarly ideas of the editor and author, and the demands of the marketplace. Admittedly, college textbooks, which Silverman edits, are under fewer political constraints than elementary and secondary textbooks are. But college textbook publishers are still interested in profit. Regarding the balance between scholarship and profit, Silverman writes, "For editors such as myself, and for numerous others who work in the industry, the 'claims of commerce' do impose limits on how free we are to pursue the 'claims of culture' . . . but within these constraints and limits, individuals can and do bring out textbooks that are scholarly, interesting, challenging, innovative."[33]

In short, the structure of the publishing industry, the existence of a national textbook market, the activities of political groups concerned with the content of textbooks, and the power of statewide adoptions result in textbooks that avoid controversy and present knowledge as neutral and official. Ultimately, students do not learn to think critically about the material presented to them in class and do not understand the controversial issues in each field of study.

THE TESTING INDUSTRY

Operating with the primary motive of profit making, the testing industry affects students' feelings of self-worth, administrators' and teachers' ratings, students' access to college, professionals' entrance into many fields, and instructional content in many elementary and secondary schools. Testing, like textbook publishing, is a big business. Pick up any educational journal, and you will find advertisements touting the value of particular tests. For instance, in keeping with the political emphasis on educational excellence in the mid-1980s, an advertisement by the textbook publisher Harcourt Brace Jovanovich for its Metropolitan Achievement Test claims, "The new era of excellence calls for more rigorous tests. The top 23 percent is the target, with programs for excellence, higher-order thinking skills, and mastery tests."[34]

Like the textbook industry, the actions of pressure groups influence the testing industry. In 1991, interest groups immediately protested President Bush's proposal for a national system of tests. Reflecting the political concerns of his administration, he justified the establishment of national tests as necessary for helping the United States to compete in international trade and for helping parents to make informed choices among schools.[35]

In reaction to the proposal for national tests, Monty Neill of the National Center for Fair and Open Testing (FairTest) pointed out, "The truth is, no other country has national exams like those the administration proposes—not Germany, not Japan, not Great Britain, not France. They don't test every child, and they don't use tests to compare teachers and schools." Neill also noted that only 15 percent of Japanese high school seniors take national college admission examinations.[36]

Fearing the negative effect of testing on dominated groups, Beverly Cole, director of education for the National Association for the Advancement of Colored People (NAACP) warned, "For African-Americans, testing has meant exclusion, rather than inclusion. The poorer the districts, the poorer the scores." Other groups objected to national testing because they would limit parental control of the content of instruction. Arnold Fege, the national PTA's director of governmental relations, said, "national testing is 'anathema to parental empowerment' and is a 'recipe for political manipulation, not improvement.' "[37]

Some educators reacted negatively to national tests because of their potential to control the curriculum and the possibility that the tests might deflect money and attention from other educational problems. For instance, Ed Keller, deputy executive director of the National Association of Elementary School Principals, objected to national tests because they "would drive classroom instruction and result in a national curriculum."[38] Michael Casserly, associate director of the Council of Great City Schools, stated this objection: "It seems to me you don't fatten cattle by weighing them. You've got to feed them. And there's a whole lot of weighing going on here."[39]

Bush's proposals for national tests occurred at a time when business was booming for the testing industry. Like the publishing industry, the testing industry is concentrated in a few major firms, some of which are also textbook publishers. For instance, Harcourt Brace Jovanovich's testing subsidiary is the Psychological Corporation, which publishes the Metropolitan Achievement Test, Stanford Achievement Test, Wechsler Intelligence Scale, and Metropolitan Readiness Test, along with nearly 100 other titles. Houghton Mifflin, one of the top seven textbook publishers, markets thirty-five major tests; and McGraw-Hill owns the California Test Bureau.

The two largest firms in the testing industry—Educational Testing Services (ETS) and American College Testing Program (ACT)—are nonprofit organizations, according to the U.S. Internal Revenue Code, because they pay no money to stockholders and reinvest income into their companies. This does not mean that they do not make a profit, however. In fact, ETS, with worldwide sales in the late 1970s of $94 million, makes a 22-percent profit on tests such as the Scholastic Aptitude Test (SAT).[40]

It is important to understand that the testing industry did not expand after World War II because of improved test construction. The expanded marketing of standardized tests was primarily a result of advances in production, computerized test scoring, and political and institutional demands for more testing. Oscar Buros, the dean of American psychometricians, and founder and editor of the *Mental Measurement Yearbook,* admitted to a gathering of his colleagues in 1977 that there had been few advances in standardized testing. He told the group, "We don't have a great deal to show for fifty years of work. . . . The improvements—except the revolutionary electronic scoring machines and computers—have not been of enough consequence to permit us to have pride in what we have accomplished. . . . In fact, some of today's tests may even be poorer [than those in 1927]."[41]

Changes in the testing industry have been compared with changes in the automobile industry. The real changes have taken place in marketing and production, not in the basic product. The changes in production can be seen in the history of ETS. Since its founding in 1949, ETS steadily improved its ability to process tests by increasing automation and improving paper-processing techniques. These developments allowed ETS to reduce the percentage of workers devoted to test development and processing and to increase the number of workers involved in management and marketing. In 1949, 80 percent of the workforce at ETS were professionals. By 1972, only 50 percent of the workforce were professionals. Only approximately 4 percent of the professional staff is involved in reviewing and writing tests. This means that more than 40 percent of the staff at ETS devotes their time to managing and marketing tests. This management and promotional staff include public relations experts, program directors, writers of corporate literature, and field representatives.[42]

Clearly, the expansion of the testing industry is the result of improved production methods and newly created markets. Companies such as ETS devote a great deal of energy to expanding and creating new markets for their tests. The classic case of marketing occurred in the early 1970s, when ETS was forced to defend in court the National Teachers' Examination (NTE) against charges of racial discrimination. Although the court opinions were mixed regarding the extent of racial discrimination in the tests, the bad publicity caused a steady decline in the use of the NTE between 1971 and 1972. Reports that there were no significant relationship between scores on the test and teacher effectiveness farther tarnished the image of the examination.[43]

In response to the decline in sales, NTE's program director, George Elford, issued an internal memo on promotional efforts for the NTE in which he admitted that a major problem in selling the tests was the "lack of data showing test validity in predicting job performance." The memo also declared, "It does seem essential that for NTE to maintain its present net income level, promotional efforts should be directed at increasing the percentage of the teacher graduates taking the NTE." Because of the teacher surplus in the early 1970s, the memo went on to suggest, "This promotional effort should first of all be directed at school district offices, taking into account the shift from a 'seller's' market to a 'buyer's' market in teacher selection which especially affects suburban districts."[44]

Elford used three major methods for marketing the NTE. The first was to promote the NTE in scholarly publications and meetings. The second was to do a more careful analysis of the market. And the third was to bring officials from institutions that might require the tests to NTE corporate headquarters in New Jersey and provide them with free housing and entertainment at its special conference center.[45]

Certainly, a free trip to ETS would impress any public school official. The corporation is spread out among buildings carefully situated on the 400-acre grounds of what was formerly the Stony Brook Hunt Club. The grounds, which include a putting green, tennis courts, jogging trails, and picnic areas, are carefully maintained to attract songbirds, waterfowl, and deer. The conference center was furnished by designer Edith Queller of New York City and includes a library, sauna, and swimming pool. Hotelier William Shearn, formerly of the Waldorf Astoria's Marco Polo Club, Laurance Rockefeller's Caneel Bay Plantation, and New York's Hotel Pierre, managed it in the 1970s. These surroundings probably favorably impressed many school administrators who were considering requiring the examination.[46]

The expansion of testing markets continually raises the question of how test content affects the instructional content in institutions that require or use particular tests. For example, I was directly involved in lobbying ETS for the inclusion of certain types of questions on the NTE. I am a member of the American Educational Studies Association (AESA), which for many years was concerned with the lack of questions about social foundations on the NTE. A major part of the concern was purely economic. With more states and school districts requiring standardized examinations for teachers, the exclusion of questions on social foundations could directly affect the profession. Since it appeared that colleges of education would increasingly teach to the test, there was the possibility that fewer social foundations courses would be required of teacher candidates. Of course, fewer required courses would mean fewer jobs available for my profession.

As representatives of AESA, Professor Peter Sola of Howard University and I went to ETS on January 3, 1986, at the invitation of Catherine Havrilesky of the NTE staff. The NTE staff in ETS's opulent conference center entertained us. Havrilesky informed us at the meeting that all projects at ETS had to show a profit within three years. They also informed us that our lobbying effort was of little value because the two teachers' unions held the major political power over the content of the NTE. It was, after all, the two unions that had the most power and greatest opportunity to drag ETS into court over the use of the examination.

As discussed at the beginning of this chapter, there is no agreed-upon standard of knowledge in any academic field—an issue that most test companies try to avoid. A good example of this occurred in 1972, when ETS released the questions on the multiple-choice Multistate Bar Exam that they had administered to aspiring lawyers in nineteen states. The faculties of two bar review courses in Washington, D.C., reviewed the test and differed on answers to 27 percent of the questions. Four other bar review faculties examined the test and differed on 35 percent of the answers. In other words, over one-third of the answers on the examination were in dispute.[47]

Besides their effect on the content of instruction, tests often place immeasurable psychological burdens on their users. Because they are used as instruments for measuring and classifying in schools—and for admission screening to colleges, graduate schools, professional schools, and occupations—tests contribute to a student's sense of self-worth. Allan Nairn and his associates present a case study of Gary Valdik. Although Valdik was in the top tenth of his high school class, he received a low score on his SATs. As Valdik told the story, students who received low SAT scores at his school tended to lie to their classmates about their test results, while they bathed those who scored high in glory. The students, of course, believed that their SAT test scores were an accurate measure of their academic worth—and, often, their social worth. Valdik believed that his score was accurate because, in his words, "It's a standardized test. It was stripping us of everything and measuring us as equals."[48]

Valdik claimed that it took him four years to recover from the psychological effects of his low SAT scores. He did not seek psychological help because he assumed that it was a valid test. The agricultural school he wanted to attend told him that his school record and outside accomplishments were impressive, but his SAT scores were too low for admission. He attended a smaller college and achieved a high grade-point average. Eventually, he could enter and succeed in the agricultural school that had first rejected him based on his SAT scores. Even after fighting a battle with hepatitis, Gary could maintain a 3.3 grade-point average on a 4-point scale. Certainly, similar stories could be told of elementary and high school students whose sense of self-worth was lowered by scores on standardized tests.

CONCLUSION

Profit is the major interest of the publishing and testing industries. The fact that the market in both industries is concentrated in the hands of a few firms reduces innovation and risk taking. In addition, political forces shape the products of both industries. Publishers fear controversy, and test makers fear being taken to court. For publishers, the possibility of harmful controversy hurting profits results in textbooks noted for their blandness and lack of a point of view. For test makers, the fear of going to court usually results in tests that please those who threaten court action.

Of considerable interest for the future is the trend for publishing houses to operate testing subsidiaries. Obviously, a company can now publish a textbook and a standardized test that are parallel in method and content. These economic interests, combined with the political pressures of state governments working together to influence textbook publishing, could cause knowledge to become standardized across the entire nation.

At this time, it is not clear how successful states such as California will be in pressuring publishers to change textbooks. Even if successful, this raises a host of questions about how legitimate it is for state governments to decide the content of textbooks. After all, Bill Honig and other elected and educational politicians have a particular political viewpoint regarding what knowledge is of most worth. It is certainly questionable whether or not they should impose their points of view on school textbooks. Even if one accepts the idea that politicians should determine the content of textbooks, there remains the question of what happens when a new set of politicians with different ideas is elected to office. Do textbooks, and possibly tests, then change with each change in political administration?

NOTES

1. Quoted in Karen DeWitt, "Bush Pushes Education Goals at Math Educators Meeting," *New York Times* (25 April 1991), p. B8.
2. Quoted in ibid.
3. Quoted in *Transcript of Proceedings before the Commissioner of Education and the State Textbook Committee, July 14-16, 1986* (Austin, Tex.: Kennedy Reporting Service, 1986), p. 182.
4. Quoted in ibid., p. 183.
5. Quoted in ibid., p. 29.
6. Quoted in ibid., p. 31.
7. Quoted in ibid., p. 169.
8. Quoted in ibid., pp. 243-244.
9. Quoted in "The Ruling in *Mozert* v. *Hawkins County Public Schools*," *Education Week* (5 November 1986), p. 18.
10. Ibid.
11. For a discussion of this case and other issues involving academic freedom, see Joel Spring, *American Education: An Introduction to Social and Political Aspects*, 3rd ed. (White Plains, N.Y.: Longman, 1985), pp. 248-257.
12. Quoted in ibid., p. 256.
13. Robert Rothman, "Wall Street 'Frenzy' Aiding Consolidation of Textbook Industry," *Education Week* (5 November 1986), pp. 1, 21.
14. Ibid., p. 21.
15. Lewis A. Coser, Charles Kadushin, and Walter W. Powell, *Books: The Culture and Commerce of Publishing* (Chicago: University of Chicago Press, 1982), pp. 23-24.
16. Quoted in ibid., p. 24.
17. These observations are the result of my own investigation of the college textbook industry in 1986. I observed the process of decision making regarding textbooks, and the interactions of editors and authors as described in the following paragraph.

18. Coser, Kadushin, and Powell, *Books,* pp. 71-92, 200-224.

19. Frances Fitzgerald, *America Revised: History Schoolbooks in the Twentieth Century* (Boston: Little, Brown, 1979), p. 37.

20. Harold Rugg, "Do the Social Studies Prepare Pupils Adequately for Life Activities?" in Guy Whipple, ed., *The Twenty-Second Yearbook of the National Society for the Study of Education—Part II: The Social Studies in the Elementary and Secondary School* (Bloomington, Ind.: Public School Publishing House, 1973), pp. 1-27.

21. Fitzgerald, *America Revised,* p. 175.

22. Ibid., p. 37.

23. Dean Jaros, *Socialization to Politics* (New York: Praeger, 1973), p. 105.

24. Quoted in *Transcript of Proceedings,* pp. 18-19.

25. Bill Honig, *Last Chance for Our Children: How You Can Help Save Our Schools* (Reading, Mass.: Addison-Wesley, 1985), p. 135.

26. Ibid., p. 135.

27. Ibid., pp. 130-132.

28. Michael W. Kirst, *Who Controls Our Schools? American Values in Conflict* (New York: W.H. Freeman, 1984), pp. 115-116.

29. Ibid., pp. 116-118.

30. Ibid., p. 120.

31. Arthur Woodward, "On Teaching and Textbook Publishing: Political Issues Obscure Questions of Pedagogy," *Education Week* (21 January 1987), p. 28.

32. Ibid., p. 22.

33. Naomi Silverman, "From the Ivory Tower to the Bottom Line: An Editor's Perspective on College Textbook Publishing," in P. Altbach et al., *Perspectives on Textbooks and Society* (Albany: State University of New York, 1995).

34. Advertisement in *Phi Delta Kappan,* vol. 68, no. 4 (November 1986), p. 265.

35. "Excerpt for Bush Administration's plan to Revamp Schools," *Education Week* (24 April 1991), pp. 24-25.

36. Quoted in Tamara Henry, "Testing Students," *Compuserve Executive News Service, Associated Press,* no. 2051 (19 May 1991).

37. Quoted in Janet Bass, "Educators, PTA, NAACP Oppose National Student Test," *Compuserve Executive News Service, United Press,* no. 1343 (27 March 1991).

38. Quoted in ibid.

39. Quoted in Kenneth Cooper, "National Standards at Core of Proposal: Model Schools Envisioned," *Compuserve Executive News Service, Washington Post* (19 April 1991).

40. Allan Nairn and associates, *The Reign of ETS: The Corporation That Makes Up Minds* (Washington, D.C.: Ralph Nader, 1980), pp. 40-41, 299, 337.

41. Quoted in ibid., p. 315.

42. Ibid., pp. 315-316.

43. Ibid., pp. 319-320.

44. Quoted in ibid., p. 321.

45. Ibid., p. 322.

46. Ibid., pp. 36-38.

47. Ibid., p. 140.

48. Quoted in ibid., p. 7.

CHAPTER 10

The Political Uses of
the Courts

In this chapter I will analyze the political uses of the judicial system rather than supply a broad review of all of the court decisions that affect public schools. Important are class action suits brought against school districts by religious, racial, language, and disabled minorities seeking protection under the First and Fourteenth amendments to the Constitution. Minority groups turn to the court system because they lack the political power to receive redress for their grievances by applying pressure on school boards, state legislatures, and the federal government. For instance, minority religious groups such as the Amish protected their religion against majority political power by turning to the courts.[1] African-American populations in the South, unable to achieve integrated education through the usual political process because of voter discrimination, were also forced to turn to the court system.[2] Lacking political power, disabled and minority language groups also used the courts to achieve political ends.[3]

The use of the courts to achieve political goals raises several important issues. One is the problem of representation in a class action suit. Is the group suing truly representative of the population it claims to represent? Consider the situation in the 1986 case *Smith* v. *Board of School Commissioners of Mobile County*, in which a group of 600 Mobile, Alabama, residents charged the local public schools with violating the First Amendment by teaching secular humanism. U.S. District Court Judge W. Brevard Hand certified the case, based on actions of these 600 Mobile residents, as a class action suit brought by all Alabama parents and citizens who believe in God.[4] Clearly, deciding it would be impossible if this group of citizens actually represented the views of all those in Alabama believing in God. In fact, the judge's decision to make it a class action suit inferred that the defendants and their lawyers did not believe in God.

The Alabama case highlights many problems in class action suits. There is the difficulty not only of determining whether or not a group truly represents a particular class of people, but also of whether or not they represent all divergent views among a class of people. For instance, probably not all people in the state of Alabama who believes in God think that the schools teach secular humanism, nor do they all believe that the content of public schooling should be changed.

Consider the same situation regarding school desegregation cases. Members of the African-American community differ sharply over court remedies. Some favor busing; others argue for community control and alternative schools. In these cases, which remedies truly represent the views of the African-American community?

In response to the issue of representation in class action suits, it can be argued that while courts initially deal with parochial interests, their final decisions have broad social implications and involve basic constitutional issues. In addition, although canvassing diverse viewpoints in a class action suit is impossible for the courts, they can rely on evidence given in the actual litigation. Nevertheless, even with these considerations, representation in a class action suit remains a problem.[5]

An issue also is the court's ability to deal with the evidence presented in education cases. Much of this evidence involves test scores, educational statistics, and research findings. Very seldom is this material presented without dispute. For instance, with standardized tests, not only are the tests themselves disputed but also the meaning of their results. The same is true of statistics and research findings. There is very little in the world of education that can be presented as undisputed fact.

Consequently, judges must rule on evidence presented in a form outside their normal training which educational practitioners contest. Historically, the courts relied on cross-examination to establish facts. In court cases involving social science evidence, judges must rely on the cross-examination of expert witnesses. In evaluating social science evidence, judges must determine which expert witness is correct. Certainly, the ability of judges to choose between social science experts and understand social science information can be questioned.[6]

A similar issue arises when courts specify remedies in their decisions because knowing the possible educational and social consequences of certain remedies is difficult for a judge. Sometimes, at least according to critics of school desegregation decisions, court decrees have affected the problems. Critics also claim that in many circumstances judges are unable to enforce their decrees.[7]

These issues are directly related to the use of the courts by political groups to achieve changes in educational policies. The problems of representation in class action suits, the ability of the court to judge educational evidence, and the ability to carry out complex remedies need to be considered in analyzing educational policies that are the result of court action. Of course, the most important issue is the protection of constitutional rights. One might criticize the political use of the courts, but one must always remember that protection of constitutional rights is an important part of the U.S. political system.

This chapter will discuss the political uses of the courts by briefly describing the major constitutional issues that affect education and by analyzing the methods used in particular class action court cases.

CONSTITUTIONAL ISSUES

The First and Fourteenth amendments to the Constitution are the focus of most class action suits in education. One major exception is the Eighth Amendment, which prohibits "cruel and unusual punishment." The Eighth Amendment was an issue in suits brought against public schools for practicing corporal punishment. In the most important of these suits, *Ingraham* v. *Wright* (1977), the U.S. Supreme Court ruled that corporal punishment was not "cruel and unusual," because it was a traditional method of maintaining discipline in public schools, and that although public opinion was divided on the issue, there may not be any trend toward eliminating its use.[8]

Suits involving religion and free speech appeal to the First Amendment. Often both sides in religious disputes rely on the First Amendment because it both protects the free exercise of religion and prohibits the government from supporting religion. For instance, those opposed to organized prayer in public schools argue that it is banned by the First Amendment; supporters argue that the Free-Exercise Clause of the First Amendment protects school prayer. In recent years, Protestant fundamentalists invoked the First Amendment in charges that the public schools teach secular humanism. The First Amendment states:

> Congress shall make no law respecting an establishment of religion, or prohibiting the free exercise thereof; or abridging the freedom of speech, or of the press; or the right of the people peaceably to assemble, and to petition the Government for a redress of grievances.

Religious minorities seek protection from public school interference with their religious practices by invoking the prohibition against government interference with the free exercise of religion. For instance, in the 1940s the Jehovah's Witnesses successfully argued before the Supreme Court that the public school requirement to say the Pledge of Allegiance interfered with their practice of religion because they believed that the obligations imposed by the laws of God were superior to the laws of government. One law of God taken literally by Jehovah's Witnesses is, "Thou shall not make unto thee any graven image, or any likeness of anything that is in heaven above, or that is in the earth beneath, or that is in the water under the earth; thou shalt not bow down thyself to them nor serve them." Jehovah's Witnesses believe that the flag is an image and refuse, for religious reasons, to salute it. In this particular case, the Supreme Court agreed that the Pledge of Allegiance requirement did interfere with the free exercise of religion.[9]

One classic case in which a religious minority desired protection of its beliefs against the public schools is *State of Wisconsin, Petitioner* v. *Jonas Yoder et al.* This case involved a group of Amish who, as a political and religious minority, had continually felt threatened by compulsory education laws. As a political minority, there was little they could do to change state and local laws regarding education. As a religious minority, they found that the public schools were teaching values contrary to their religious beliefs. For instance, one objection of Amish parents to compulsory high school attendance was the requirement that young women wear shorts for physical education, which is a serious violation of Amish beliefs. The Amish also objected to the public high school's broad curriculum and its vocational and college preparatory courses. (The Amish do their own vocational training within their communities.) In addition, the Amish objected to an education that stresses critical thinking and asking questions.[10]

Unable to achieve their goals through normal political channels, the Amish community in New Glarus, Wisconsin, went to court in 1968 to fight state compulsory education laws. School authorities argued that compulsory education laws were necessary to protect the general welfare of the state, while the Amish argued that such laws were a violation of their free exercise of religion. The Supreme Court ruled in favor of the Amish, arguing, "We can accept it as settled, therefore, that however strong the State's interest in universal compulsory education, it is by no means absolute to the exclusion or subordination of all other interests."[11]

Groups invoke the First Amendment prohibition against the establishment of religion seeking to change religious practices in the public schools or the values being taught. Again, the courts are used to effect changes in educational policies. The classic case is the school prayer decision in *Engel* v. *Vitale* (1962), in which the New York Board of Regents granted a local school district the right to a brief prayer in each class at the beginning of the school day. The prayer was voluntary and considered denominationally neutral. The prayer stated, "Almighty God, we acknowledge our dependence upon Thee, and we beg Thy blessings upon us, our parents, our teachers, and our country." The Supreme Court ruled that this was a clear violation of the First Amendment prohibition against the establishment of religion because a government official had written the prayer. The Court stated, "In this country it is not part of the business of government to compose official prayers for any group of the American people to recite as a part of the religious program carried on by government."[12]

The Free-Speech Clause of the First Amendment is used to protect student rights. In the most famous case, *Tinker* v. *Des Moines Independent School District* (1969), a group of students was suspended from school for wearing armbands in protest against the Vietnam War. The Supreme Court, ruling in favor of the students, stated that a student "may express his opinion, even on controversial subjects like the conflict in Vietnam. . . . Under our Constitution, free speech is not a right that is given only to be so circumscribed that it exists in principle but not in fact."[13]

Minority religious and language groups use the Fourteenth Amendment to pressure schools for equality of educational opportunity. In addition, the Fourteenth Amendment is used to protect due process rights. The Fourteenth Amendment states:

> All persons born or naturalized in the United States, and subject to the jurisdiction thereof, are citizens of the United States and of the State wherein they reside. No State shall make or enforce any law which shall abridge the privileges or immunities of citizens of the United States; nor shall any State deprive any person of life, liberty, or property without due process of law; nor deny to any person within its jurisdiction the equal protection of the laws.

The clause in the amendment stating "nor shall any State deprive any person of life, liberty, or property without due process of law" is used to protect a student's right to an education and a teacher's right to employment. The courts consider state provisions of schooling and employment of teachers to be property rights that cannot be taken away without due process. So, for instance, in *Goss* v. *Lopez* (1975), the Supreme Court argued that suspension from school involved a property right. The Court ruled that due process "requires, in connection with a suspension of 10 days or less, that the student be given oral or written notice of the charges against him and, if he denies them, an explanation of the evidence the authorities have and an opportunity to present his side of the story." The Court based its decision on "legitimate claims of entitlement to public education" as given in state law.[14]

Politically, the most important part of the Fourteenth Amendment is the Equal-Protection Clause, which states, "nor deny to any person within its jurisdiction the equal protection of the laws." Under the Equal-Protection Clause, if any state government provides a system of education, then it must be provided equally to all people in the state. Certainly, one of the most fundamental and revolutionary concepts of the eighteenth and nineteenth centuries was the idea that the law must treat all people equally.

Concerning education, the concept of equal treatment is extremely complex. Consider the issue of segregation. The Supreme Court ruled in the nineteenth century that school segregation was constitutional if equal facility and instruction was provided. In 1954, the Supreme Court reversed the ruling by arguing that segregated schools were inherently unequal and, therefore, violated the Equal-Protection Clause of the Fourteenth Amendment.[15]

As another example, consider the issue of language. Does the fact that a child does not speak English deny the child an equal opportunity to gain the advantages of a state-provided education? The Supreme Court answered yes to that question in *Lau et al.* v. *Nichols et al.* (1974). The case was a class action suit brought for non-English-speaking Chinese students in the San Francisco School District. The complaint was that no special instruction for learning standard English had been provided to these students. The Supreme Court ruled that special aid had to be provided for students for whom English was not a standard language; otherwise, the school system was not providing equal educational opportunity. The Court based this ruling on Title VI of the 1964 Civil Rights Act, which bans discrimination based on "race, color, or national origin."[16]

The concept of the state providing equal educational opportunity is used to question educational practices ranging from tracking to school finance. Any practice that appears to exclude an identifiable group of children from equal participation in education is open to question in the courts. In some situations, such as school finance cases, actions are limited to state courts. In *Rodriguez* v. *San Antonio Independent School District* (1978), the Supreme Court ruled against the plaintiffs, who were arguing that unequal educational funding was violating the Fourteenth Amendment. In its decision, the Court stated, "The consideration and initiation of fundamental reforms with respect to state taxation and education are matters reserved for the Legislative processes of the various states."[17] This meant that school finance issues related to equal protection would have to be decided on a state-by-state basis within state court systems.

In summary, although a wide range of legal issues exists in education, the First and the Fourteenth amendments of the Constitution are the primary concern of groups using the courts to achieve changes in educational policies. As mentioned in the chapter introduction, these types of court cases require (a) an analysis of the representativeness of the plaintiffs in class action suits, (b) an analysis of the ability of the courts to understand testimony based on educational research and statistics, and (c) the ability of the courts to determine remedies.

THE OTERO *CASE*

Otero v. Mesa County Valley School District No. 51 is a case study used by Michael Rebell and Arthur Block in their national study of the effects of courts on educational policy making.[18] This case provides an example of the problems of plaintiff representativeness and the capabilities of the courts. It is one of the four major case studies that Rebell and Block use to explore the general debate about the role of the courts in determining social policy. Besides the four case studies, they analyze sixty-five federal court proceedings that deal with educational issues.

The overall goal of Rebell and Block's research is to determine the legitimacy of judicial action on social policy issues. As for representativeness, in 71 percent of the cases, the plaintiffs requested class action status. In 36 percent of the cases, the court ignored or neglected to determine whether the group was truly representative of the class it claimed to represent. "Thus," Rebell and Block write, "although plaintiffs purport to speak for broad classes, available judicial mechanisms for verifying claims of representativeness are not applied with regularity."[19]

In analyzing the ability of courts to deal with evidence from the social sciences, Rebell and Block found that most judges avoid basing judicial decisions on social science evidence. In their study, judges did not decide complex social issues, though social science facts were introduced in forty-two of the sixty-five cases. In half these situations, judges based their decisions on legal issues, not on social science evidence. Rebell and Block found, however, that most judges had a reasonable working knowledge of social science concepts and language.

Rebell and Block found that in thirteen of the fifteen cases in which the judge ordered a remedy that involved major reform of an educational system, defendants and public agencies had played a major role in drafting the court decree. This participation involved the basic drafting of orders and the negotiation of details. In only one of these fifteen cases had the judge assumed sole responsibility for drafting the court order.

Overall, Rebell and Block found that the courts' involvement in social issues created a political role that was not considered in the traditional judicial system. Important is that the courts' method of political involvement is quite different from that of a legislative body. For instance, judges use an analytical fact-finding method that depends on the weighing of evidence from experts. On the other hand, various interest groups achieve political decisions in legislative organizations through compromise and accomodation. In other words, judges reason about evidence while politicians strike bargains.

In this political role, Rebell and Block were favorably impressed by the ability of judges to gather and evaluate social science evidence and to deal with diverse interest groups in class action suits. Consequently, these researchers did not believe that the real issue is whether or not courts are capable of dealing with social problems, but rather whether or not a given political decision should be made by a judge or by legislators.

Formulating the issue in this manner leads to a different set of considerations. On one hand, judges can be considered rational decision makers who decide based on an analytical judicial process. On the other hand, elected political officials can be viewed as decision makers who depend on bargaining and compromise. Within this framework, the question becomes "whether particular aspects of social problems should be handled through the principled, analytical judicial process or through the instrumental, mutual adjustment patterns of the legislatures."[20]

Given this orientation, Rebell and Block use the *Otero* case study to illustrate problems faced by the judiciary when dealing with social issues. The case highlights the problems of the representativeness of plaintiffs and the capabilities of courts to deal with social science evidence.

When the *Otero* case was initiated in 1974 by lawyers from the Mexican American Legal Defense Fund (MALDEF), the Chicano Education Project (CEP), and Colorado Rural Legal Assistance (CRLA), there was an immediate conflict over the issue of representation. Based on an analysis of test scores and personnel records, the plaintiffs accused the local school district of not providing equal educational opportunity for Chicano children and demanded bilingual educational services. The local school board expressed its strong hostility to the legal action because it believed that it represented the interests and needs of local Chicano children, and that the plaintiffs were primarily outside agitators. Not only did the school board dismiss most of the plaintiffs as not representative of the local Chicano community, but it also accused one local Chicano leader of using the case to advance his political fortunes.

In certifying the case as a class action suit, District Court Judge Fred Winner ignored arguments given by the defense that none of the plaintiffs were deficient in English and that some had achieved high levels of education. Indeed, at the beginning of the case, there was little support for the suit in the local Chicano community. But the fact that it was declared a class action suit made it possible for the plaintiffs to present the case as a crusade for the entire local Chicano community. As part of the crusade, the plaintiffs believed that one of their goals was educating the local community to the educational problems in the local school system.

Therefore, as the case began, the whole issue of representation was thrown open to question by the public. Although the court recognized it as a class action, the public debated how well the plaintiffs represented the local Chicano community.

The major legal issue in the case forced the court to deal with social science evidence. The focus was on the Supreme Court decision in *Lau et al.* v. *Nichols et al.* The plaintiffs wanted to prove that Anglo children in the school district substantially outperformed Chicano children, and that bilingual education services therefore needed to be established. On the other side, the defendants (the local school board) argued that it had met the requirements of the *Lau* decision by providing transitional English instruction for students with language problems.

Specifically, the plaintiffs claimed that all Chicano children were discriminated against by an Anglo-oriented curriculum. The curriculum, the plaintiffs argued, resulted in lower academic achievement scores. To achieve equal educational opportunity, it was argued, the local school district would be required to consider cultural differences in the planning of educational programs. Given this legal argument, the plaintiffs needed to establish in court that Chicano students did have lower academic achievement scores as compared with Anglos, and that the differences in test scores were the result of cultural bias in the curriculum.

In deciding the case, Judge Winner had to consider highly controversial social science evidence dealing with test validity and educational programming. The case opened with the plaintiffs claiming that 80 percent of the class they represented were proficient in Spanish, while the defendants argued that only 19 percent came from Spanish-speaking homes and that none were fluent in Spanish. The plaintiffs claimed that 54 percent lacked ability in English; the defendants claimed that only 5 percent had difficulty with English.

To support their case, the plaintiffs introduced information from three school surveys. Teachers had taken one survey on whether or not Spanish was spoken in students' homes. The second survey had examined student records to find remarks regarding language problems. And the third survey had been done of the homes of Spanish-surnamed students to determine whether Spanish was spoken in the household. As noted by Rebell and Block, none of these surveys had dealt directly with the language proficiencies of the students. The survey evidence was presented for the plaintiffs by an expert witness and psychologist, Steve Moreno. He claimed that it demonstrated that 80 percent of the Spanish surnamed children had significant Spanish-language abilities.

The real debate over social science evidence was opened when the defendants introduced test data, which they claimed showed that only a few Chicano children were proficient in Spanish. Consequently, the defendants argued that only remedial education courses, not bilingual education, were needed. The plaintiffs countered by arguing that the test lacked content validity. In response, the defendants brought in an expert in sociolinguistics who argued that the test did have content validity. The plaintiffs then introduced an expert witness who claimed that the test was not valid in that part of Colorado because it had been standardized in El Paso, Texas, where Mexican-Americans spoke a different dialect. The plaintiffs then questioned the ability of the testers, who admitted that they were unfamiliar with the testing guidelines of the American Psychological Association (APA). The defendants countered by claiming that the formulators of the APA standards had an ax to grind and compared the standards to an automobile manufacturer's recommendation to use a certain brand of oil in a new car.

The problems faced by judges in dealing with social science evidence are exemplified by the testimony given by the defense's star expert witness Gene Glass, a professor of education at the University of Colorado. Glass testified that the differences in achievement test scores between Anglo and Chicano students in the school district were not a result of an Anglo-dominated curriculum. He argued that the explanation could be found in differences in intelligence (IQ test scores) and socioeconomic status.

Marshaling a whole range of social science studies, Glass maintained that all research showed that IQ and socioeconomic status were the best predictors of achievement test scores. Therefore, he asserted, one must control for socioeconomic status and IQ before one can determine the impact of cultural and linguistic differences. This could be done, using his methodology, by classifying students according to ethnicity, IQ, and socioeconomic status. If IQ and socioeconomic status were similar for Anglo and Chicano students, and achievement scores were different, then, Glass argued, one could ascribe the differences to cultural or linguistic causes. After grouping the school district's students by ethnicity, IQ, and socioeconomic status, Glass concluded that the differences between Anglo and Chicano students were only minor. Anglos were one month ahead of Chicanos in reading and 1.8 months ahead in language, while Chicanos were 3 months ahead of Anglos in mathematics.

The plaintiffs attacked Glass's testimony by arguing that IQ tests are culturally and linguistically biased. Glass countered that his method compensated for bias in both IQ and achievement tests. The only problem that could exist, Glass claimed, is if the IQ test were more biased than the achievement test. Glass also argued that IQ tests were geared to the language proficiency demonstrated on other tests by Chicano students in the school district.

According to Rebell and Block, the fact that the judge accepted Glass's evidence is a good example of the difficulty the judiciary has with social science evidence. From their perspective, Glass's evidence was full of methodological and logical errors. They demonstrate how Glass's data could be manipulated to show significant differences in language and reading performance between Anglos and Chicanos. In the end, the major failure was that the plaintiffs did not adequately analyze and respond to Glass's findings.

In this situation, the court failed to provide an adequate arena for the judgment of social science data. The legal process depends on an adversarial relationship in which evidence is adequately evaluated by expert witnesses representing both sides of a case. If one side does not prepare adequately, then the whole process fails as a mechanism for dealing with research information. In the words of Rebell and Block, "What is pertinent here is that the mechanisms of adversarial presentation of social science data apparently did not, on this occasion, elicit a well-balanced perspective on the critical issues."[21]

The lawyers for the defense were given a better understanding of social science methodology than the lawyers for the plaintiffs. Glass spent many hours coaching the lawyers for the school board on social science methodology. The lawyers for the plaintiffs, on the other hand, apparently had little training for cross-examination on social science issues. Furthermore, Glass proved to be a very good witness who could steer the plaintiff's lawyers away from the greatest problem in his data—namely, that Chicanos in his classification did better than Anglos in mathematics but not in language. This opened the possibility (which was never taken by the plaintiff's lawyers) of using Glass's results to prove the linguistic bias of the curriculum.

In his decision in favor of the school board, Judge Winner stated that the expert witnesses for the school board had made more sense than had the expert witnesses for the plaintiffs. In fact, Judge Winner presented his own detailed analysis of the comparative validity of the plaintiff's surveys and the defendant's standardized tests. He dismissed the failure of the school district to follow the testing guidelines of the APA as being merely a technical issue.

The *Otero* case provides a good example of the problems faced by the courts in dealing with social science evidence, and it demonstrates the problem of the representativeness of a group suing. It was never established that the plaintiffs did in fact represent most of the local Chicano population. There is also the larger issue, raised by Rebell and Block, about whether the courts, with their adversarial means of handling social science evidence, is a better place for certain types of political action than are legislative bodies, which operate on compromise and accommodation.

HOBSON *V.* HANSEN

The case of *Hobson* v. *Hansen* exemplifies the difficulties faced by courts in providing remedies for social problems. It is one of the four detailed case studies used by Donald Horowitz in his book *The Courts and Social Policy.* Horowitz is highly critical of court involvement in social policy issues. He finds that differences between the methods of legal inquiry and social science inquiry create major problems in litigation. For instance, because they rely on an adversarial relationship to gather information, the courts do not go directly to the source when dealing with social science evidence, but rely on the hearsay evidence of expert witnesses. This situation, Horowitz argues, leaves judges at the mercy of advocates and interpreters of social science data and restricts the sources of their information. "So far," Horowitz writes, "expert witnesses have had too much latitude to parade their own preferences as science." The previously discussed *Otero* case provides evidence of this problem. Horowitz proposes, "It would be far preferable to admit books and articles on matters of social fact directly into evidence as exhibits, not require as a precondition that an expert refer to them in his testimony, abolish the favored position of government reports, and permit counsel to attack the reliability of studies directly."[22]

Courts also have difficulty handling social science data in the implementation of remedies. Very often, courts are unable to predict adequately the ultimate consequences of a judicial plan to remedy a social problem. In trying to predict the outcome of a remedy, courts must rely on predictions made by competing social science experts. The same types of problems occur in court remedies based on social science information. In addition, Horowitz argues, courts are often limited in their ability to supervise their remedies and monitor the consequences: "The record suggests that the courts are better equipped with machinery to discover the past than to forecast the future."[23]

Hobson v. *Hansen* is Horowitz's prime example of the problems of judicial implementation.[24] Julius Hobson in 1966 initiated the case against the Washington, D.C., schools system for denying African-American and poor children equal educational opportunity. Before the suit, the District of Columbia had, until the 1954 *Brown* decision, maintained a racially separate, dual school system. In response to the requirement to end the dual school system, the school board tried to find other means of maintaining segregation. One method was to allow students to transfer from one school zone to another with lower enrollments. These transfers, it was determined in court, usually favored whites and maintained segregated schools. In addition, Superintendent Carl Hansen introduced a tracking system in 1957 that resulted in further segregation. Circuit Court Judge J. Skelley Wright identified both the transfer system and the tracking plan as fostering segregation.

Of major concern to Judge Wright, and eventually the central feature of the court's plan to end inequality of educational opportunity, was the unequal distribution of financial resources in the Washington, D.C., school system. Judge Wright argued that if whites and African-Americans, or the rich and poor, were in separate schools, then there had to be a measurable means of maintaining equality between schools. For Judge Wright, this measurable means was financial expenditures.

In 1967, Judge Wright issued *Hobson I*, which abolished optional zones and required faculty integration and voluntary busing. The decision also abolished the tracking system. It was assumed that expenditures among schools would equalize because of these actions.

In 1970, Hobson again returned to court with claims that school expenditure had not been equalized. In fact, there were few positive results under the decree from *Hobson I*. Both voluntary busing and voluntary teacher transfers for integration proved ineffective. Large financial differences between schools still existed.

In *Hobson II*, Judge Wright decided to focus on the issue of unequal expenditures. The major question to be answered was what should be equalized. The court now entered the tricky arena of educational research to establish a link between educational expenditures and equality of educational opportunity. For instance, equal amounts of money spent on cafeterias or maintenance might not result in equal educational opportunity. In fact, at the time, more money was being spent on building new schools in African-American neighborhoods than in white neighborhoods.

The court therefore had to go through the process of narrowing the issue of unequal expenditures. In this regard, the lawyers played an important role. Initially, the court considered a wide range of resources that could be equalized between schools, including equalization of teachers according to their measured verbal abilities and years of experience, equalization of all resources, and equalization of pupil–teacher ratios. The final decision was to focus on per-pupil expenditures in each school. Per-pupil expenditures provided a measurable standard that the courts could administer.

The court further narrowed the issue of per-pupil expenditures to teachers' salaries, although one option had been to consider per-pupil expenditures in a school according to the total sum spent on textbooks, library resources, and salaries of the entire staff. The court held that there was a right to an equal per-pupil distribution of teacher services and that the best measure of this was teacher cost. The court, in its decree, chose not to classify teacher costs according to different components. For instance, no distinctions were made between the costs of classroom teachers and special subject teachers. Nor were teacher costs adjusted for pupil–teacher ratios.

One problem with narrowing the issue of equality to teacher costs per pupil was the lack of agreement that inequalities in this cost factor were related to race or income. Lawyers for each side argued over whether the correlation between parent income and per-pupil costs of teachers was weakly positive or weakly negative. Like many social science disputes, the issue hinged on methodology, with one side using a rank-order correlation and the other a Pearson product-moment correlation. Reflecting the problems courts have with this type of dispute, Judge Wright dismissed the whole debate as an abstruse statistical dispute.

Judge Wright avoided the entire issue of the relationship between parent income and per-pupil teacher costs, and focused on the wealth of the neighborhood surrounding each school. Wright also refused to accept arguments dealing with the size of the school. For instance, the plaintiff's lawyers used the testimony of an expert witness in economics to establish that the size of a school accounted for one-third of the difference in per-pupil teacher costs between schools. This economic argument raised the issue of economies of scale. In larger schools it is easier to establish optimal pupil–teacher ratios. In smaller elementary schools fewer students absorb the costs of special subject teachers in art, foreign languages, music, mathematics, physical education, reading, and science. Therefore, the costs of teachers per pupil tend to be higher in smaller schools.

Trying to establish the value of narrowing the remedy for inequality of educational opportunity to teacher costs per pupil increased the complexity of the court's consideration of social science data. In Horowitz's words, "Data were available on the issue of economies of scale, but important factual and legal gaps remained. Each legal question turned on the resolution of an empirical question, which then turned out to have another legal question embedded within it." From Horowitz's perspective, "The legal question of inequality depended on the empirical question of economies of scale."[25]

Part of the court's justification for using per-pupil teacher costs was the belief that experience was related to teacher quality and that teacher costs were dependent on a pay scale that rewarded seniority. In his summary of the case, Horowitz did not find this assumption substantiated by research literature. For instance, after looking at the studies cited by the economists for the plaintiffs, Horowitz found research to support the theory that verbal scores on standardized tests are better predictors of performance than experience is. In addition, hiring teachers with higher verbal scores is less expensive than hiring teachers according to experience. Teacher experience, according to the research explored by Horowitz, helped the achievement scores of white students but not of African-American students.

In his criticism of the court's use of social science data, Horowitz argues that if research is to be believed, then the court's remedy could not promote equality of achievement between African-American and white students. He believes that the problem is even more fundamental. The available research on the relationship between costs and student achievement, Horowitz claims, is not substantial enough to draw any meaningful conclusions about the effect of financial changes on equality of educational opportunity. In other words, the research in this area of education is not complete enough to support legal remedies based on changes in educational expenditures as related to student achievement.

If one accepts Horowitz's argument, then the use of social science data in court proceedings can be criticized on many points. One criticism is that most social science data are open to dispute by other social scientists. Another criticism is the court's difficulty in deciding academic disputes. In addition, there is a problem with court remedies that have no support in social science data or for which the data is open to dispute. This means that court decisions can be based on disputed data and that the remedies for those decisions can be based on equally disputed data.

As mentioned in the *Otero* case, a major difference between judicial decision making and normal political decision making is that politics depend on compromise and accommodation of conflicting interests, while judicial actions require judgments about evidence given in an adversarial relationship. Therefore, if a judicial decision is made based on faulty evidence or is the result of poor judgment, then the consequences of the decision might not be related to the court's intentions. Of course, the same situation can arise in a political struggle among different sets of interests in which one or more parties miscalculate the best way of achieving their interests. In *Hobson* v. *Hansen*, the final court decision caused unexpected results.

After the court's decision, the school board, as it considered the political consequences of its actions, further narrowed the remedy. According to Horowitz, the school board had several options for achieving equality among schools in per-pupil teacher costs. It could have moved teachers by compulsory transfers, moved students by compulsory busing, or done both by closing schools and changing school boundaries. Because it believed the measures were unpopular with the public, the board rejected changing school boundaries, closing schools, and mandatorily busing students. This left only the transferring of teachers, and, of course, union seniority rules discouraged the mass transfer of teachers. The school board therefore had to comply with the remedy by devising a scheme that minimized teacher transfers. It accomplished this by focusing adjustments on special subject teachers. Whenever a school's per-pupil teacher costs were high or low according to systemwide standards, special subject teachers could be added or removed. Administratively, the transfer of special subject teachers was easier than transferring regular teachers.

In other words, the court's need to find a measurable remedy worked with the political process of the school system to reduce the issue of equal educational opportunity for African-American students in the Washington, D.C., school system to the transfer of special subject teachers. The major effect was to make the special subject program in the schools a function of per-pupil teacher costs in each school. In turn, the per-pupil teacher costs in each school depended on pupil–teacher ratios and the seniority of the school's teachers. This meant that the special subjects program in the school system did not operate according to the educational needs of the students, but according to pupil–teacher ratios and teacher seniority.

Because of this strange turn of events, the final remedy did not affect the equality of educational opportunity between African-Americans and whites. In fact, the remedy might have had the opposite effect. In the early 1970s some primarily African-American, low-income schools in the district experienced a rapid decline in enrollment. This caused the virtual elimination of special subjects programs at those schools. During the same period, a large white school in a high-income neighborhood experienced an increase in students, which caused an expanded special subjects program. In fact, the school, because of its lower per-pupil teacher costs resulting from an increased pupil–teacher ratio, received extra funds to hire a second music teacher to establish a school orchestra and a teacher to provide French instruction beginning in the third grade. In addition, other schools attended by children from high-income families maintained special subjects programs through outside funding. In the end, this meant that the final decree in *Hobson* v. *Hansen* caused the closing of special subjects programs in some African-American elementary schools.

Hobson v. *Hansen*, Horowitz argues, is a good example of the difficulty the judiciary faces in decreeing remedies for social problems. Not only must the courts deal with highly debatable social science data in making a decision and planning a remedy, but they often also have little control over the actual process of implementation. Here, the political process of the school system reduced the already narrowed remedy of equalizing per-pupil teacher costs to the transferring of special subject teachers. Therefore, the problem is not only with the judicial process, but also with the political forces outside the judiciary that effect the implementation of judicial remedies.

CONCLUSION

Analyzing judicial involvement in educational policy making requires consideration of the following:

1. the representativeness of the individual or group initiating court action;
2. the type of evidence presented by plaintiffs and defendants;

3. the ability of the judge and lawyers to understand and use evidence based on social science data;
4. the relationships between the original complaint, the goals of the judge, and the court's remedy;
5. the effect of political forces outside the court on the implementation of the court's remedy; and
6. the actual results of the implementation of the court's decree.

Otero and *Hobson* provide good examples of issues surrounding representation and the capabilities of the courts to deal with educational issues. *Hobson* also shows what an impact court decisions can have on educational policies. In *Hobson*, the court's decree affected the budget, teacher transfers, and the curriculum in special subject areas.

Overall, court decisions touch a broad range of policy issues. In some situations, court decisions directly affect the political process by requiring election (for assuring minority group representation) to local school boards by district, as opposed to at-large, elections.[26] In New Jersey, the actions of the state supreme court in trying to assure equality of educational spending resulted in the creation of a new layer of state bureaucracy to monitor compliance. In this situation, one result of court action was a change in the state educational bureaucracy.[27] Also, in most cases dealing with inequality of educational funding, the result is a change in state financing methods.[28]

Desegregation cases affect the curriculum, school assignments, teacher transfers, administrative organization, tracking, ability grouping, and transportation.[29] Cases brought by religious groups effect religious practices in schools, textbooks, the curriculum, and state laws.[30] Free-speech issues involve the courts in methods of book selection and in the treatment of students and teachers by school systems. Due-process requirements can formalize the relationships between students, teachers, and administrative staff.[31]

There is virtually no area of educational policy making that is not touched by court action. Primarily, judicial action is taken to protect religious and free-speech rights under the First Amendment, and equal-protection and due process rights under the Fourteenth Amendment. The major problems faced by the courts in the protection of these rights are (a) the introductions of evidence based on often-confusing and contradictory results of educational research, and (b) the implementation of decisions in the complicated arena of educational politics.

NOTES

1. *Wisconsin* v. *Yoder,* 406 U.S. 205 (1972).
2. *Brown* v. *Board of Education of Topeka,* 347 U.S. 483 (1954).
3. *Pennsylvania Association for Retarded Children* v. *Commonwealth of Pennsylvania,* 343 F. Supp. 279 (E.D. Pa 1972); *Lau* v. *Nichols,* 414 U.S. 563 (1974).
4. Tom Mirga, "On Trial—'Secular Humanism' in Schools: Federal Judge Considers Arguments in Alabama," *Education Week* (15 October 1986), pp. 1, 13, 18.

5. Deborah L. Rhode, "Conflicts of Interest in Educational Reform Litigation," in David Kirp and Donald Jensen, eds., *School Days, Rule Days: The Legalization and Regulation of Education* (Philadelphia: Falmer Press, 1986), pp. 278-302.

6. Michael Rebell and Arthur Block, *Educational Policy Making and the Courts* (Chicago: University of Chicago Press, 1982), pp. 11-14.

7. Ibid., pp. 14-15; Lino A. Graglia, *Disaster by Decree: The Supreme Court Decisions on Race and the Schools* (Ithaca, N.Y.: Cornell University Press, 1976).

8. *Ingraham v. Wright*, 430 U.S. 651 (1977).

9. *West Virginia State Board of Education v. Barnette*, 319 U.S. 624 (1943).

10. Albert Keim, ed., *Compulsory Education and the Amish* (Boston: Beacon Press, 1972).

11. *State of Wisconsin, Petitioner v. Jonas Yoder et al.*, 406 U.S. 205 (1972).

12. *Engel v. Vitale*, 370 U.S. 421 (1962).

13. *Tinker v. Des Moines Independent Community School District*, 393 U.S. 503 (1969).

14. *Goss v. Lopez*, 419 U.S. 565, 581 (1975).

15. *Brown v. Board of Education of Topeka*, 347 U.S. 482 (1954).

16. *Lau et al. v. Nichols et al.*, 414 U.S. 563 (1974).

17. *Rodriguez v. San Antonio Independent School District* 411 U.S. 1 (1973).

18. Rebell and Block, *Educational Policy Making*, pp. 123-147.

19. Ibid., p. 43.

20. Ibid., p. 215.

21. Ibid., p. 164.

22. Donald L. Horowitz, *The Courts and Social Policy* (Washington, D.C.: Brookings Institute, 1977), p. 281.

23. Ibid., p. 264.

24. Ibid., pp. 106-170.

25. Ibid., p. 133.

26. See *Sierra v. El Paso Independent School District*, 591 F. Supp. 802 (W.D. Texas 1984).

27. R. Lehne, *The Quest for Justice: The Politics of School Finance Reform* (White Plains, N.Y.: Longman, 1978).

28. R. Elmore and M. McLaughlin, *Reform and Retrenchment: The Politics of School Finance Reform* (Cambridge, Mass.: Ballinger, 1982).

29. R. L. Crain et al., *The Politics of School Desegregation* (Chicago: Aldine, 1968).

30. Keim, *Compulsory Education and the Amish*.

31. For coverage of legal issues affecting teachers and students, see Louis Fischer, David Schimmel, and Cynthia Kelly, *Teachers and the Law* (White Plains, N.Y.: Longman, 1987).

CHAPTER 11

The Political Control of Education in a Free Society

Who should decide what knowledge is of most worth? This question assumes that the major function of schools is the dissemination of knowledge. In contemporary times, the dissemination of knowledge is linked to giving individuals credentials for entry into the labor market. Any answer to the above question must consider the effect of the knowledge disseminated by schools on the student's mind and on the student's ability to compete in the labor market. The decision about what knowledge is of most worth occurs in an arena of conflicting interests.

Groups and individuals are in conflict over influencing the ideas disseminated to students. They also compete to enhance the opportunities for their children to compete in the labor market. Also, professional educators want to improve their status and income. This results in struggles among professional educators for power and money. In addition, politicians demonstrate a propensity to turn to the schools to solve social and economic problems. They try to use educational issues to win votes.

For a free society to exist, I would argue, requires the free dissemination of ideas and information. For equal opportunity to exist requires that schooling is not used to give some individuals a privileged position in the labor market, while reducing the ability of other individuals to compete. There are certain elements in the current political structure of American education that inhibit the free flow of ideas and information through the schools and allow certain individuals to gain privileges over others. They include:

1. the problem of majoritarian control
2. the power of special-interest groups
3. the political use of schools
4. the economics of education

THE PROBLEM OF MAJORITARIAN CONTROL

Majoritarian control of American education does not exist. However, the idea continues to influence those wanting democratic control of the schools. Under majoritarian control, a majority of the people determine what knowledge is of most worth. The problem with majority control is that minority viewpoints regarding politics, culture, and social organization are excluded from the curriculum. Thus the parameters of political dialogue are narrowed, and political learning is reduced to consensus values.

Rather than being arenas for the free exchange of political ideas, the public schools are institutions for the imposition of values and ideas that do not offend most people. Horace Mann, the father of the American common school, predicted this outcome. Mann argued that political controversy, including controversial ideas, had to be excluded from common schools because including it would cause warring public factions to destroy the schools.[1]

Ironically, therefore, democratic, or majoritarian, control of public schools limits the free political dialogue that is necessary for the maintenance of a free society. Thus, democratic control of public schools could be said to contain the seeds of destruction of a democratic society.

On the other hand, some people argue that the limitation of political dialogue by democratically controlled schools creates political and social stability. From this perspective, narrowing the parameters of political dialogue reduces the possibility of political conflict. Some people might argue that this places necessary curbs on the potential for democratic societies to create excessive political activity.

There are sharp differences in concepts of citizenship. Some people believe that a wide-ranging political dialogue is necessary for maintaining a democratic society. Others believe that limiting such dialogue is essential for political stability. One side wants the schools to produce active citizens who have the intellectual tools to participate in democratic control. The other side wants citizens who are educated to obey the law and assume the responsibilities of government. One group emphasizes an active concept of citizenship; the other, a passive concept.

Political philosopher Amy Gutmann believes that the free flow of ideas in public schools is essential for the maintenance of a democratic society. Consequently, she argues that the principle of nonrepression should be a guiding standard for public schools in the United States: "The principle of nonrepression prevents the state, and any group within it, from using education to restrict rational deliberation of competing conceptions of the good life and the good society."[2]

I agree with the importance of the principle of nonrepression for a democratic society. However, I do not agree with Gutmann's proposal for ensuring nonrepression in U.S. schools. She believes that teachers' professionalism is key to maintaining nonrepression in the schools. She wants teachers to assume a professional responsibility to maintain the principle of nonrepression and cultivate democratic deliberation in the classroom.

How does one ensure that teachers will assume the professional responsibility of upholding the principle of nonrepression in the schools? Gutmann's answer is teachers' unions. She writes, "The principle of nonrepression defines the democratic purpose of teachers' unions: to pressure democratic communities to create the conditions under which teachers can cultivate [a] critical reflection on democratic culture."[3] In fact, she considers upholding the principle of nonrepression as the democratic concept of professionalism in American schools.

I would like for teachers and teachers' unions to uphold a principle of non-repression. However, the reality is that teachers do not have that type of power under the current political system. Freedom of expression in the classroom is limited by the power of school administrators, curricula mandated by state governments and school boards, pressures from special-interest groups, the activities of politicians, standardized testing, and mandated textbooks. Teachers' unions do sometimes attempt to protect classroom activities, but their primary concern is with wages and working conditions.

How can Gutmann's principle of nonrepression be incorporated into the public school system? One way to ensure freedom of ideas in school is an amendment to the U.S. Constitution. This amendment could give courts the power to protect the exercise of the principle of nonrepression. Achieving this amendment to the Constitution is as unlikely as teachers' unions making the principle of nonrepression the centerpiece of their activities. In reality, it would appear that restrictions on freedom of ideas in schools will increase, and schools will continue to function as ideological managers.

THE POWER OF SPECIAL-INTEREST GROUPS

Despite discussions of majoritarian control, my analysis demonstrates that public schools are a battleground for groups seeking to have knowledge serve their interests. Important are the continual attempts by business interests to shape the schools to meet their economic needs. During the 1980s and 1990s, business interests assumed ever-greater control of state educational policies; local school districts signed compacts with private industry councils; and corporations participated in adopt-a-school programs. This pattern represents a continuation of the human capital theories that fostered the rise of vocational education in the early part of the twentieth century. Since then, the educational goal of preparing citizens for participation in a democracy has been replaced by that of preparing them for employment.

In keeping with an economic system based on the pursuit of profit, business interests are primarily concerned that public schools serve their needs. But business groups are often preoccupied with short-range goals, and one of their overriding concerns is to reduce employment costs to increase profits. The short-range economic goals of business cause constant changes in educational policies. One needs only to contrast the major goals of schooling in the 1970s with those of the 1990s. The career and vocational education thrust of the public schools of the 1970s was replaced in the 1990s by the demands of business interests for more scientists and engineers. In fact, the business goals of the 1990s were similar to those of the 1950s, when it was considered necessary to have more scientists and engineers to win the technological race with the Soviet Union.

In addition, unexpected events upset economic predictions. The Vietnam War in the 1960s, the energy crises of the 1970s, and international competition in the 1980s and 1990s are some unforeseen factors that have shaped the U.S. labor market. It is difficult for economists to predict future events and include them in long-range economic forecasting.

Therefore, educational goals derived from projected economic needs could actually have a negative impact on students. Consider a situation that might have occurred for many students in the 1950s and early 1960s: A student enters the first grade in 1955 at a time when business is proclaiming a shortage of scientists and engineers. The student remains in school, including college, for approximately 16 years. However, economic conditions change dramatically during this time. The student graduates from college in 1971, near the end of the Vietnam War and the beginning of the energy crisis, just when demand for scientists and engineers is at its lowest. Consequently, the student cannot find a job.[4]

A student's future career can be damaged not only by educational goals derived from the predicted needs of the labor market, but also by the desire of business interests to reduce labor costs. If labor costs follow the law of supply and demand, then business has to be interested in maintaining a large labor supply to keep wages and salaries down. In fact, business is in the most advantageous position, regarding labor costs, when there is an oversupply of workers in needed job categories.

When business interests claim, therefore, that there is a shortage of trained workers in a particular job category, it may be because they are being forced to pay higher salaries. In other words, business interests, feeling the impact of increasing wage costs, might declare a shortage of workers in order to ultimately reduce those costs. The public schools might respond by training more workers, and the labor market might be flooded with workers trained for that particular job category, which in turn might cause salaries and labor costs to decrease.

It is difficult to determine to what degree the declared shortage of scientists and engineers in the 1950s and 1980s was the result of business feeling the pressure of increased labor costs. One could hypothesize the following scenario. In the 1950s, business interests, in reaction to increasing costs for engineers and scientists, put pressure on the schools to increase training in those areas. As a result, the labor market was flooded with scientists and engineers by the late 1960s, which drove down salaries and labor costs. Consequently, business stopped pressuring the schools for training in those areas, and, because of reduced salaries and employment problems, fewer students chose to enter those fields. As a result, by the early 1980s the supply of engineers and scientists was low, and business, beginning to experience rising labor costs in those areas, began again to pressure the schools to emphasize science and mathematics.

Of course, business is not the only interest group seeking to have the schools serve its needs. The most powerful interest groups other than business are politically conservative and right-wing religious organizations. Since the early part of the twentieth century, these groups have censored teachers, curricula, and textbooks to ensure that their points of view dominate public school classrooms.

Protecting the schools from these pressures is as difficult as ensuring the principle of nonrepression. One possible solution is to make public schooling, through a constitutional amendment, the fourth branch of government with the same protection from outside influences that is given to the Supreme Court and the Federal Reserve Bank.

Obviously, no branch of government can be completely free of outside influences. The Supreme Court is politicized by the process by which its members are appointed. The administration in power fills vacant seats on the Supreme Court with justices attuned to the administration's political philosophy. The same is true of the Federal Reserve. While complete freedom from outside influences is impossible, a structure could be created that would minimize the influence of special-interest groups. In addition, this new branch of government could be organized to protect and support the free expression of ideas.

Like the proposal for an amendment to assure the principle of nonrepression, making public schools a fourth branch of government does not seem very likely. The reality is that business and other interest groups want to keep the school doors open to outside pressures. In the present climate, it appears most likely that public schools will continue to serve the interests of the business community and to have their curricula narrowed by conservative political and religious groups.

THE POLITICAL USE OF SCHOOLS

The education system is in constant change as a result of pressures from elected politicians and educational politicians. Such continual change creates unknown costs that never seem justified by the results. Education, despite endless new programs, has not eliminated poverty, solved problems of national defense, ended unemployment, or resolved any of the other social problems foisted on the schools. Some might argue that because of the constant state of change, the schools never have sufficient time to solve any single economic or social problem. The goals of the system change so swiftly that nothing is ever given a chance to work. On the other hand, it could be argued that schools cannot solve major social and economic problems. From this perspective, it is not that the schools fail, but that they truly do not have the power to reform society and save the economic system.

Measuring the economic costs of change in education is a complex job. At the federal level, one has to consider the actual costs of developing and implementing new programs, along with the money spent on the programs themselves. The same is true at state and local levels. Each change in national and state educational goals breeds a new crop of administrators in state departments of education and the central offices of local school systems. And, as we have seen, these administrators form their own interest groups to fight for more funding.

There are also the costs of financing the research programs that usually accompany each new direction in national and state education policies. One cost is the funding of the great army of educational researchers that inhabit colleges of education around the country whose professional lives depend on each swing of the policy pendulum. It would certainly be interesting to do a cost-effectiveness study to see whether or not educational research has improved student learning. For instance, has all the money spent on reading research since the 1950s produced any improvement in students' reading skills?

EDUCATORS AND SOCIAL IMPROVEMENT

Often, educators are the last to admit that schools cannot solve the world's problems. It is in the interests of educators and educational researchers to accept and promote the idea of schooling being a panacea for society's problems. Educators can demand more financial support by claiming that schools can solve economic and social problems. The idea of education as a social panacea enhances educators' feelings of self-worth.

One difficult solution is limiting educators' perspectives on what schools can accomplish. In addition, politicians and the public must be convinced that schools are not a panacea for social and economic problems. The propensity of politicians constantly to turn to school as politically safe solutions to social and economic problems makes it difficult to change images of schools as a means of social improvement. Educators will probably continue to boast about the social power of schooling. Consequently, schools will continually be tied to policy goals.

THE ECONOMICS OF EDUCATION

Often, people seek the maximum benefits from education at the minimum cost. In the 1990s, the financial crisis is caused by the loss of revenue to schools caused by reduced taxes for business and the wealthy. While business gained greater control of schools, it reduced its financial support.

The solution to the financial crisis is simple, but achieving that solution will be difficult. Business and wealthy individuals must be forced to pay higher taxes to support education, and the practice of giving local and state tax abatements to business must end. The business community and the wealthy must not be allowed to withdraw their financial support from the infrastructure of the nation. As documented in Chapter 3, business and wealthy individuals paid a higher rate of taxes in the 1950s and 1960s than they now pay. They can be taxed at a higher rate.

CONCLUSION

This final chapter does not present a positive view of the future politics of education. If current trends continue, then public schools will primarily serve the interests of business and politicians; the curriculum will be narrowed and ideas restricted in the classroom by pressures from interest groups; and education will be in continual financial crises.

One possible direction for schools is privatization. Proposals to use education money to provide a choice between private and public school offer an opportunity for the expansion of private education. Schools may be marketed in a manner similar to fast-food chains. For-profit schools will not be interested in controversy and they will limit their discussions of economics and politics. If this is the future, then it seems very unlikely that schools will promote the tenets of a free society.

NOTES

1. For a discussion of this political dilemma, see Joel Spring, *The American School 1642-1990*, 2nd ed. (White Plains, N.Y.: Longman, 1990), pp. 83-93.
2. Amy Gutmann, *Democratic Education* (Princeton, N.J.: Princeton University Press, 1987), p. 87.
3. Ibid., 79.
4. For a discussion of the problems of linking schooling with labor market needs, see Richard Freeman, *The Overeducated American* (New York: Academic Press, 1976).

Index